The Life and Times of a Ska Man

To John

An Offbeat Trip

Keep Blowing !!

Nick Welsh

Nick Welsh
_2017_

NEW HAVEN PUBLISHING LTD

First Edition
Published 2017
NEW HAVEN PUBLISHING LTD
www.newhavenpublishingltd.com
newhavenpublishing@gmail.com

All rights reserved
The rights of Nick Welsh, as the author of this work, have been asserted
in accordance with the Copyrights, Designs and Patents Act 1988.
No part of this book may be re-printed or reproduced or utilized in any
form or by any electronic, mechanical or other means, now unknown or
hereafter invented, including photocopying, and recording, or in any
information storage or retrieval system, without the written permission
of the Author and Publisher.

Front cover photo©Heather Michelle
Back cover photo©S. Elfie

Cover design©Pete Cunliffe
pcunliffe@blueyonder.co.uk

newhaven
publishing

Copyright © 2017 Nick Welsh
All rights reserved
ISBN: 978-1-910705-29-2

FOREWORD

Punter: "I bet you got some stories, you should put out a book."
Me: "Who the fuck would wanna read that?"
Punter: "Well, I would for a start."

I've had that conversation at gigs of mine a hell of a lot over the past ten years. Alright, the punter might not have sounded quite so much like a low rent Alfie Bass, but I'm sure you get the picture.

I began thinking he could be right though, maybe there were a few people out there who might want to know a little bit more about me, my music and some of the shenanigans I've got up to over the years. And so, a little seed was sown. I knew writing a book would be a lot harder than writing a song, but I started putting pen to paper, scribbling down a few memories, and promising myself if it was gonna end up as a book, it had to be one of those that once you put it down you can't pick it up again.

I started with the punk era, because as any old punk rocker who was there in 76/77 will testify the memories from those days are locked in your mind forever, and no matter how much whizz you may have done back then, you'll never forget it.

When I looked at what I'd written I have to say it impressed me, so much in fact I gave a couple of 'teaser' paragraphs to a few websites and the response they received was really good, but even more importantly it aroused the interest of a publishing company (they will remain nameless) who approached me to say they were interested in my book, but would I consider 'slagging off' this singer or 'dishing the dirt' on this artist that I'd worked with in it?

"Fuck me," I thought to myself. "These people are even worse than some of the music business shysters I've had to deal with, and that's saying something."

And with that my interest in writing a book stopped and I went back to doing what I think I do best - writing songs.

A year so later another publishing company got in touch, but this time it was the good people of New Haven asking me if they could see a section of the book. This proved a little difficult though because I'd deleted everything I'd written and the only thing I could get hold of was those few punk paragraphs that had been posted online.

Anyway, long story short, I sent that 'teaser' off to them and they loved it, and the added bonus was they had no interest in me writing a 'slagfest', they just wanted MY story which is why you're reading this now.

Let me just explain a couple of things about the book...

I chose the picture for the cover because, although I was a bit pissed when it was taken, I wasn't so drunk that you'd walk away from me. I think it has a 'have I told you this one?' kind of quality to it.

And as for the title, well it's a bit of a personal joke because I've never considered myself to be a ska or reggae artist, it's just something I use as a canvas to make my music on.

On reflection, maybe "Random Ramblings" would have been more suitable, and as for the language used in it, well, it might be a little bit 'fruity', but I'm sure you've all heard worse.

I'm not a famous musician with untold hit records to his name and millions in the bank, far from it. I'm just a guy with music running through his veins, who for forty years has tried to follow a dream. If that's good enough for you then sit back and let me tell you about my 'offbeat trip.'

Nick Welsh, September 2017

Content

THE LIFE AND TIMES OF A SKA MAN

I was born in London in 1962,
When the world was black and white,
And smoking was good for you.
Mama was an angel, my daddy was a music man,
And with big brother they worked so hard,
To get out of the caravan.
This is the life and times of a ska man,
The life and times of your friend and mine.
I used to play my records on a red Dansette,
There was bluebeat and reggae ska and rocksteady,
Some of it I had on cassette.
And that's what kept me dancing all through my teenage years,
Those days of wild confusion,
Those days of have no fear.

I got myself a guitar and learned a lick or two,
So, I could play The Roxy maybe The Vortex too.
Well music's been my first love, an occupation too,
It's just as well because to tell the truth,
There's nothing else that I can do.
But blink and you will miss it, so many years have gone,
But I've still got my mojo, man, I've still got my song.
This is the life and times of a ska man,
The life and times of your friend and mine.

Full time recreational drug taker.

Social and anti-social drinker.

Serial bird bandit (in my younger days)

These were just three of life's little treats I had to look forward to when I entered this world on the 23rd April 1962, which was a Monday; so that apparently makes me a child that's 'fair of face'.

Well what a load of bollocks that is for a start.

I was born in The Bearsted, a Jewish hospital in Stoke Newington, which makes me a Londoner, but not a cockney (you'd have to have fucking large ears to hear Bow Bells from there) and for the first two years of my life I lived in a caravan, so there you have it... I'm proper trailer trash!

I suppose this would be a good time to tell you about the people I shared this home on wheels with:

Mother: **Rosemary Jacqueline Francesca Maria Cyster**
Father: **Nicholas Peter Welsh**
Brother: **Richard Nicholas Welsh**

I have a bit of a problem telling you about both my parents' early days, because the information I received from them was shall we say a little bit 'sketchy' to say the least, but here we go:

Mum was born in the poor house and as a child was brought up on a farm in Buckinghamshire by her aunt. In her teens, she lied about her age to get into the WRAF, and then after suffering a life-threatening car accident later on in life she couldn't actually remember how old she was.

A few years later she moved up to Scotland and worked in a biscuit factory for a while, before she jacked it in to try and make a name for herself as a singer on the ballroom circuit, where she performed the popular songs of the day like "I Only Have Eyes For You" and "Misty" to the great unwashed.

One day she went for an audition to sing with a band, and after getting the gig she received some advice from the band leader: "Watch out for the pianist hen, he's a wee bit of a ladies' man."

Meet Nicky Welsh.

She told me she looked over to see a tall, handsome man sitting behind the Joanna, wearing shades and a dark pinstripe suit and that was it.

The old man was from Lanarkshire. He told me that when he left Catholic school he became a butcher and then a miner, but that could all change depending on how many drinks he'd had that day, and if he was really steaming he would go into great detail about how he'd fought the Germans in the Second World War.

I can remember spending many afternoons listening to him telling me about this or that battle he'd been involved in and like a mug I bought it, but as I got a little older and better at maths I began to realise he would've been about fourteen when it was all kicking off, and when I asked him exactly what war it was that he was involved in his reply was: "A war you don't know about son."

And to think he used to call me Tam Pepper!

One thing that is true though, is that he was a brilliant musician, who'd learned to read and write music without ever taking a lesson.

After spending a year or so together on the road Dad decided they should get married and he should leave the band to concentrate on his dream of becoming a musical arranger. That only meant one thing: they had to move down to London, which was the home of the big, bad music business; and so off they went. By the time I arrived on the scene a few years later they were living, along with my big brother, in a run-down caravan site just behind Harringay Stadium, where all of our neighbours were 'theatricals'.

Now, from what I understand, this means that they were mostly down-on-their-luck music hall artists who because of the rise in popularity of television and rock'n'roll were now spending most of their time performing to all the other artists who lived on the site while they waited for the offer of work.

> **"I'm Popeye the sailor man,**
> **I live in a caravan,**
> **When I go swimming,**
> **I kiss all the women,**
> **I'm Popeye the sailor man."**

Many years later Mum showed me some photographs of what life around the trailer park was like and it mainly seemed to be a lot of women in head scarves hanging out washing on makeshift lines outside their caravans.

In one picture, me and Richard are being held by men who looked like they were more interested in acquiring the contents of a recently widowed lady's savings book and going on the hoof. They were all bow-ties and Terry Thomas moustaches and so from what I could see we were living in our own personal Ealing comedy. Imagine *The Lavender Hill Mob* meets *Freaks* and you're getting close.

Mum always spoke about them affectionately but personally I would have thought more than twice about leaving my child in the care of an unemployed clown or a down-on-their-luck knife throwing act, but hey maybe I'm just being a little bit over protective.

One thing that I could never work out though was how Dad managed to work his way up the music business ladder so quickly and successfully. I know he was a man of considerable talent, but we lived in a fucking caravan with no phone. Now that's what I call networking.

But the important thing was he was earning a good reputation in the industry as a great musical arranger/director, which created enough work to help the Welsh family say goodbye to the caravan park and move five hundred yards down the road to a basement flat with a garden at 366a Green Lanes N4.

Now, I'm not one of those people who claim to remember coming out of the womb or any of that old bollocks, but I can say that my first real memories are from when we moved into our new gaff. Nothing special, just ordinary little things like going shopping with Mum in Harringay. She seemed to stop every five minutes to talk to someone about the weather or who was shagging who in *Peyton Place* while I would impatiently shuffle behind her, but I was always on my best behaviour because I knew at the end of their natter the person she'd been talking to would usually give me a sixpence for my pocket; in my mind they immediately went from zero to hero in just a few short seconds.

See how easy I can be bought!

A word of advice though: don't bother doing that today, because you will more than likely be hunted down as some kind of serial nonce case and have your house burnt down by some psychotic lynch mob.

We used to put our shopping into a big brown wicker basket that you had to pull behind you, but of course being an adventurous young boy, I would always try to wheel it in front of me, and it always ended up the same way…

The basket would topple over and the shopping would go all over the pavement, earning me a firm tongue lashing followed by a quick slap across the back of my knees. Those were the days eh?

The Beach Boys   **"God Only Knows"**
The Beatles   **"Eleanor Rigby"**
The Kinks   **"Sunny Afternoon"**

But my tears would soon disappear when Mum took me to the sweet shop, and bought me some fruit salads or black jacks to stop my whinging.

When I wasn't experimenting with shopping baskets, I spent a lot of time with Richard in our garden playing 'keepie-uppie' or 'three-and-in' and of course, on the many occasions when the ball would fly over the wall into our neighbour's garden, we'd take it in turns to knock on their door to say those immortal words every kid has said at one time in their life: "Can we have our ball back please?"

Now what other random things spring to mind?

Well, I was very keen on dressing up as a cowboy, standing by our front gate and firing my cap gun at everyone who passed by. I'm sure that's exactly what the good people of Haringey wanted to endure after a hard day's work and if I was caught doing it, guess what I got?

A firm tongue lashing and a quick slap across the back of my knees.

Every morning I would have porridge for breakfast served in my much loved Beatles bowl (which I still have) followed by chucky egg in my Beatles cup (sadly long gone). As far as TV goes I was a big fan of *Bill and Ben*, *Tom and Jerry* and *The Magic Roundabout*.

Fuck me! Dougal, Florence, Dylan and Zebedee - that was some spaced-out shit.

Another unmissable show was *Batman*. I used to watch it every week with Dad laughing his head off while I spent all my time worrying how The Dynamic Duo would get out of their weekly tight spot and it wasn't until I was a few years older that I realised just how much grown up humour was in it. R.I.P. Adam West. You will always be the real Caped Crusader x

And then there was Butlins.

I have quite a few photographs of the Welsh family enjoying themselves at this paradise for the working-class, but my favourite has to be the one of me sitting next to a beautiful lion cub and by the look on

11

my face I can only assume that someone must have airbrushed all the shit that was running down my leg at the time.

But I had no fear the day I was chosen to chase Long John Silver all over the camp on a pirate hunt and push him off a diving board into the swimming pool. The whole camp cheered when I did.

My first round of applause.

I got the chance to do it because the pirate, John O'Mahoney, was a friend of my dad's. And as everyone knows in showbiz, it's all about who you know. John worked at Butlins as a comedian, but on this day was moonlighting as 'Long John O'Mahoney' the evil monster of the high seas. His brother was also a comedian, the brilliant Dave Allen, but sadly John wasn't to follow him on the road to fame and fortune, because it wasn't too long after this that he committed suicide.

From holiday camps to suicide in just a few seconds. Fuck me Nick, you're a right bundle of laughs.

There were no holidays abroad for us in those days, just two weeks in some windy British seaside town like Bridlington, Scarborough, or Ramsgate, and do you know what? I loved every fucking minute of it. What kid wouldn't? You were entering a magical kingdom of candyfloss, amusement arcades and Punch and Judy shows.

When I was five I joined my brother at Woodberry Down Primary School, which was about a half mile walk from our house. Now I can't remember if having an elder brother there helped me in any way, but I do know that on one particular day having my mum working as a dinner lady there didn't. I was being particularly annoying to a kid who was in the year above me but instead of just giving me a well-deserved back hander, he went up to Mum who was on playground duty and said: "Excuse me Miss, Nick's really annoying me. What can I do about it?"

Her reply: "Ok, well bring him over and I'll hold him so you can hit him, but only once mind." Thanks Mum! Just the once eh? That's fucking nice of you. I tell you what, why don't you just invite him round to the house to take a big shit in my bed? And so I had to go through the humiliation of being held by my mum while this boy punched me in the stomach but you'll be glad to hear that I took my punishment like a man.

Well, actually that's a lie. I took it like the young boy I was and ran off crying and shouting: "I hate you Mum! I hate you!" (I'll let you into a secret: I didn't.)

My teacher Miss Westfield was a right bitch. No, let's make that a right cunt. How come the other two classes in my year were taught by young blonde birds in miniskirts, who wouldn't have looked out of place in Pan's People, but I got lumbered with some fucking old spinster with thick rimmed glasses who loved to pull me around by my hair and hit me for whatever reason she could think of?

I didn't take it personally though, because she did it to near enough every kid in my class and when I told my brother about it, he told me that it had been exactly the same for him when she was his abuser. Sorry, I mean teacher. Yes, boy or girl, it didn't seem to matter to this vicious little fucker; as long as she was making your life a misery she was a happy old bag.

Keith West	**"Excerpt From A Teenage Opera"**
The Monkees	**"Daydream Believer"**
The Beatles	**"Hello Goodbye"**

While Mum was on playground duty, Dad was going from strength to strength on his chosen path so let me fill you in on what happened to him after moving to London. For a couple of years, he sang with the close harmony vocal group The Fraser Hayes Four, who were very popular mainly due to having a regular guest spot on the radio show 'Round The Horne' but it's the period between the mid 60s until the late 70s, when he worked constantly as a live and a studio musician, that I'm going to focus on.

Let me begin by telling you a little bit about some of the records he made during that period that I really love. No bollocks, I'll just make a list and then fill you in on them.

NICK'S TOP TEN BIG NICK RECORDS.

Dorothy Squires	**"Is That All There Is?"**
Cilla Black	**"Sing A Rainbow"**
Levi Jackson	**"This Beautiful Day"**
London All Stars	**"Stop The Drums"**
Oscar	**"Over The Wall We Go"**
Fraser Hines	**"Who's Dr Who?"**
Rolf Harris	**"'Ave You Got A Loight Boy?"**
Gerry & The Pacemakers	**"Girl On A Swing"**
Jimmy James	**"Red Red Wine"**
Don Fardon	**"I'm Alive"**

We live in a celebrity age where you only have to come third in some heap of shit TV talent show and the title of 'star' is immediately bestowed upon you, but if you wanna know about a real star, then look no further than the woman who's at the top of my list: Dorothy Squires, or as I used to call her 'Auntie Dot.' Dot was exactly that, a real star, in a career lasting over fifty years. In the late 40s she was the highest paid female singer in the UK, but after marrying the actor Roger Moore in 1953 she spent the next few years of her life in Hollywood trying to help the future James Bond break into the film industry. She split with Roger in the early 60s and went back home where she found out that her star was not shining quite as brightly as it had been before she'd left. You could say that it was definitely a case of 'out of sight out of mind' but Dot being Dot it wasn't long before her fortunes changed and at the end of the decade, after teaming up with the old man, she made a surprise return to the charts with her version of 'My Way' (produced by Dad) and then in 1970 made the brave move of hiring The Palladium with the show selling out in just a couple of hours.

Whenever I listen to the album of the show I always get a tear in my eye when I listen to the introduction that Dot gives to Dad: it's extremely loving and very funny.

In 1974, Dot's Bexley mansion burned down. You can hear her lamenting that sad day on my chosen track "Is That All There Is?" from her 1977 award winning album "Rain, Rain Go Away". I was lucky enough to spend a lot of time at that beautiful house with her but unfortunately not at any of her legendary parties she used to throw there. I did get to run wild in her enormous garden and bang the keys on the huge white grand piano that was the centrepiece of her front room. Her kitchen was bigger than our fucking house! I can remember sitting in there watching her cooking me breakfast, singing "For Once In My Life" at the top of her voice.

She was an amazing woman, and "Is That All There Is?" is an amazing record.

Dad made a lot of records with Cilla Black that could've made my top ten: "For No One", "Don't Answer Me" or "The Right One Is Left" for starters but "Sing A Rainbow" has a unique and almost disturbing vibe to it. A couple of years ago, a DVD "Cilla At The Savoy" was released and there he was conducting the orchestra, looking splendid in his tux, in the first half of the show; but when George Martin takes over for the second half, I can clearly see him standing at the side of the stage chatting up some right tasty looking dolly bird. I don't know which one makes me feel prouder.

I'm told "This Beautiful Day" is a bit of a northern soul classic, although I can't see it myself, to me it just sounds like a great slice of 60s orchestral pop. What I can tell you is that the same record was released twice under two different names. One was credited to Levi Jackson and the other to the slightly better-known Solomon King, but besides being exactly the same record, they also share something else: they both go for much moolah on the rare occasions that they show up on eBay. Through the wonder of Wikipedia, I've just discovered that Solomon King not only had a big hit with a song called "She Wears My Ring" in 1968 but was also the first white singer to tour with Billie Holiday; but like I say that snippet did come to me via Wikipedia, so it might just be a load of old bollocks.

The sleeve notes on the back of The London All Stars' "Percussion" that features the track "Stop The Drums" makes for a very interesting read: "On the cold and frosty morning of the 23rd of February 1965, twenty-five musicians assembled at Pye recording studios in London for what was to be one of the finest recording dates of the year. Flexing his not inconsiderable muscles, arranger Nicky Welsh set to work one month after Christmas 1964 to arrange the music for a powerhouse line up of the finest musicians in England." Well, I suppose any line up that has Jimmy Page and John McLaughlin on guitar is worthy of the description 'powerhouse'! Jimmy played guitar on many of my old man's sessions, but I can remember him telling me that he had to stop using him because he was considered 'too wild' for some of the MOR artists he was working with by the 'powers that be'. If you can find a copy of the original album, your pockets will be lighter to the tune of £300, which is probably more than all the musicians got paid collectively for the recording.

"Over the wall we go, all coppers are nanas." Now, I'm sure we'd all agree that this is not David Bowie's finest lyrical moment, but I think I'm also right in saying that Oscar's "Over The Wall We Go" was one of the first Bowie songs to be covered by another artist and although the record flopped, the writer did go on to make a bit of a name for himself. Oscar was the middle name of Paul Beuselinck, who, I can only assume, after realising he wasn't going to climb the showbiz ladder with a surname better suited to a mad professor, changed it to Nicholas, and it worked because within a few years he was onstage playing Jesus Christ and having hit records like the classic "Reggae Like It Used To Be", which was a regular feature of early King Hammond setlists. "Over The Wall We Go" is a bit pants though.

Another actor Dad made a record with was Fraser Hines. Fraser played the character Jamie McCrimmon in *Doctor Who* from 1966-69 and it was during this period that he released the novelty psych/pop single "Who's Dr Who?" in an attempt to cash in on his role. Unfortunately for him, even though the song was written by the hitmaking machine of the time, Barry Mason and Les Reed, it turned out to be a commercial flop, which I have to say surprises me, because not only was Fraser's star shining brightly at the time due to the TV series but also because I actually happen to think that it's a really good track. Fraser went on to play Joe Sugden in the series *Emmerdale Farm* and I often wonder if it ever crossed his mind during those twenty-three years spent in the Dales to give the pop world another shot... Probably not.

Rolf, Rolf, silly old Rolf. I think out of all the Yewtree nonces who've been 'outed' in the last few years he was the one that surprised and saddened us the most. When I found out that when Rolf wasn't playing the role of a friendly children's entertainer making young kids happy with his paintings and novelty records he was also putting in a shift as a as a serial sex beast, it did make me think twice about putting him into my top ten; but because "'Ave You Got A Loight Boy?" was not only arranged by Dad, but also features him laughing all the way through it, I have to admit that the record still has a very special place in my heart.

I met Rolf in the West End not long after my old man passed away but for some reason when I introduced myself to him and he asked about Dad I told him that he'd just died in a motorbike accident while off his tits on smack. Rolf's face was a picture: "No? Not Nick! Yeah, we all used to have a drink back then, but not heroin." He looked so upset that I had to come clean with him before he made his way up Chancery Lane in his ridiculous poncho looking nothing like Clint Eastwood.

Rolf, Rolf, silly old Rolf.

Let's move on a bit sharpish to the much more wholesome and always overly optimistic world of Merseybeat. Besides working with Cilla, Dad also made records with most of the artists on Brian Epstein's roster: David & Jonathan, Billie J. Kramer and the band I've chosen to represent this golden era of pop... Gerry & The Pacemakers. "Girl On A Swing" is a beautiful record that makes you feel like a warm summer day filled with love and hope, especially when he sings the line: "Take all the hate from the world that we're in."

16

Only a fool would underestimate Neil Diamond as a songwriter. We'd be here all day if I had to list all my favourite songs of his but "Red Red Wine" would have to be right up there and the only way to describe the version by Jamaican soul singer Jimmy James is sublime. When Jimmy and his band, The Vagabonds, relocated from JA to the UK they released "Ska-Time" for the Decca label, which was one of the first ska songs to be recorded in England. They toured the UK constantly, sharing bills with The Who, Rod Stewart and Jimi Hendrix and in 1968 Jimmy had a hit with "Red Red Wine" and the track is the centrepiece of his wonderful "Open Up Your Soul" album, which I would advise you to check out. I guarantee that you'll never listen to the UB40 version in the same way again.

Last but not least is a record that even fifty years after it was released can fill any dancefloor. Don Fardon started his career in the Coventry band The Sorrows alongside my future good friend Roger Lomas, before going on to achieve considerable solo success with singles like "Indian Reservation", "Belfast Boy" and of course "I'm Alive" on the Young Blood label. When today's record collectors are trying to flog a copy of "I'm Alive" they describe it as 'freakbeat' and from what I understand this is basically anything recorded from the mid to late 60s that features a Hammond organ and a bit of fuzz guitar, and although the track does tick all those boxes I prefer to stick with my description: it's fucking great.

Well that's my personal top ten, pop-pickers, but I do have to point out that it will change from day to day. I'm a regular visitor to the wonderful world of eBay and will spend a couple of hours a week searching for my old man's records, and it never ceases to amaze me what comes up. The biggest shock to me was finding out he'd made a record in 1970 with The Artie Scott Orchestra called "March Of The Skinheads" released on the Major Minor label, because I had recorded a song in the late 80s with the same title, on my first King Hammond album "Revolution 70", and I swear that I never knew anything about his track.

Surely that must make us the rudest family in town.

He made a lot of records for that label, some good, some bad and some that were just fucking bizarre, like Pat Campbell's "The Deal" which made it onto the 1978 Kenny Everett compilation album "The World's Worst Record Show." And how can I not mention the tracks he recorded with Freddie 'Parrot Face' Davies, that really do make me feel "sick, sick, sick up to here" (if you're old enough you'll remember that was his catchphrase), or the tearful saloon-bar classic "Nobody's Child" that gave Karen Young a huge hit in 1969.

Here's a quick list of just some of the other artists he worked with:

Long John Baldry
David Essex
Gilbert O'Sullivan
The Nolans
Geno Washington
Mac & Katie Kissoon
Dominic Behan
Jimmy Powell
Maxine Nightingale
Janie Jones
The Grumbleweeds
Lena Martell
Jimmy Witherspoon

And how about this? I recently found out he made a single with Eve Plumb from The Brady Bunch! Fuck me I nearly pissed myself thinking about him working with this kid and having to keep his language in check that day for what must have seemed like a very long three hours. The reason I say three hours is because that's how long a session lasted back then: 10am-1.00pm, 2.00pm-5.00pm, 7.00pm-10.00pm.

"He reads the dots and plays each line and always finishes on time"

With all of this going on in Dad's life, I suppose it would've been a bit strange if I hadn't started taking more than just a passing interest in music, especially because I was lucky enough to be taken by him to some of the great studios like Pye, Olympic Sound, and probably the best and most famous of them all, Abbey Road, to see how it was all done. I can vividly remember looking down through the windows of Abbey Road's Studio Two control room, watching Dad conduct a huge orchestra, feeling so high up and far away from where all the action was, but when it was all over he'd come up and get me and we'd go for something to eat in the studio canteen where I'd get to meet all the musicians who'd been on the session, and they would always make a big fuss of me.

18

Another plus for me was that he used to bring home lots of record company promos that he'd give to me and Richard to play, and I must've had good taste for a young kid because the record I remember playing all the time was The Zombies' classic "Odessey And Oracle" album, but before I give it large the first single I ever bought from a shop was Val Doonican's "The Straight Life".

Here's a touch... In 1978, I was cleaning out a cupboard in my bedroom that I'd never been into before mainly because it was right behind a big fuck off wardrobe. Anyway, besides all the usual bedding and shit like that, I found about fifty unopened envelopes all containing acetates that had been sent to Dad by various publishers, artists and record companies that he obviously couldn't be fucked to open. I'm glad I did though because amongst a whole load of artists I'd never heard of was one whose name did ring a bell... David Bowie.

I was now in possession of an un-played acetate of "Love You 'Til Tuesday" with a spoken intro from the man himself and a handwritten letter from his publisher asking if Dad would be interested in doing something with his artist. Ka-ching! I think it took less than an hour from me discovering this little bit of stardust to it leaving my house in the hands of a Bowie collector I knew, after parting with £80 for it. Good money in those days.

I made my stage debut in 1968 at the tender age of six playing the part of a shipwrecked sailor in a school play. As I walked to school on the evening of the show, I was full of nervous excitement. Thinking about it now I had a very good reason to be nervous, although I didn't know it at the time, and it wasn't because I was about to tread the boards for the first time, it was more to do with the fact that I was an unaccompanied young child dressed up like a paedo's dream in a sailor's top and tight little blue shorts!

Now I know people my age say things like: "Oh, it was a different time back then." And maybe it was, but the idea of letting your kid walk down the road on their own dressed like that for me is fucking frightening.

Apart from that I have to say I really loved the experience of performing in front of an audience, even taking the liberty of straying from the script and ad-libbing a little bit (nothing's changed) and for the next few weeks the only thing to come out of my mouth was: "When I grow up I want to be an actor."

It didn't last too long though, because this was also the year that I fell in love for the first time, and it wasn't with a pretty girl in my class, but with a football team… West Bromwich Albion.

If I had a pound for every time I've been asked: "Why do you support West Brom?" I'd be a millionaire.

So, for hopefully the last time in my life, here's the answer: the first Cup Final I watched all the way through was West Bromwich Albion v Everton and the simple truth is as I watched both sides being introduced to some Royal who obviously didn't give a fuck about football, I decided that WBA had a better name and kit than Everton.

I'd tried showing some interest in the previous year's final between Spurs and Chelsea, but I kept on getting up every few minutes to go and play with my Action Man, which at the time seemed a lot more interesting to me, and even though that match was a lot better than the Albion game, as boring as it was it infected me with the dreaded football bug which is why nearly fifty years later I still suffer from that awful pain and anguish any true football fan gets every time he watches his team play.

The game also presented me with my first bona fide hero: Jeff Astle. Not because he scored the winning goal that day but because I was really impressed with his heading ability and his continuous work off the ball. Are you swallowing that one? Ok, it was all down to the goal, but what the fuck do you expect? I was only eight years old. I knew he was no George Best, but then again who was?

And from that year Cup Final day was all about sitting in front of the TV not just to watch the match but also the build up to it, because through the wonder of TV we could now follow the teams making their way up Wembley Way and playing cards on their coach, or marvel at some celebrity fans' unique footballing insights; and when there was a bit in the programme that I found boring I'd swap the box for that week's edition of *Shoot!* magazine, which I would buy every week, reading it cover to cover before cutting out any pictures or articles that had anything to do with Jeff or The Albion. I especially liked pictures with a domestic theme, you know the kind of thing, showing one of the players at home washing up, or putting up a new pair of curtains in the front room with his wife. Now you never saw Georgie Best doing that!

A couple of weeks after Albion's cup win I was allowed to stay up later than usual so I could watch the Man Utd v Benfica European Cup

Final go into extra time and witness Georgie 'dummy' their keeper and slide the ball into an empty net.

"Georgie Best, superstar, walks like a woman and he wears a bra"

The next day at school, all the kids tried to repeat his little bit of footballing genius in the playground, with varying degrees of failure.

I loved all the Albion players but it was usually more to do with their name than their ability on the pitch. For example, for a couple of seasons I had a thing about the Welsh midfielder Dick Krzyswicki. Now he was not a great player, in fact not even a good one, but in my mind he had a world class name.

A few years later, my attentions turned to another midfield man Asa Hartford although this little Scotsman really could play, which is why I got so upset when I found out that he wanted to leave the Baggies and sign for every football fan's enemy, Leeds United. The hurt didn't last too long though, because the transfer broke down when his medical showed that he had a hole in his heart. When I asked my dad what that meant he told me: "It means they've found a polo mint in his waistcoat pocket." Smart arse.

Saying that, being a smart arse obviously ran in the family, because that's exactly what I was at school, which meant that I was no stranger to being thrown out of a lesson and sent to the Headmaster to get the cane. While I sat outside his office waiting to receive some punishment to my bottom, I would pass the time by looking at all the Lowry prints that hung on the wall. I seriously thought they'd been drawn by a former pupil. And I don't know who was responsible for the sculpture that stood in the entrance to the school, but whoever it was had a very warped mind indeed. In the Infants I thought it was a man sitting with an animal on his lap but as I grew older it became obvious to me that it was some zoophile giving a pig one up the arse!

Now I don't say this for some kind of shock value, and I will of course try to provide some photographic evidence to back this up.

The Move	**"Fire Brigade"**
Louis Armstrong	**"What A Wonderful World"**
Honeybus	**"I Can't Let Maggie Go"**

The school had a really big playground that was perfect for all the frantic and frankly sometimes violent twenty-aside football matches it hosted every break time accompanied by the sweet and slightly sickly aroma floating across the reservoir from Maynard's wine gum factory. Maybe that's what drove us all crazy. Maynard's was where our teachers said we'd spend the rest of our lives working if we weren't good students, which when you think about it is a bit of a stupid threat because to a young kid that sounds like the best fucking gig in the world.

One of my class mates was a boy called Dean Waters who used to go on and on about how he was gonna be a great boxer when he grew up. I suppose that's why he used to go running three times a week around Finsbury Park with his dad. Because Dean was my friend I'd sometimes join them even though I never really took to his dad, mainly because I thought he looked like a criminal I'd seen in a Laurel and Hardy film who'd wrapped their legs around their heads and I didn't want that to happen to me!

Dean and I used to play a game in the school toilets, where we would hang onto a pole that ran along the ceiling and kick each other until one of us fell off onto the piss stained floor. Pretty soon the word got around that this was the place to be and before long there were large queues of young boys waiting for their turn to try and become the new Champion of the Bogs.

That's not why I'm telling you about Dean, it's because a few years later he emmigrated to Australia, and guess what? He only went on to become the Heavyweight Boxing Champion of the country! Unfortunately, it wasn't to be all glory for him, because after his career ended he was involved in a high-profile murder trial. While I was searching the internet for information to find out what had gone on, I began to see lots of reports of how badly Dean's dad had treated him, and that may have been one of the reasons he went 'off the rails'.

Dean, you may have had your troubles but at least you achieved your childhood dream and how many people can say that?

Who remembers Alf Tupper?

Alf was a working-class runner known as 'The Tough of The Track' who lived on a diet of fish and chips and always arrived for his races just in the nick of time, usually after helping some poor sod out of a tight spot. Well, every day after tea, I would go to the sweet shop with Richard and on our way home we'd always have a race. I would be Alf Tupper and he was Wilf Willoughby, one of Alf's arch rivals. No matter how hard I tried that cunt would always beat me. Even now it winds me up, especially when I think about when he used to let me lead for most of the race, but as soon as we got near to our house he would overtake me with his arms in the air and a big fucking smirk on his face. And don't even think that I've forgotten about all the times he used to push the glass in my mouth when I was gargling water after brushing my teeth. Richard, you were a top tosser, but I love you x.

By the way Alf Tupper was a cartoon strip in *The Victor*.

Like any kid, I loved my comics, but I was an avid book reader too, following the escapades of my schoolboy heroes Jennings and Darbishire and Just William or spending hours thumbing through my collection of biblical Ladybird books with one in particular, *The Lost Sheep*, being read, re-read and re-re-read.

Right here we go, there's no easy way to say this but…

Although my old man might have a been a very talented musician, he was just as useful at getting pissed and indulging in the odd bit of the old domestic violence. It's not nice when you're a kid lying in bed and then it starts:

The shouting.

The screaming.

The fucking horror.

All you can do is put your head under the eiderdown and hope that it all goes away.

I never ever saw any of the physical abuse with my own eyes and so I didn't know the severity of it and the thing is at that age you think that maybe it's 'the norm'. Maybe everyone's Mum and Dad argues like that; don't they?

Well, don't they?

This went on for a few years, until one night our bedroom door opened and Mum told me and Richard to get ourselves dressed. She put a few of our bits and pieces into a suitcase, before taking us into the front room where the old man was sitting in his chair with his head down.

Mum: "We're going away for a while, so say goodbye to your Dad."

Boys: "Bye Dad."

Dad (to Me): "Here's something for you son."

And he hands me a book.

I know what you're thinking: he's giving me a copy of the bible to give me a little inner strength to help me through what was obviously going to be a rough time for me. Wrong. It was a copy of the Glasgow

Celtic 1967 yearbook, giving you all the information you'd ever need on their fantastic five trophy winning season and just in case you're interested they were:

European Cup
Scottish First Division
Scottish Cup
Scottish League Cup
Glasgow Cup

But hold on a minute, if you include the Di Stefano Trophy that makes six, so maybe it could've been helpful to me. I mean who knows, in thirty years' time I might be part of a pub quiz team and one of the questions could be: "How many trophies did Glasgow Celtic win in the 1966/67 season?" And because of that book I would have a slight edge over all the usual pissed up football enthusiasts who would think it was only five. Wonderful, truly wonderful.

"Love grows where my Rosemary goes and nobody knows like me"

We were driven by my cousin Peter to my uncle Bill's house in Enfield, where he lived with his Barbara Windsor lookalike wife Jill and their three kids Lorraine, Anita and Stephen.

From what I can remember Bill and Jill were ok, although he was quite strict with his kids. No, let's make that very strict, and he treated us in exactly the same way. As for Jill, well she just seemed to spend a lot of time in front of a mirror doing her hair into what I would have to say was the most perfect beehive that I have ever seen, although I'm sure she did a lot more than that. But if having Mum and Dad breaking up wasn't bad enough, it was about to get a lot worse for me because I was about to enter a brand-new era of sadness that I can describe in just four words...

Bush Hill Park School.

From the moment I started at my new school, my life became one of pure and utter misery. Not one fucker would speak to me and to this day I still have no idea why. It was silence in the classroom, which I suppose I can understand, but why the fuck was it silence in the playground as well? I would spend every break and lunchtime on my own, wondering why no one liked me, and after a while I got it into my head that maybe it was because my mum and dad weren't together, which made me some kind of freak in their eyes.

Now this may sound stupid, but you have to remember I was only eight years old.

The funny thing is though, I can't remember any of the teachers trying to help the situation by asking some of my fellow pupils to mix with me, or vice versa. Surely, they must have noticed there was something going on because we are talking about months and months here.

I suppose sometimes, just sometimes, kids can be little cunts.

Blue Mink	**"Melting Pot"**
Kenny Rogers	**"Ruby Don't Take Your Love To Town"**
The Archies	**"Sugar Sugar"**

Christmas 1969 was a weird one. Not because Rolf Harris was number one in the chart with a song about "Two Little Boys", but because I had to spend the whole of the holiday period with my Auntie Brenda and Uncle Roy at their house in Harringay, just FOUR DOORS AWAY from where my dad was.

I seemed to have a lot of relatives in those days. "Come on, we're going to your Auntie this or your Uncle so and so's." But even though they weren't my real relatives, I liked Brenda and Roy a lot, they were nice people. Brenda was always on hand with a plate of cakes, and Roy, well I thought the pipe-smoking Roy was a fucking star, because I'd seen him untold times on TV in some of my favourite programmes like *The Saint* and *The Champions*. I don't quite know what to call him, because although he never had a major part in anything, you definitely wouldn't call him an extra. His gig seemed to involve walking up to someone like Simon Templar in a bar and saying, "Nice to see you Simon, fancy a drink?" And then he'd be off.

I've just looked him up on the IMDb site and I was even more impressed to find some of his film credits so here's another little list:

NICK'S TOP FIVE FILMS 'UNCLE' ROY APPEARED IN

1.	'Cromwell'
2.	'10 Rillington Place'
3.	'On The Buses'
4.	'Frenzy'
5.	'Stardust'

25

I went to see *Cromwell* at the cinema when it came out (maybe it was with Roy?) and I loved it even though it's a fucking long film for a seven-year-old to sit through. I was totally absorbed by it, and afterwards went straight to the library and got a book out on the geezer (the geezer? Cromwell?) and although I can't imagine that I understood a lot of it, it probably kept me occupied for a bit while all my school mates were busy avoiding me.

Let it go mate, it's nearly fifty years ago!

Anyway, back to that year's Christmas. Just when I thought my mind couldn't get fucked with anymore... it did. As I was saying goodbye to my make-believe-relatives, Mum ushered me and Richard towards the car that was taking us back to Enfield, and told us to get in and lock the door.

I looked up towards Manor House, and through the fog I could see a lone figure heading down the hill towards us. It looked like a gunfighter on his way to a shoot-out in some old western, but as it got closer to us I realised that it wasn't a cowboy at all.

It was my dad.

Mum walked away from the car and had a short conversation with him, after which he came over to say hello to the two of us sitting in the back of the motor. I was totally bemused about what was going on, because, although I can't talk for my brother, I certainly didn't know the full strength of what had gone on between the two of them. I couldn't understand why I wasn't allowed to spend more time with him, and I know this probably sounds a bit fucked up, knowing what I do now, but I will always love my mum and dad exactly the same, even though he behaved like an absolute cunt towards her. Sorry, it's just the way I am.

Fuck, I'm depressed now.

Never mind, I'm off to the studio to hopefully try and record a little bit of magic, but when I return I will tell you all about my lip-smacking, thirst-quenching, ace-tasting, motivating, good-buzzing, cool-walking, high-talking, fast-living, ever-giving... 70s!

Cilla's Hits
CILLA BLACK

* *With accompaniment directed by Nicky Welsh*
† *With accompaniment directed by Burt Bacharach*

GEP
8954

SIDE ONE	SIDE TWO
*1. DON'T ANSWER ME *(Zambroni-Enriquez-Callander)*	†1. ALFIE (Inspired by the Paramount Film 'Alfie') *(Bacharach-David)*
*2. THE RIGHT ONE IS LEFT *(Arnold-Morrow-Martin)*	*2. NIGHT TIME IS HERE *(Willis)*

OTHER ENJOYABLE EPS BY CILLA BLACK . . .	IT'S FOR YOU
ANYONE WHO HAD A HEART Love of the loved; Shy of love; Anyone who had a heart; Just for you. GEP 8901	He won't ask me; You're my world (Il mio mondo); It's for you; Suffer now I must. GEP 8916
AND LPs . . .	CILLA SINGS A RAINBOW
CILLA Goin' out of my head; Every little bit hurts; Baby, it's you; Dancing in the street; Come to me; Ol' Man River; One little voice (Uno di voi); I'm not alone anymore; Whatcha gonna do 'bout it?; Love letters; This empty place; You'd be so nice to come home to.	Love's just a broken heart; Lover's Concerto; Make it easy on yourself; One two three; (There's) No place to hide; When I fall in love; Yesterday; Sing a rainbow; Baby I'm yours; The real thing; Everything I touch turns to tears; In a woman's eyes; My love come home.
PMC 1243 (mono) PCS 3061 (stereo)	PMC 7004 (mono) PCS 7004 (stereo)

 45 EXTENDED PLAY | **E.M.I. RECORDS** (The Gramophone Company Ltd.) HAYES · MIDDLESEX · ENGLAND Made and Printed in Great Britain G & L 6609 VM

EMITEX
RECORD CLEANER
The use of NEW EMITEX
provides an effective means of
ensuring groove cleanliness so
essential to good reproduction.
Its regular use will heighten the
life of the record and reduce
its static charge. Available
from Record Dealers.

The old mans name above Mr Bacharach!

WHEN WE WERE YOUNG

When we were young,
When we were young.

It only seems like yesterday,
The days were there for fun,
Do you remember you would say?
Let's burn by twenty-one.

When we were young,
When we were young.

You're acting so restless,
Maybe you're confused,
You dress to impress,
And don't care what you lose.

It only seems like yesterday,
Your money was to blow,
Do you remember you would say?
The line is not to toe.
When we were young,
When we were young.

The 70s began with the three of us still living in Enfield, which for me meant going through my day-to-day misery at Bush Hill Park, but luckily it wasn't to last for much longer because in March we went back to live in Harringay, because Dad moved out of the family home. He went to stay in the Redmond Hotel opposite Finsbury Park, which once again was a bit of a mind fuck for me, but it did mean I was now going to be back amongst all my friends at Woodberry Down; and the other good news was I was no longer going to be taught by the psychotic bitch from hell because I now had a new teacher, who by complete contrast was young, likeable and had the ability to actually make you want to learn something.

Say hello to Mr John Watts.

Hey, do any of you remember when you used to play football in the playground and all the kids would line up against a fence to let the two captains choose the players for their teams and there would always be some poor kid (usually fat) who'd be picked last and then stuck in goal to keep him out of the way of outfield play, or, thinking about it, to use his extra girth to block off most of the goal?

Well, it was during a game like this that Mr Watts noticed I had some considerable footballing talent and went out on a limb to start the first football team Woodberry Down had ever had and what's more: he made me the captain.

I couldn't speak highly enough of the man.

When he used to take the odd day off (probably nursing a hangover because he was a bit of a piss artist) it made me sad, because it meant we wouldn't be having one of our chats about the beauty of Ajax FC or his love for Rod Stewart and The Faces that day.

I just took a quick break from writing this to go for a piss and remembered mid-slash about the time there was a big splash in all the newspapers because some Andy Warhol film was going to be shown on TV.

Of course, with all the publicity it got, I had to stay up and watch it, which was something I'd only do for *Monty Python's Flying Circus* or *The Old Grey Whistle Test*. Naturally, it was the big talking point at school the next morning, although to be honest I don't think many of the pupils in my class had actually seen it. When Mr Watts asked if anyone had watched it and what their opinion was of it, mine was the only hand that when up in the air.

I asked if it was ok to use a swear word to try and describe what I thought of it and he said: "Yes, if you really feel that you need to."

And so I stood up and said: "Sir, I think it was the biggest load of bollocks that I've ever seen in my life."

Fuck me did he laugh!

If I was ever out of order in a lesson, he would take me into the stock room under the pretext of giving me the cane, but after closing the door instead of hitting me he would hit the big sheets of art paper kept in there telling me to scream on impact. The geezer was a gem.

Mr Bloe	**"Groovin' With Mr Bloe"**
Tom Jones	**"Daughter Of Darkness"**
T.Rex	**"Ride A White Swan"**

I can still picture it in my mind. It's 1970 and I'm making my way up Green Lanes to Manor House. There's about ten of them, all with shaven heads, Levi's and big boots and they're running down the hill towards me chasing four geezers running for their long-haired lives. I did a quick David Hemery and jumped over the fence into the safety of a small grass bank in Rowley Gardens where I got my first ever sighting of: SKINHEADS!

And fuck me did they look scary.

If you'd told me at that moment that skinheads were going to play a big part in my later life, I probably would've run for my life and shit my pants. Who knows? Maybe that was the reason why I decided to follow in my brother's footsteps and join the 12th Stoke Newington Scout Group the very next week so I would always be prepared.

It turned out that the pack I joined was a little bit different to the others. Yeah, we did all the usual things that other packs did to earn their merit badges, but when Akela used to fuck off home early for his bangers and mash, leaving our pack leader (who was also his son) to take over for "exercise time", you began to see why so many kids in our area wanted to join up.

It was all down to a little game called "British Bulldog in The Dark".

For those of you who don't know the rules of British Bulldog it goes something like this:

- **Choose a couple of nutcases to become bulldogs and stand them in the middle of a big play area.**
- **All the other nutcases have to try to run from one end of the area to the other, without being caught by the bulldogs.**
- **If a bulldog catches you, you become a bulldog.**
- **The winner is the last one to be caught.**

Easy.

Oh and no prizes for guessing that we played it in the dark.

Sometimes our leader would change the game to "Piggy Back British Bulldog in The Dark". Once again there are no prizes given for why. At the end of the evening there would be fucking claret everywhere, and the more there was the more this Baden Powell psychopath seemed to like it. I'd go as far as to say that the sight of a lot of kids with bloody noses and cut legs seemed to excite him a great deal because the bloke was a little unhinged, I think due to a few years of excessive amphetamine intake. Even though I couldn't see it at the time, the clues were all there: he was a long haired bearded man who used to arrive on a huge Harley Davidson and over the top of his uniform he wore a cut off Levi jacket with the words 'HELLS ANGELS' on the back... oh and he was very aggressive. Which I suppose is why all the kids loved him, because he brought an element of danger and excitement to an otherwise mundane world of learning how to administer first aid or tie a reef knot.

Personally, I think the Scouts provided quite enough danger when they sent us out on our own to take part in the weird and definitely not wonderful world of something they liked to call 'Bob-A-Job'. Even the name of it sounds a bit noncey to me. If you don't know what it was all about, let me go over all the ins and outs of it with you. For the princely sum of five pence (a 'bob') a young child, dressed in a smart green uniform, would be asked to knock on a complete stranger's door and say: "Is there anything I can do for you for a bob?"

And so besides having a fifty-fifty chance of actually making it back out of there with your shorts still on the right way, I really don't think a bob was a good enough payment for washing some pensioner's shitty underpants, or weeding an old biddy's garden, no matter how many fucking glasses of Tree Top they might have given you.

But being in the Scouts did provide me with another opportunity to play football, because unlike my school they had a team who played in a proper league, and even though I was a year younger than you were supposed to be to join, I was improving so fast I got put into the first team and told to say that I was a year older.

Hold on a minute. Aren't the Scouts supposed to be an honest bunch?

Anyway, I didn't give a fuck about being honest, because I was now getting to play in competitive matches, not just playground stuff. Also, I don't think you can apply the term honest to a boy who, like a lot of kids his age, was coming to terms with being in the first throes of an evil and deadly addiction called... Knock Down Ginger.

Tell me, has there ever been a better game?

And it was made even better if you knew the occupant was shall I say a little bit slow on their pins, or even better/worse on crutches or wheelchair bound; but you could always justify this to yourself if the person behind the door was one of those miserable old gits who'd made you clean their dirty windows for a measly fucking bob.

Now being the creative type I always tried to add a few extras to this already brilliant game. For example, I came up with the idea of putting lots of drawing pins on the door mat. Or my personal favourite: take a fat kid along with you, and just as the door's about to open get him in a bear hug and see if he possesses the necessary strength and speed to get away.

I've just realised that's the second time I've mentioned fat kids in this chapter.

Who knows, maybe it's fat boy karma that I grew up to become a man of considerable size.

In other words I'm a big fat bastard.

I spent a lot of time with Dad that summer, either going to see him at his hotel opposite Finsbury Park or at our house, where I can clearly remember him making me cry one night when Jeff Astle missed that 'sitter' against Brazil in Mexico 70. It was the kind of chance he'd normally put away on any Saturday afternoon, and I tried to argue his case by saying that he had just come on, but the old man wouldn't let it go and the tears soon started. Right from the start of Mexico 70 the bastards tried to mug off us by getting the old bill to stitch up Bobby Moore on some trumped up theft charge. Can you believe that? They tried to convince the world that our golden boy was nothing but a common tea-leaf, accusing him of half-inching a bracelet and putting him under house arrest in an attempt to try and unsettle him, and did it?

Did it fuck!

After a few days, he was released without charge and went on to produce some of the best performances of the whole competition, which I have to say was some fucking going, because there were so many great players and teams on show that year; but as good as Mooro was, it has to be said no-one came anywhere near the beautiful football that Pele and Brazil gave the world in that tournament.

But I'm English so fuck Brazil and their silky samba skills.

Who had the best fucking world cup song? We did, and it got to number one.

"Back home, they'll be watching and waiting and cheering every move,

Back home, though they think were the greatest, that's what we've got to prove"

I still get a tingle whenever I hear it, because it is, without doubt, the best football record ever made, and if that isn't good enough they made an album "The World Beaters Sing The World Beaters" released in a football shaped sleeve featuring twelve tracks of pure magic. Besides the hit single, you get Bobby Moore's versions of The Archies "Sugar, Sugar" and Lennon and McCartney's "Ob-La-Di, Ob-La-Da", both of which, in my opinion, are better than the originals. Then you have Jeff Astle's sentimental ballad "You're In My Arms", but the highlight of the album has to be the stirring rendition of "There'll Always Be An England" where the listener is treated to a few gems of wisdom from some of the squad, with the most informative being Alan Ball who lets us know that: "The climate and conditions will be against us."

He forgot to mention the old bill as well.

Staying with the beautiful game, I finally got to see West Brom in the flesh on 19th September 1970, when Dad took me to Highbury to see Arsenal humiliate us 6-2. The result didn't really matter to me that much, because the day was all about being close to the players that I'd only previously seen on TV or in magazines.

On the Monday after the game I took my match programme into school to show it off to my mates, but my balloon soon burst when one of them said: "Big deal, I get them all for nothing off of the dinner lady Mrs Friar."

Who turned out to be the mum of the Arsenal's director Ken Friar.

See what you get for showing off?

So, everything was going along quite nicely, when once again life decided that it should go tits up for me: Mum got offered a job running a cafe in Burnt Oak along with the chance of a nice place to live in the nearby Jewish paradise of Stanmore. I know at the start of the book I said I was trailer trash, but this particular piece of trash didn't really fancy moving again; but Mum thought it would be good for all of us, and so once again we moved. She was right about one thing, our new house in Du Cros Drive was a bit tasty, and had the added bonus of having Rabbis living either side of us, who took it in turns to invite us for dinner on Friday nights. Great food and such big portions.

Moving again meant I had to go through all the old bollocks of having to try and fit in at a new school, and this time I really was a fish out of water, because this one was posh. Fucking posh. I turned up for my first day at Aylward Primary School in my best psychedelic paisley shirt and matching cravat with Mum by my side doing that embarrassing thing that mums like to do, slicking your hair down with their freshly licked palm. The school's car park was full of Jags, Bentleys and Rollers, which was a bit of a culture shock for me because I was only used to seeing some geezer giving a pig one up the shitter. Once again I didn't really speak to anyone for the first few days, and I began to worry that it was going to be the same old story, but pretty soon things began to change when some of the kids started to mix with me, and within a couple of weeks I'd made quite a lot of new friends who didn't even seem to care about my disgusting taste in shirts.

I'd also arrived at the school at the right time because they'd just recently opened a brand new swimming pool funded by parent donations, which was a right touch because I loved swimming and I could now go whenever I liked. Then things got even better for me when the manager of the school football team saw me playing and immediately put me into the first team giving me the role of (in his words): "An aggressive midfield playmaker in the Nobby Stiles mode."

I'm not sure that's the best brief to give a young boy desperate to impress everyone in his new surroundings, and I have to say for a while I did go a little over the top, but after a couple of games I calmed it down a bit and started concentrating on more important things, like improving my passing and timing my runs into the box a little better. In no time I began to shine and at the end of my first season I was given the player of the year award.

I would train for an hour or so after school, before coming home to help myself to a couple of slices of Bakewell tart and then going back out again for a kickabout with my mates until 7.00pm, when Mum would come home from work to make me my ham, beans and chips.

One day while I was midway through my slice I turned on the radio to hear a song that would change my life forever: "Ride A White Swan" by T.Rex.

"Wear your hair long babe, you can't go wrong"

I'd never heard anything like it before.

I began putting on the radio as soon as I got in from school, in the hope that I would hear it again, but I needn't have worried because it seemed to be on all the time. Although I'd already bought lots of records I'd never felt the same kind of excitement of wanting to get those seven inches in my hand, and so when I woke up on Saturday I emptied my money box and went off to buy it. When I got back home I think I must have played it about twenty fucking times on the trot or at least enough for Mum to say: "Yes, it's lovely, but can't you play something else?"

And when I saw Marc Bolan singing it on *Top Of The Pops* it was a done deal. Not only did he have a unique sound, he also looked like no other pop star I'd ever seen before and so along with my friends from the Black Country it was the beginning of a lifelong love affair.

One of the kids I'd made friends with at my new school was a little Jewish kid called Lawrence Wainman. Now, I won't make any bones about it, I only became his mate because he was the owner of two full size goalposts in his very large garden. And while I'm being Mr Honest here, I might as well tell you that if I'd also known that this annoying little git's brother Phil (who would occasionally come out for a kickabout with us) was the same Phil Wainman who was producing The Sweet at this time and would later go on to work with The Sensational Alex Harvey Band and Generation X, well, I might not have been such a nasty little cunt towards him and maybe would've eased up a little bit on all the chopping and elbowing on him that the Aylward manager encouraged me to indulge in. But I didn't. Sorry mate x.

Every Saturday morning I'd sit looking out of my front room window like some ornamental cat, waiting for Dad's grey Vauxhall Viva to pull into our driveway to take me and Richard out for the day. When he arrived we would drive over to Harrow to watch Richard play football and afterwards go off to Edgware for a Wimpy and an afternoon's bowling.

I wasn't gonna mention this, but fuck it, I will. When we used to go for a Wimpy I would always have Wimpy and chips that cost 21p, but you could also get something called a Wimpy Brunch for 20p, which was the same thing but without the bun. Now, you tell me, what kind of tight bastard would go for that just to save a fucking penny? There, I've done it.

That's got me thinking, I wonder if there's ever been a Wimpy related anecdote/complaint/rant in any other ska/reggae musician's memoir?

Somehow, I doubt it, but I think now's the time for a food list...

NICK'S TOP TEN GRUB AS A KID.

1.   **Wimpy and Chips.**
2.   **Fish and Chips.**
3.   **Pie and Mash.**
4.   **Fray Bentos Steak and Kidney Pie.**
5.   **Birds Eye Crispy Cod Balls.**
6.   **Apple Fritters.**
7.   **Mince and Tatties.**
8.   **Fish in Milk.**
9.   **Beans on Toast.**
10. **Heinz Kidney Soup.**

Bollocks.

I've just read online that Manzes in Chapel Market are closing down after 106 years due to the crippling high business rates, and so they're doing what a lot of cockneys do and that's move to Essex (Braintree to be exact). That's a fucking long way to go to feed my pie and mash addiction, 48.7 miles to be exact. I know I could go to another of these emporiums of working class nosh that's a lot nearer but none of them are as good as the place I've been going to for fifty years.

"Goodbye to you my trusted friend"

There was one Saturday (24th April 1971 to be precise) when we changed our routine. It was the day after my birthday and Dad arrived slightly earlier than usual with an armful of presents for me that included:

A pair of brown hushpuppies.

Some brown French-pleat hipster trousers.

A cream and brown jumper.

Of course, I had to put them all on straight away, giving me a look I would describe as 'Jack Wilde's cooler younger brother' and then we were off, not to meet Richard, but to receive my biggest and best present of the day: a trip to The Hawthorns to see the Baggies play title chasing Arsenal.

The week before we'd turned over Leeds United at their own ground with Jeff scoring the winning goal, and so I was feeling pretty optimistic about the game.

I didn't know where I was going until we were halfway up the M1 and Dad pulled an envelope out of his pocket (which I was half hoping was an information pack on how to avoid getting secondary cancer because I could barely see the fucking thing in the smoke-filled motor) but eventually I saw the letter was on West Bromwich Albion headed notepaper and went something along the lines of: "Thanks Nick, I'm sorry, but it won't be possible for you and your son to meet Jeff and the boys after the game but here's a couple of complimentary tickets for the match."

I wasn't even that sad that I couldn't get to meet my idol (he was probably too busy dashing off home to put up a garden shed with his missus) because I wasn't expecting any of it, I was just happy with having some WBA headed notepaper.

We arrived at the ground about an hour before the game and parked up outside the pub opposite the stadium, but disaster struck when I stepped out of the car straight into a great big puddle staining and ruining my brand spanking new hushpuppies I'd had on for less than three fucking hours.

The old man could see I was upset and tried to console me, only I don't think that "It's only a pair of shoes, you wee poof" was the way I would've gone about it.

I suppose I could have taken a youthful first stab at self-harm, but at ten years old what the fuck was I gonna do? Listen to Uriah Heep while freebasing a Curly Wurly?

37

We went for something to eat in a cafe and bumped into another one of my so-called 'Uncles' Clem Cattini, one of my dad's best mates and a lifetime Arsenal supporter. Clem is one of the greatest drummers ever and for those of you who don't know him he was a member of The Tornados, who had a number one hit in 1962 with the wonderful Joe Meek produced single "Telstar" and was the session drummer of choice in the 60s and 70s, playing on hundreds of top thirty records, many of them number ones.

Do you wanna know a few of them?

Johnny Kidd	**"Shaking All Over"**
The Walker Brothers	**"The Sun Ain't Gonna Shine Anymore"**
Tom Jones	**"Green, Green Grass Of Home"**
Chris Farlow	**"Out Of Time"**
Love Affair	**"Everlasting Love"**
Chicory Tip	**"Son Of My Father"**

And the list goes on and on…

Clem was another one of those grown-ups who'd always slip me a little bit of silver whenever I saw him and since it was my birthday (ish) I think I may have got 50p that day. Even though he's now in his 80s he still does the occasional gig, and a couple of years ago he turned up playing on Paul Weller's brilliant "Wake Up The Nation" album.

Anyway, back to the game, what can I say about it? Well, how about this: it was so good that for ninety minutes I forgot all about my devastating shoe incident, but I still feel the 2-2 score line flattered the Gunners a little bit. Jeff gave their defence a really hard time that day and was responsible for what they call in modern day football speak the 'assists' on both of our goals, one for Asa Hartford (who also scored at the wrong end) and the other for the legend that was and is Tony 'Bomber' Brown.

On the way home, this tired but extremely happy nine-year-old fell asleep for the whole journey, and if you're wondering how I can remember the match so well after all these years, it's not because I've got a great memory it's just in the last few years there's been a wonderful new invention called YouTube.

My own football 'career' took a big step forward when I signed for Tansley FC, a local club formed in 1887, who had quite an illustrious history; well, that's what their manager told me. We trained on Thursday nights and played our matches on Sunday mornings. Once again, I was playing with and against players a little bit older than me (some even had pubic hair!) but I never ever worried about that, I just saw it as a challenge that I had to overcome and I settled into the team quickly and soon started adding goals to my game. I moved from midfield to play up front, given the number 9 shirt just like my hero Jeff, except he didn't have to play in a hideous orange kit that looked like a household duster.

My goals helped the team to second position in the league that year but that's not what sticks out in my mind from my time at Tansley. This is:

One night after training me and Richard began our usual mile long walk home from the club up Honeypot Lane which would usually take us about fifteen minutes, but on this night, it would end up being nearer two hours. Why? Well let me tell you. It was pissing down. And I mean seriously pissing down. I don't know why we didn't just ask one of the coaches to give us a lift home, which I'm sure wouldn't have been a problem, but we didn't. Youthful enthusiasm, or just a couple of mugs, you decide. Anyway, we were a couple of minutes into our journey when Mr Thunder and Mr Lightning decided to show their unwanted faces and that's when things started to get really scary because every time we saw a flash of lightning we ran and hid under the nearest tree we could find, shitting ourselves in the process.

I'm now reliably informed that this is the worst thing you can do when lightning-strikes. Not shitting yourself but standing underneath a tree.

The only thing going through my mind that night was how the Spurs player, John White, had died after being struck by lightning on a golf course.

Long story short, we eventually got ourselves safely indoors and I have a crystal-clear recollection of drying myself off in front of the fire watching Rod Stewart and The Faces kick a ball around the *Top of The Pops* studio performing "Maggie May".

"All I needed was a friend to lend a guiding hand"

It's funny how music always seems to play the biggest part in any of my memories.

Marmalade	"Cousin Norman"
Labi Siffre	"It Must Be Love"
John Kongos	"Tokoloshe Man"

Then, out of the blue, I was on my way back to Harringay to live with my dad. For fuck's sake, how many times do you want me to move? Nick, Nick, the yo-yo kid. Apparently, he'd convinced Mum that we'd have a better standard of life with him, and so wanting the best for us she let us go.

Well, now my mind was all over the fucking place. I had kind of settled in Stanmore, but I have to say the idea of going back to Woodberry Down was a buzz for me and so once again, and thankfully for the last time, I packed my bag and headed back to what turned out to be the beginning of a quite unconventional life with the old man.

Things started really well when I received an unbelievable reception from all my mates who were waiting at the school gates for me to arrive. I was greeted with what we used to call 'a bundle', which basically means everyone jumps on top of you, getting in as many punches as they can before you either manage to break away or they just start feeling sorry for you. I have to say, I don't remember the latter ever happening.

Mr Watts was also happy to see me again. He shook my hand and said: "Right, now you're back we can have a decent bloody team again."

And from the look in his eyes I could that tell that he meant every word of it.

To rubber stamp the deal, a few days later he pulled me out of a class and drove me to Harringay, in his slightly less than mint condition red E-type Jag, to Duvall's, which was a great little sports shop, to help him choose a new kit for the team. Now, I bet you all think that I chose a blue and white striped kit, so we could be just like the Baggies, but you'd be wrong. Woodberry Down would now be playing their games in a beautiful claret and blue shirt, with white shorts and claret socks with blue hoops. Think West Ham away, with a hint of Burnley home (both circa 1970/71) and you're there. The honour of being made team captain, and being asked to make a big decision on something like the choice of our kit, really did make me feel special and I think it showed in my performances on the pitch.

And so, the lesson is?

Treat people well, and they should respond positively.

When I said that this was the start of an unconventional life, what I meant was that with Dad working away a lot we could now do whatever the fuck we wanted. I have to point out that he didn't just leave us on our Jack Jones to fend for ourselves. We were left in the care of our Auntie Claire (another false relative), a proper old cockney, who lived on the tenth floor of a tower block in Rowley Gardens with her son George. Anytime Dad was away, Richard and I would stay there with her.

Although Claire's son's name was George, everyone on the manor called him 'Georgie Boy'. I can only imagine this was because he was a young, long-haired, randy milkman, who would stand at the bar in the Finsbury Park Tavern telling anyone who'd listen all about his sexual conquests with all the 'well up for it' housewives on his milk round.

I'd like to say that Georgie boy was just a sad cunt, dishing out a load of old cobblers, but he wasn't, and how do I know that?

Because Georgie Boy gave me a job helping him on his round and there were many occasions when I would have to sit in the float, waiting ages for him to go and 'collect some money' that was apparently owed to him. It's funny how all his debtors looked like clippies from *On the Buses*, but I suppose it was 1972 and the whole of Britain was bang at it. The streets of London were full of a never-ending stream of crumpet in hot-pants, riding on chopper bikes. Really? Don't be a cunt.

America	**"A Horse With No Name"**
Colin Blunstone	**"Say You Don't Mind"**
Gilbert O' Sullivan	**"Alone Again (Naturally)"**

Let me tell you about my near miss with Big-Time Showbiz:

One day my old man asked if I would be interested in singing on stage at one of his shows. "Anytime you fancy," replied the cheeky little cunt in blue-tartan flares and a penny-collared shirt.

"It's with Dot at The Palladium."

Gulp.

The next word to come out of my gob was the considerably less cheeky sounding: "Fine."

And so, for the next few weeks, I sat at the piano with him rehearsing for something that would have been the biggest moment in my life. As much as I try, I can't remember what song it was I was going to be doing. It may have been "Send In The Clowns", but don't hold me to it. I must have nailed it though, because I got a rare compliment when Dad said he thought I was good to go.

A couple of days later I received what was to be my first, but by no means last, kick in the bollocks from that world we call show. After another day of boring everyone at school stupid, with boasts of how I was gonna go on to a life of fame and fortune, I was brought right back down to earth when he told me that my services were no longer required. To be fair, he did look as gutted as I felt, but at the time that really wasn't much of a payoff. I found out that my place was to be taken by an annoying little Scots bastard, by the name of Neil Reid, who had won *Opportunity Knocks* the year before and had a record, "Mother Of Mine", riding high in the charts. Obviously, I can see why they chose him over me, bums on seats etc, but it was the start of a dark couple of weeks for me. Even when Dad bought me the pair of ridiculous green platform shoes I'd been going on about for ages, as some kind of runner-up prize, I was still down in the dumps, and just to twist the knife a little more, when I went along to watch rehearsals for the show, guess who was sitting in front of me?

You got it. Hughie Green's little pal.

It did cross my mind to give his seat a good kick, but fuck it, he wasn't to blame, was he? I was just about to slip out and take a walk down Carnaby Street, which was something I used to do whenever I went to The Palladium with the old man, when I witnessed Dad doing something that, even as a young boy, I found really embarrassing.

He was taking the orchestra through another run through of "My Way" or some other big ballad that Dot's mostly gay audience would lap up when he gave the signal for them to stop playing. He turned to the only female musician on the firm, a cellist, and asked her: "Tell me darling, do you just play that thing to have something to rub between your legs?" Cue for the whole orchestra to have total hysterics.

You're a class act Dad. A class act.

Of course, when I heard Neil Reid sing that night I thought he was a pile of shit, and that I would've been a million times better. But then I would, wouldn't I? No offence mate, I'm sure you're a nice guy.

Showbiz Fact 1... Neil Reid now lives in Blackpool and works as an Independent Financial Advisor. Showbiz Fact 2... I still have never performed at The Palladium.

I'm in shock. Double shock.

I've just heard that the actor Geoffrey Bayldon, who played *Catweazle* and appeared in Marc Bolan's film *Born to Boogie,* has just passed away at the age of ninety-three, which is a pretty good innings, so maybe shocked isn't quite the right way to describe my feelings on his passing, but it certainly is for the next bit of tittle tattle I've just received: Holloway Prison is no more.

"They took my baby to Holloway jail"

Just in case you don't know, Holloway was an all-female prison just up the road from my house, and any time I've gone past the place in the last forty years I can't help but think about another pearl of Scottish wisdom Dad passed on to me in my youth: "If you ever need your hole, go and stand outside Holloway Prison at eight in the morning, because that's when they release the prisoners and they're fucking desperate for it."

Some top quality parental advice there.

Anyway, back to the world of precocious showbiz talent.

The year ended with another horrible little brat, Jimmy Osmond, grabbing the Christmas number one with his "Long Haired Lover From Liverpool" pile of shit keeping Marc's "Solid Gold Easy Action" off the top spot, but who ever said there was any justice in pop music? The public gets what the public wants.

Now, pass me a Caramac and a copy of *Popswop*.

Time machine please…

43

(I WISH IT WAS) 1973

I wish it was 1973,
I-Roy, U-Roy, Byron Lee, Al Capone and Lee Perry on my
radio,
I wish it was 1973,
Harry J and Dennis Brown, The Pioneers go round and round
on my stereo,
On my stereo.

Put the needle on the track,
Let the music take you back,
To a place I wanna go with you.

I wish it was 1973,
I-Roy, U-Roy, Byron Lee, Al Capone and Lee Perry on my
radio,
I wish it was 1973,
Harry J and Dennis Brown, The Pioneers go round and round
on my stereo,
On my stereo.

It's a 45 attack,
Let the music take you back,
To a place I wanna go with you.

I wish it was 1973,
I Roy, U Roy, Byron Lee, Al Capone and Lee Perry on my radio,
I wish it was 1973,
Harry J and Dennis Brown, The Pioneers go round and round
on my stereo.

I could've just included a few memories from 1973 in the previous chapter, but as my song "(I Wish It Was) 1973" is a favourite of mine, I thought it deserved one all of its own. It's funny to think that Britain joined the Common Market on the first day of that year, and, as I'm sitting here today, our unelected, leather trousered sourpuss Prime Minster, Theresa May has just triggered Article 50 to begin our 'Brexit' from the European Union.

Although this is all very important stuff, it's not as important as me getting dipped for my iPad by some thieving little cunt on the bus as I made my way back home from the studio today. I had untold precious memories on that thing.

Forget it mate, let's go back to an easier and more gentler time.

Hold on Nick, you say that, but wasn't 1973 when you got mugged? The year when four lads from Clissold Park School stole your Rolf Harris Stylophone? Yes, that's true, you heard right, I was mugged for a fucking Stylophone!

I took it to school that day because the instrument had become so popular with all the kids there that a club for owners of this state of the art machine was now being held in the music room every Tuesday lunchtime, and so of course, after I got mugged, I could no longer be a member, and who knows what might have been if I hadn't? Maybe a few of us would've got together and gone on to form a band called The Stylotones and have a few novelty chart hits, but now thanks to that thieving gang of four, another one of my early breaks into Showbiz had been thwarted.

I'm joking of course.

I have to say writing this book is certainly good for jogging my memory, because I've just remembered I wasn't mugged once that year, it happened twice; however, on the second occasion, I did manage to get back what was taken from me. Here's what happened...

I was on my way home from Roy's Records with a copy of "Aladdin Sane" on the day of its release under my arm. I can only assume I must've turned down the offer of a plastic bag to put it in because I wanted to walk the streets of Harringay holding it like some sort of hip badge of honour to show everyone what a rebel I was, but all it succeeded in doing was to encourage some lanky, skinny, greasy ginger-haired fucker on a chopper to cycle up beside me and say: "Oi is that the bum-boy's record you got there? What are you? A fucking queer or what?"

"Nah mate. I just like Bowie."

"Well, I'm having it."

I tried to leg-it, but he grabbed hold of me and gave me a dig that put me on the deck.

When I got home, Dad could see I was in pieces and so I told him what had happened. His response was: "You wee poof, you couldn't fight your way out of a paper bag."

So, in what? Ten minutes? I'd been robbed of my album and had my sexuality questioned twice! In the old man's defence, he did offer to buy me a replacement, which was an improvement on the previous year when he wouldn't give me the money to buy "Metal Guru" until I could tell him what a guru was. It was a mental torture that went on for a couple of days until he eventually handed the money over to me, but thinking about it, if I was as smart as the teachers at school said I was, why didn't I just look it up in a fucking dictionary?

Anyway, he told me he was going out to meet a mate at a boozer in Newington Green, so I went for a ride with him in the motor to try and forget all about it, and guess what? On our way there, I spotted that thieving little cunt with my album in his hand sitting on a bench with a couple of his mates, laughing their heads off. "Dad that's the kid that mugged me!"

He looked over at them and started laughing.

"Can't you go over there and get it back for me?"

His laughter continued.

A few minutes later I was sitting at a table in The Royal Oak on Green Lanes, with a Coke and a packet of crisps chaser, while my old man chatted away to his pal behind the bar. The pub door opened and in walked my teenage ginger mugger, straight into the arms of his extremely pissed off landlord father, who took him upstairs (by his hair) and gave him a hiding that you could clearly hear downstairs even with The Dubliners' "Seven Drunken Nights" playing loudly on the jukebox, and that's when the penny dropped why Dad was laughing so much when I pointed the kid out to him.

As we were leaving the boozer Dad's mate handed me back my copy of "Aladdin Sane" along with a quid telling me his mugger son wouldn't be getting his pocket money that week. When I got home I sat cross legged in my bedroom and played the album over and over again, something I'm still doing forty-four years later.

"It's a crash course for the ravers"

46

1973 was also the year I began a one-man crusade of trying to impress the girls at my school by standing on a bench in the playground at break times, doing impersonations of Marc Bolan, Noddy Holder and Gary Glitter. At first, I was just playing to a handful of gigglers, but word quickly spread about this idiot pop offspring of Mike Yarwood, and pretty soon my numbers were well into double figures. It was on one of my bench performances that I came up with my first original composition: "Dume Batty". On second thoughts, original might not be the best way to describe it, because it was just my bastardised version of the French song "Mammy Blue", but it became so popular with my fellow pupils that it became an after lunch ritual for them to march around the playground singing it, with the "Dume Pussy" verse always being sung the loudest.

NICK'S TOP FIVE GLAM ROCK SINGLES

Before I give you my glam rundown, I have to let you know that I don't consider Bolan, Bowie, Roxy or Mott to be in any way glam: in my book, to qualify as a serious glam artist you have to look like a brickie in drag.

1. Slade   "Squeeze Me Pleeze Me"
2. The Sweet   "The Ballroom Blitz"
3. Gary Glitter   "I'm The Leader Of The Gang (I Am)"
4. Iron Virgin   "Rebel Rule"
5. Jook   "Bish, Bash, Bosh"

I finally got the chance to be like David Watts and lead the school team to victory, when we played Tyssen in the Gaffney Trophy, a cup named after the bloke who designed it. The final was held over two legs, the first at our home ground in Finsbury Park, played on the same day T.Rex released "20th Century Boy". The whole school turned out to see the game finish 2-2, with yours truly grabbing a brace. It would've been a hat-trick if the scissor kick I attempted in the last few minutes had connected with the ball instead of some poor bastard's head, leaving him on the deck with untold claret running down his nut.

At the end of the game, their manager ran on to the pitch and started pushing me and accusing me of dangerous play, which encouraged all his team to come over and encircle me giving it the big-un about what they were gonna do to me in the next match. Let's just remember that we are talking about eleven-year-olds here, and for fuck's sake I never did it deliberately. Their centre half was just doing what he was supposed to, which was be brave and get his head in where it counted. Only the month before, it had been me on the receiving end of a boot that caused my eye to swell, and I never complained like a pussy, even though I had to walk around for a couple of weeks looking like Johnny fucking Kidd!

To calm the stormy waters, Mr Watts made the decision to put me on the bench for the return leg two weeks later on the cinder pitch in Springfield Park. I told him I didn't think it was fair and even tried to play the 'I'm the captain' card, but none of it seemed to work even though I knew he wanted me to play.

"Look, I've been told by the Headmaster that you have to be punished and that means you being sub, but listen, no matter how the game's going I will bring you on at half time."

I'm gonna spare you all the *Roy of the Rovers* stuff and just give you the result.

Second Leg - First Half: Woodberry Down 0 - Tyssen 2
Second Leg - Second Half: Woodberry Down 3 - Tyssen 2

Fuck it I can't!

They were all over us in the first half, and the kid brought in to replace me was rubbish. It wasn't his fault; he obviously wasn't going to have the same understanding I had with my striking partner Peter Hines, who I played alongside not only for the school, but for the scout team as well. I say partner, but to be honest Peter was no team player, he was a boy who was very much out for himself. Fuck it, let's be absolutely honest here, Peter was a greedy little bastard, who would only ever pass the ball when he absolutely had to, but I will also say he had skills way beyond his years and when he had the ball no one could get it off of him.

So, I came on for the second half and we were 4-2 down, sorry I meant 4-3, because after only two minutes on the pitch I broke through their defence and around the keeper to side-foot it into the net, a move that in my mind was just like Bestie had done five years before against Benfica. Now, before you think I'm gonna tell you that I banged in another couple and was carried off the pitch on my team-mates' shoulders at the end of the game, well sorry, I'm not. Peter scored the other two goals that won us the Gaffney Cup, which meant as team captain I got to receive the trophy in assembly from the same wanker who'd made me miss half the fucking match just because he didn't understand the way the games played.

By the way, after a short spell in the army Peter went on to play for Dundee United before going on to play in Japan, which I think is pretty impressive! Wherever you are Peter, I love you mate even if you did like to keep the ball to yourself x.

Now, what else was happening at this time?

Well, Mum left Burnt Oak and opened 'The Butty Bar', a sandwich bar underneath The Arches in Charing Cross, which meant I got to see her more than just on her Sunday visits to the house.

And oh yeah, I went away with the school for two weeks to Marchants Hill in Surrey and as soon as I arrived I fell in love with the place, which was described to me as an 'adventure centre.' It looked exactly like the camp 5C went to in the *Please Sir* film: lots of wooden huts surrounded by some really beautiful woodland; and because three other schools were staying there at the same time as us I had plenty of Sharons and Maureens to try and grab hold of.

"Cum on feel the noize, girls grab the boys"

Away from all the flower-spotting and bird-watching a football tournament was arranged for all four schools to take part in, but our matches were so one sided (in our favour) it actually started getting a bit boring for me. Cut to the chase: we won the tournament and I scored lots and lots of goals.

When I wasn't being Woodberry Down's very own *Roy of the Rovers* in the day at night I was playing the role of 'disc jockey' at the camp disco. Yeah, I was a right little Peter Marinello, with a touch of the Tony Blackburn's.

Fucking hell it took me minute there to think of a DJ who hasn't been 'outed' in the last few years for some kind of sexual nastiness.

While I was spinning the discs, boys would come up and ask for requests: "Have you got any Gary Glitter?" "Play some Slade mate."

I think what they really meant was: "Will you stop playing T. Rex all the time!"

The girls were a completely different gravy though. I can safely say it was through their requests that I noticed the big difference between black

49

and white girls and it was as simple as this:

Black girls liked The Jackson 5.

White girls liked The Osmonds.

Now, I wouldn't normally generalise like this, and obviously there were girls who crossed over to the other camp, but to me that seemed to be the way it was.

In every other department, they were exactly the same. They all bought *Jackie* and *Mirabelle* magazine and dressed in smock tops and wore platform shoes but, when it came down to their musical affections, as that annoying old bastard used to say at the start of the TV show *Hart to Hart*: "It was murder!"

I know where I stood though, and that was firmly in camp Jackson, although I have to say, in hindsight, The Osmonds weren't half as bad as I thought they were back then, and while "Crazy Horses" might not be "I Want You Back", it's still a great track, especially Donny's wild futuristic synth sound (which I sampled and used twenty years later), and in fact, a year later, I made a few bob out of those smiling Mormons when me and a couple of mates managed to 'obtain' two hundred tickets for one of their London shows. I think they might have been on the wane by then, because we only managed to sell a few before we dumped them. Whereas, when we pulled the same stunt a few years later for a Bay City Rollers gig we got rid of all them within a few days.

Anyway, back to the black/white thing.

If you ask me about where I was brought up and what my school life was like, I'm happy to say that it was a very mixed area, which culturally played no small part in helping me do what I do today.

"I was well into reggae back then." Over the years I've had a million and one people telling me that but my experiences of the time was that it was actually quite hard to get to hear much of it back then. Of course, the odd chart hit would get radio play, and you had magazines like *Black Music* and *Blues & Soul* where you could find out what Dandy Livingstone or Nicky Thomas were up to that week, but the truth was that in the mainly-white-run media, reggae was considered novelty music, to be filed next to Clive Dunn's "Grandad" or "Ernie" by Benny Hill.

I mean why would anyone want to sit and listen to that when you have 'proper music' like Black Sabbath's "Paranoid" to freak out to? Why indeed…

And so, although I didn't know it at the time my future was being shaped by where I lived amongst friends who were giving me a musical education I was never gonna get from *Melody Maker* or the *NME*. My mates were my mates and the colour of their skin wasn't important and thankfully, because of that upbringing, I'm still like that today. If you're a cunt, you're a cunt, not a black cunt or a white cunt, you're just a cunt.

Cunts aside (that sounds like an old Leslie Phillips film), playing DJ gave me a head start over all my mates when it came to chatting up birds and on the last night of the trip I just bunged on an Al Green album that allowed me enough time to get my arse out from behind the deck (note the word deck; my equipment was an old Dansette with a huge speaker attached) and get in a few slow dances with some of the girls who'd been giving me the eye. Looking back at it now it really was a lovely time, where every innocent kiss you stole counted as something very special.

And then the dream was over.

Because it was now time for me to leave the warm, friendly, loving environment of junior school and make the giant step up to the big bad Secondary Modern.

On my last day there I took part in all the usual fun and games. You know the sort of thing; uniforms being destroyed, kids pelting each other with flour and eggs, and the one that always makes me smile, girls hugging you saying their tearful goodbyes: "I'm really gonna miss you Nick." Well, that's sweet of you, but it is only gonna be six weeks before we all see each again, and come to think of it, we'll probably meet up in the holidays.

The person I was really going to miss though was my teacher and guiding light John Watts who just a year later tragically passed away after falling under a train late one night at Manor House station. God bless you sir you were my kind of teacher x.

Linda Lewis	"Rock A Doodle Doo"
Medicine Head	"One And One Is One"
First Choice	"Smarty Pants"

And so I had six weeks, six long, hot, summer weeks to get used to the idea that things were going to be a little different from now on, especially when I received all the usual elder brother scare stories: "Look, if you're lucky on the first day the fifth-formers will maybe just stick your head down the bogs. It happens to everyone, it's a kind of initiation ceremony, but I've gotta tell you, that if they don't like the look of you, there's a chance you might get a bumming from some the prefects."

I'd already heard all the 'head down the loo' stuff from some of my older mates, but a bumming? That's upping the game a little bit, isn't it? Don't get me wrong, I wasn't that stupid, I'm sure that if there was a bit of underage anal going on in the toilets of a London Secondary Modern I would've read about it in *The Sun* or seen it on *Nationwide*, but you never know do you…

It was bad enough that I couldn't get the Barathea blazer I thought would make me look like the ultra-smooth Dick Stuart-Clark from *Doctor in Charge* in my size but instead had to make do with some fucking old woolly rent-a-tent thing ("You'll grow into it son"). It certainly looked like the next few months were going to be a very long uphill climb for me.

Here's a couple of summer holiday randoms:

I bunked in to see the film version of *Love Thy Neighbour* at Turnpike Lane ABC. I think it was also the same day I went to see Arsenal beat Man Utd 3-0 at Highbury but one thing I'm definitely sure about is that it was a very hot Saturday morning in August. After the first film (oh yeah back then we used to get two films, and an usherette) I went for a quick slash, before settling down to watch what was billed as 'The funniest film ever to hit the big screen.' Why do the words 'trades description' quickly spring to mind?

Anyway, I was mid-waz, when a young black kid came up and asked me if I was looking forward to seeing the film, but before I even had the chance to answer, he put his face close to mine and said: "Do you wanna kiss me?"

I tried to make a joke of it and said: "Can't you wait until after I've finished having a slash before asking?"

He didn't look that threatening, or aggressive. Truth be told he looked like he had learning… no, fuck all that that PC shit, he looked fucking mental.

After zipping up my bright yellow dungarees I made my way towards the door (I must have been shitting it a bit because I didn't even stop to wash my hands) at which point he put his arm on my shoulder and repeated his question… twice. Now in my book, that's taking 'love thy neighbour' a little bit too far.

I could say I turned around to gave him a 'Clint Eastwood' stare, telling him to get out of town, but that would be fibbing, because the truth is... I screamed in his face: "Fucking leave me alone!"

And ran out of the door, back to my seat, not the seat I was in before, but one next to someone who I thought looked like a responsible grown up!

"Love thy neighbour, walk up and say, 'How be ya?'"

I mentioned Arsenal a minute ago; well how about this for a sporting event that would never be allowed to happen in today's fat-cat, big-money world of premiership football. Less than twenty yards from my front door stood Finsbury Park, and that summer some bright spark came up with the brilliant idea of holding a charity cricket match between Arsenal and Spurs there, giving the fans a chance to mingle with all the players and get their autographs.

But that's not all, because, get this, we were also promised there would a handful of stars from the world of showbiz in attendance, with Mike and Bernie Winters' names being mentioned as a definite possibility.

See what I mean? Close your eyes and try to imagine Olivier Giroud and Harry Kane having a drink with Ant and Dec in a beer tent chatting to a load of pissed-up fans about their team's chances in the forthcoming season. I bet you can't. But that's what I saw Charlie George and Pat Jennings doing that afternoon, because it was me they were doing it with. The only difference being, I wasn't pissed, but there were plenty of supporters there who were, and it didn't just stop with them, because after the match (I can't remember who won) I saw the players getting stuck into the odd bevvy or four. When John Radford obliged me with his autograph he had a pint in one hand and a fag in the other, but we are talking about a time when there was a good chance you might bump into one of your heroes on his way to the match on public transport!

It was a day I'll always remember although one thing has been on my mind ever since then... Where the fuck were Mike and Bernie Winters?

So, do you want the good news, or the bad news?

Let's go for the good news first. I didn't get my head stuck down the bogs on my first day at 'big school' or more importantly my bottom interfered with.

The bad news?

From the moment he set eyes on me my new form teacher Mr O' Hagen treated me like a complete and utter cunt, and I think it had something to do with the fact that he'd also been Richard's teacher a couple of years before. He definitely gave me the impression that maybe my big brother hadn't exactly been the model student he'd led us all to believe he was. So right from day one my card was well and truly marked.

Another downer for me was that Woodberry Down was very much a rugby school, with football coming in a very poor second. Rugby didn't interest me at all, but how about this for some fucked up teacher logic? When the head of the sports department heard that I was a talented footballer the wanker put me straight into the school rugby team, and even though I tried to convince him that I was totally shit at the game, he wasn't having any of it. As far as he was concerned, a ball was a ball, whatever the shape, and if you can kick and run with it you can hold and run with it.

What a stupid prick.

But at least I still had the scouts to play for, and I'd also been asked by Parkside, my local youth club, if I was interested in playing for them. The problem was, I'd already been asked by another team, Clissold Rangers, to join them, and I'd said yes, and as Clissold played in the same league as Parkside, this was to cause me untold grief at home, because when I told the old man I'd said yes to playing for a team called Clissold Rangers he went fucking mental: "No son of mine will ever play for a team called Rangers, not Clissold Rangers, Queens Park Rangers or the fucking Texas Rangers!"

Something told me I may have touched upon a slightly delicate subject close to his heart.

Our conversation went something like this... "There is another side that wants me to play for them."

"Who are they?"

"Parkside, you know, the youth club at the top of Rowley Gardens."

"Well that's who you're going to play for laddie."

And he was right, because that's exactly who I ended up playing for, and here's the reason why: on most days, if the old man wasn't working, you'd usually find him in the Finsbury Park Hotel, getting pissed with a few of his drinking buddies, and one of them just happened to be the Parkside manager, and it was on one of these days over a few afternoon whiskies that Dad told him his team were going to change their name to

Parkside CELTIC, and from now on were going to be playing in green and white.

This wasn't just pissed talk. The old man had the bit between his teeth and it wasn't long before Parkside took delivery of twelve brand new green and white kits, courtesy of Dad's old friend Jock Stein, and so Parkside F.C. became Parkside Celtic F.C.

It wasn't hard to attract players to play for us, because I invited all my mates from the school team along to the trials and pretty soon it was: North London League here we come. Our matches were played on Sundays in Regents Park, either at 11.00am or 3.00pm. I preferred a morning kick off, because Mum came to see me on Sundays and if the game was in the afternoon I didn't get to spend very long with her.

Most of our team were under the illusion that we'd stroll through all our games just like we'd done as juniors, but we couldn't have been more wrong. The difference now was we were playing teams aged between eleven and fourteen, and at that age there can be a huge gap physically, and so it took us a few weeks to get into our stride; but when we did we began climbing up the league, finishing third in our first season.

Unfortunately, at the same time as this, I was becoming a junkie...

A vinyl junkie.

I started bunking off school just so I could spend endless hours browsing, buying and nicking from every record shop I went to. It was an addiction that started off as a local one, but it wasn't long before I started taking regular red-rover trips into the West End, which also meant me having to forge all my teachers' signatures on the report form I always seemed to be on, but it was well worth it. I mean, why the fuck would I want to be stuck in a classroom learning French, when I could be out trying to have it away with the latest Roxy Music album?

"Your skin is like vinyl, the perfect companion"

There were quite a few places in Harringay where you could pick up vinyl and none were better than Divine Sales, a gaff run by the Divine Light Movement. It wasn't just a record shop though, it was more of a glorified junk shop selling anything from books and clothes to furniture and of course everyone's favourite bric-a-brac. But what I was interested in was the contents that were for sale in the dark and grubby room at the back of the shop... records.

Divine Sales was like no other shop I've even known. For a start when you took your purchases up to the counter they would actually try and barter you down! And how about this for a touch? In one afternoon there, I picked up "Desdemona" by John's Children, the 1972 T.Rex Christmas flexidisc and a handful of Who singles on Track, all in mint condition, for a pound! It almost made me feel bad about all the stuff I had tucked away in my jumper!

My next port of call would be Berry's, which once again wasn't a record shop: it sold musical instruments (we had one of their pianos at home), but they did have five or six racks full of mid-price compilations like "Motown Chartbusters", "Tighten Up" or the latest *Top of The Pops* album that no self-respecting music fan would ever buy, not even to knock one out over the bird on the cover.

The one proper record shop in Harringay was Roy's and fuck me was it tiny. I think the only smaller one I've ever seen was just down the road in Finsbury Park, but I'll get to that place later. The owner of Roy's was a lovely guy called… Roy (no surprise there), and let me tell you the man was an absolute diamond. He knew I was Bolan freak and so he let me have all the promo posters of Marc the reps gave him, giving him immunity from my thieving little hands.

Anyone of my age who shares my addiction will know that back then a record shop wasn't just somewhere where you bought music, it was a community centre for the kind of people (I say people, but I mean men) who wanted to spend hours talking to strangers about their favourite band or gigs they'd been to. I tried to join the club but to be honest with you, back then I was the sort of cunt who'd spurn possible friendships just because he didn't like what he saw in their record collection.

"But why don't you wanna be mates with me?"

"I just can't be friends with someone who owns a New Seekers album."

Dad had begun dating some toffee-nosed, middle-class bint called Iris who was Dot Squires' chiropodist, and I didn't take to her at all. What's that old saying? 'Opposites attract.' Well fuck me, you couldn't find two more different people than those two; maybe he was her bit of rough. And of course, I didn't want any Mum replacements hanging around. I suppose, at that age, I just didn't understand that in life people do split up and go on to have new partners.

I'll tell you another thing as well…

I certainly didn't fancy spending Christmas with her, but that's what I had to do that year. She had two sons a bit older than me whose only topic of conversation seemed to be about joining the old bill as soon as they left school, so it's safe to say that they weren't really the kind of people I wanted to share a turkey leg with or sit with watching the Christmas edition of *Top of The Pops*. Not even Noddy shouting "It's Christmas!" could cheer me up that year.

School sucked, WBA were relegated and the old man had a new bird. I wish it was 1973... well, maybe not.

It's the future

ROCKING ON RIDLEY ROAD

Put on your hat and don't be late,
Let's take the bus ride to E8,
Down to a place where time's stood still,
If you want some lime and fish to grill.

You can hear the music play,
All night and all day,
I can hear Rupie say,
SKANGA!

We're rocking on, rocking on Ridley Road.

I used to go back in the day,
To get my soul and my reggae,
As I walked along my Orange Street,
I look 'pon dem girls that looked so sweet.

We're rocking on, rocking on Ridley Road.

Asian, African and Jamaican,
Come together in Ridley Road,
Curry goat, swordfish, ackee and yellow yam,
You can get them in Ridley Road.

Mmm, the pleasure of sharing a candlelit bath with my brother.

No, that's not some kind of incestuous weirdo perversion of mine, it's just the first thing that springs to mind when I think about 1974.

Why?

Don't tell me you can't remember the three-day-week?

We had striking miners, a lack of fuel, and the most important thing, no fucking TV after 10.30pm. I could say that all these had some effect on my worsening behaviour at school, but that would be a load of old bollocks, although I do think you should hear the reason I gave for trying to murder ten of my classmates in Wales though, because it's a good 'un.

We were all in a minibus on our way to do some abseiling, when our teacher decided he needed to get something from the only shop in the area we were staying in, so he parked up at the top of a hill and told us he'd be back in a couple of minutes. For some reason, I thought the best way for me to spend this unsupervised time was to jump into the driver's seat, let the handbrake off and jump out to watch the vehicle travel down the hill and smash into a wall at the bottom, to the soundtrack of screaming children.

What the fuck was I thinking about?

And that was the question I was asked, not just by the teacher with us, but by our Deputy Headmistress, who wasn't best pleased that she'd had to leave the comfort of her London home to schlep up to some remote village in the middle of Wales. "Why did you do it, Welsh?"

"Well, last night I was watching this band called Sparks on *Top of The Pops* and they had a guy on keyboards who looked like Adolf Hitler and I think he may have taken over my brain."

I told you it was worth hearing.

"This town ain't big enough for both of us"

They didn't send me home, but they did book me an appointment with a child psychologist and when I went to see him it got me into even more shit. After we'd done the preliminaries, he invited me to lie down and so I did, choosing the floor over the bed he obviously meant, which definitely got the response I was quite obviously looking for: "Do you know anyone who takes drugs Nick?"

"Of course I do."

"Stay here, I'll be back in a minute."

And when he returned he had a couple of London's finest with him, who began questioning me, going around the houses for a bit before going for the money shot: "So, Nicholas do you know anyone who takes drugs?"

"Yeah, of course I do."

"Well, can you give us a few names?"

"If you want." (I gave it a few seconds before answering.)

"Mick Jagger, Jimi Hendrix, Janis Joplin."

They gave me the impression this was not what they wanted to hear, and proceeded to give me what used to be called a 'flea in the ear' and the psychologist never did manage to find out why I tried to kill everyone, although the answer was easy... I just liked acting like a stupid cunt.

It wasn't long after this that the school began suspending me on a regular basis for all my fun and games, and after the third time they called Dad up to tell him they wanted to get rid of me, leaving him with the choice of either packing me off to a boarding school or sending me to something called an Educational Guidance Centre in Hoxton. With a little help from me he chose the latter.

Hoxton in 1974 was nothing like it is today. It was a tough working-class area that was probably best known for its market and boxing club, and in those days there wasn't a fucking cereal café in sight. I quickly learned 'Educational Guidance Centre' meant 'school for nutters'; compared to these kids I was a fucking angel, but after a few weeks there I realised I'd had a touch.

This is how it worked: for every piece of good work you did there you were given a gold star, and at the end of the week the person with the most stars got a fiver. A fucking fiver! And because all the other kids there could barely read or write, I was walking home every week with a ching in my bin.

It was the easiest gig in town.

Besides gold star lessons, we'd also go on regular trips to the cinema, museums and twice a week to the Sobell Centre in Finsbury Park for ice-skating and football! I was only supposed to go there for a few months until I calmed down a bit, but let me tell you I didn't ever want to leave.

1974 was the year I really got the reggae bug.

I was now beginning to dig a little deeper into the genre and I started checking out the shops that sold more than just commercial reggae music. The place I went to most for this was Paul's For Music, opposite

Finsbury Park tube station, which without doubt was the smallest record shop that I've ever been to in my life. It was about the size of the bogs in The Tottenham pub in Oxford Street. No, hold on, let me think about that for a minute, no, it was a lot smaller than that.

I'd be there every Saturday afternoon, not just to buy the latest tunes, but to enjoy the excellent cabaret provided by the locals. I still can't understand how all the geezers in there could tell the good records from the bad so quickly and I would stand and watch in amazement as some rude boy, decked out in a polo neck and high waistband trousers, would ask the face behind the ramp to put a record on, and within seconds could decide if it was worth buying or not.

And do you know what?

They were always right. These people definitely knew their I-Roys from their U-Roys and so I would seek out their advice on what was what.

Another shop with a similar vibe was Rita and Benny's in Stamford Hill, which wasn't just a record shop because the lovely couple who ran it also had their own label; but I have to say the place that was the guv'nor for all things reggae was somewhere I stumbled upon by accident shortly after returning from that Marchants Hill trip. When I say stumbled upon, what I mean is I was on my way to meet a girl I'd met down there and when I jumped off the 141 I took a wrong turning and somehow ended up in the busy but wonderful world of Ridley Road market. Obviously I didn't want to be late to meet her but I kept on stopping at every stall that had reggae music coming out of what looked like huge homemade speakers. It was a little slice of Kingston just off the Kingsland Road.

Max Romeo	**"Sixpence"**
Matumbi	**"Funky Stuff"**
Dennis Alcapone	**"Wake Up Jamaica"**

Now I know you probably think that I forgot all about the girl and went shopping for vinyl instead, but you'd be well wrong because, boys and girls, I did the right thing and went straight round to pick her up for our date. Only now, the plan of going for a Wimpy had been replaced with me taking her back down to the market to watch me spunk the £4, or whatever it was that I had on me, on new singles; but as she was a big soul fan she didn't seem to mind that much.

I've gotta tell you this though…

When I was looking for her flat, a little girl stopped her skipping to ask me: "Are you looking for my sister Kim?"

"Yes, I am. How do you know that?"

"Because she told me to keep an eye out for a boy who looks like David Cassidy."

"I'm just a daydreamer walking in the rain"

My visits to Ridley Road became more and more frequent, because it was only a fifteen-minute walk to there from the 'Guidance Centre'. I began finding myself getting completely sucked in by the market's atmosphere, even though it wasn't all Orange Street because at least half the stalls down there sold fruit and veg run by either Cockneys or Africans.The only problem about going there after school was that it made me very late getting home, which I used to blame on the buses. My old man must've thought London had the worst bus service in the world!

By now I'm sure you've worked out that I had a fairly major obsession with records and record shops in general, and with that in mind allow me to tell you about two shops in Dalston Junction that stood next door to each other but in every other sense were worlds apart. Mr Music was where you went to buy chart music, but it also carried a huge selection of albums catering for every musical taste which I suppose was why it was always full. The shop next door (sorry I can't remember the name) was run by a lonely old hippie smelling of patchouli oil and had racks and racks full of unsold Byzantium, Snafu and Fumble albums, which I think gives you the main reason why it was always empty. To be honest I only went in there because I felt sorry for the geezer; alright, he may have stunk a bit, but he was obviously very committed to the progressive rock cause.

I think the lesson here is...

You can't make a decent living selling shit.

I now started bunking off from the Centre as well; even though I knew the consequences of doing it and being caught were a lot more serious at this last chance Educational Guidance Centre saloon than at Woodberry Down, I still did it. And when I got caught here was one word they always liked to throw at you...

Borstal.

But even the threat of that didn't seem to deter me. As far as I was concerned I was gonna do whatever I wanted to and fuck everyone. It wasn't that I missed my friends at Woodberry Down or anything like that, in fact I didn't care if I ever went back there again.

I dunno, maybe it was the glue.

The glue?

Maybe you don't know, but back in 1974, the hip thing to do was stand in a phone booth smelling of piss and stick your hooter into a crisp bag full of Evo. Now I'm not saying I was the big Evo Kinevel, to add a little bit of shock value to this book, I just tried it a couple of times and that was only because a lot of my pals were bang into it at the time.

So to recap: my life in the mid 70s mainly consisted of me bunking off school, indulging in casual solvent abuse, talking to lonely hippies in smelly record shops and finally, chatting up any bird that came within two feet of me. Which brings me nicely on to this slightly delicate subject...

Although I'd snogged loads of girls, and sometimes had even ventured the odd finger 'down south', I can tell you the exact date when I COULD have lost my virginity.

August 10th 1974.

While the football world was rocking to the news that Billy Bremner and Kevin Keegan had become the first players to be sent off at Wembley after a having a 'handbag' moment in the Charity Shield I was in Margate camping with some of Parkside's older boys and a youth leader that's just about to become an entry into this book and and a youth leader who I will call Mr X.

When you say 'could have' Nick, why didn't you?

Well, because I'd always imagined that when that big day eventually came, it was going to be with a girl I was going out with, or even just someone I really fancied, but it was definitely not going to be with Mr X, a youth club leader/stationery salesman in his early forties.

So, it was Saturday night and because most of the lads there were 16/17 they all went out to the nearest pub for a couple of beers, leaving me alone with Mr X. I'd been told that because I was the youngest one there I'd have to share a tent with him and so when the time came for me to get my head down for the night (slow down, this is serious) I jumped into my sleeping bag to try and get some kip. About twenty minutes later Mr X came in to the tent, got into his bag and put his arm around me with the words: "Give me a cuddle then."

I froze.

Now, this was someone I'd been alone in the company of quite a few times and he'd always been as good as gold; maybe the sun and sea air had fried his fucking brain a bit. Memory tells me I said, "No thanks" or something like that, and he took his arm off me, but a couple of seconds later it was back on again, only this time he was a lot closer to me and I could now feel something very hard poking near to my arse. Now it could've been his knee, but I'm pretty fucking sure it was his cock. I jumped out of my bag and ran into the field where, as luck had it, some of the lads were just returning from the pub; and do you know what the first thing one of them said to me was?

"Cuddles ain't been trying to snuggle up to you, has he?"

"No mate we were just having a laugh."

So there you have it: even though it seemed to be common knowledge amongst my 'mates' that the geezer was a fucking wrong 'un, and they all knew that I was sleeping in the same tent as the nonce, they never even bothered to tell me. They'd even given him the affectionate nickname of 'Cuddles'. It was just like that 'Pedo Kennedy' character in *The Inbetweeners*. A couple of them did say they'd give the cunt a kicking for me, but I just wanted to forget the whole thing, although I did take them up on their offer to stay with them in their tent; in fact, if I remember right, I don't think I left their side for the next two days.

I'm sure you won't be surprised to hear that Mr X left Parkside soon after that.

I was just happy that he'd pissed off, but thinking about it, there's no doubt in my mind that he probably just went on to another youth club and tried the same thing on with some other kid. But I'm not going to beat myself up about it, I was only twelve at the time so I wasn't to know that the right thing to do was tell to someone about it. And I never did tell anyone about it until thirty years later when I mentioned to Richard what had happened that night and his reply was a beauty: "Don't worry mate, he tried it on with me as well."

Fuck me that's weird, I just stopped writing for a minute to have a look on my Facebook page and the first thing I see is: "Colin Gregg, the bakery heir, has been jailed for thirteen years for abusing young boys over a period of thirty years, starting in 1963 while he was working as a teacher in the North East."

It's not just the act that repulses me, it's the abuse of privilege and position of trust. Stealing away a child's innocence. Cunt. That's the last fucking time I will ever buy a pasty from there.

Well, that's the obligatory 'I was nonced' story out the way, well not entirely, because I have another one coming along soon. I was also to be the receiver of even more cruelty in the form of 'Elder Brother Syndrome.'

EBS is a cruel disease that can creep up and strike its victims down virtually overnight, with the two main symptoms being 'hand-me-downs' and 'suffer-my-shit-music'. One minute you can be lying on your bed listening to "1000 Volts Of Holt", and the next your lugholes are being tortured by a triple album of complete bollocks courtesy of Yes. I can't tell you how many nights I spent crying under my eiderdown while big brother tried to molest and rape my musical taste-buds with Leo Sayer, Heart or The Alan Parsons Project, but somehow I managed to find the inner strength to fight the bastards off.

Even though the age-old ritual of receiving your big brother's hand-me-downs wasn't quite as bad as the music, it did mean that sometimes I became the owner of some faded, sweat-stained cheesecloth shirt, or a pair of flared Wrangler jeans, completely covered with apparently humorous slogans like: SMILE IF YOU'VE HAD IT TODAY.

While I was playing for Parkside Celtic, I would spend most nights of the week hanging out in the back room of the club where the girls danced around to the sound of Philadelphia on the juke box. All innocent stuff, but everyone knew as soon as the club leaders weren't around the lights would go down and the snogging would start.

"While the juke box plays our favourite songs"

I've gotta tell you this…

Parkside received some complimentary tickets from Radio One to go to a recording of *Quiz Kid*, which was a very popular music based quiz show at the time hosted by Alan 'Fluff' Freeman; exciting or what? On the evening of the show, the youth leader who was supposed to take us rang in ill. So, foolishly, we were trusted to go to the show on our own. Yes, that's right, unaccompanied by an adult, which I saw as my chance to become group leader for the night, which in my eyes meant…

"Let's see how much trouble we can cause in a rival youth club."

We were about ten-handed, and when we arrived we made sure we took the front row. When Fluff made his appearance, we greeted him with wolf whistles and he told us to: "Get it out of your system, because we have a show to record."

Of course, Mr Freeman.

So, the show starts and we're being good little boys, just like we were told, but then I suddenly started taking a dislike to one of the contestants, not just because he looked like that horrible little git Tristan from *George & Mildred,* but also because he didn't seem to have any musical knowledge at all, which I saw as a major crime that deserved a verbal kicking. Come on, how can you not know which two members of The Move left the band to go on and form ELO?! So is it any wonder that I started shouting out all the answers to the questions before anyone on the panel had a chance to? I thought it would make for a more interesting show, but 'Fluff' didn't, and after stopping the recording I earned a stern reprimand from him, which only made me want to do it even more.

And so once again it was a case of pain stops play. "Do that one more time kid and you're out." This time he sounded remarkably like the man I'd heard advertising Brentford Nylons on TV.

The next question...

Fluff: "Who sang "Everlasting Love" a number one in 1968?"

Me: "Love Affair"

Fluff: "Right! That's it! Get him out!"

And so I was led out of the club by two Radio One security guards shouting, "Alright, not 'arf." Over and over again.

I began hanging around with kids a little bit older than me who had a club of their own, but it had nothing to do with playing table tennis, or going camping with perverts, because these boys called themselves 'The Little Highbury' and the only activity they were interested in was sticking the boot in on some poor cunt's head. The only drawback of being an Albion fan (besides them being shit) was it was too far and too expensive to get there every other weekend, and because I needed my regular football fix, I started going to the Arsenal instead. I would pay the ten-pence or whatever it was to get into the boys' enclosure back then, and once I was inside I would jump over the small fence that separated it from the North Bank and run right to the back of the stand to join my mates for a Saturday afternoon of coin throwing, fighting, and of course, football.

Whenever I go to The Emirates these days and I'm standing in a queue for twenty minutes just so I can spend a fucking tenner on a couple of watered down drinks I always think about what the facilities were like back then, when the fans' refreshment was provided by a smoke-filled bar behind the stand that resembled a concentration camp. And this was where a thirsty fan could buy a dodgy light ale, or if you were hungry a packet of out of date crisps or a stale pie that after one bite would usually end up becoming a savoury grenade to chuck at the old bill at some point during the match.

'The Little Highbury' usually entered a bundle after all the real damage had already been done by the older proper firm, so you were basically giving someone a 'dessert hiding' after he'd just received his 'main course kicking'. It wasn't all one-way traffic though. I can remember a time when a West Ham fan ran through the North Bank with an axe, trying to slice up anyone in sight.

Fuck me, I've never seen so many people move so quickly.

Thankfully psychopaths wielding axes were not a regular sight on the terraces back then. You were much more likely to see a hooligan wearing a budgie jacket throwing a dart in some poor bastard's face. It's the bullseye!

To tell the truth I didn't really enjoy all the violence, I think I just wanted to belong to some kind of gang, which looking back now is a little strange because I've always been a bit of a loner; but hey, I guess I was just young and dumb.

On one of my many visits to the West End, I met a guy called Adrian, who worked in the Vintage Magazine shop in Earlham Street next door to the Marquis Of Granby pub. Adrian was another big T.Rex fan, and so a couple of times a week I would pop in to see him for a few hours to talk about Bolan. It was through one of these chats that I found out that Marc had an office in New Bond Street, and so the very next day I went down there in the hope of seeing my idol; and I got lucky on my very first visit. I'd only been there about twenty minutes when a Mini pulled up and Marc got out, and instead of just rushing in to the building, he spent time posing for pictures and chatting to all the fans hanging around.

Beginner's luck eh?

And so, the start of my three-day-week spent outside 69 New Bond Street had begun. Some days I'd wait all day and he wouldn't show, and although you might get to see Keith Moon, Linda Lewis or a member of Pink Floyd (who all rented offices off him) coming in and out of the building it just wasn't the same as seeing Marc. But it was all worth it on the days he turned up. I couldn't believe how open he made himself to the fans, and when I got a tip from someone that he also often frequented the offices of his record label EMI in Manchester Square, I started going there too, and the tip was right because I met him there many, many times.

By the way, a few years later, Adrian changed his name to Nikki Sudden and formed a fucking brilliant band, Swell Maps ("Midget Submarines" is one of my favourite songs, ever) but sadly, I lost touch with him and was extremely saddened to hear of his early passing in 2006.

1975 was the year I started going to lots of gigs, with The Marquee being my venue of choice for spending many nights standing bored shitless nodding my head pretending to like shit bands like Stackridge, Babe Ruth or FBI.

It wasn't all dross though.

I got to see the mighty Gong, Van Der Graaf Generator and Medicine Head who I fucking loved and it was also the year that I started following T.Rex on tour. Marc did a small tour of seaside ballrooms around the country to promote his single "New York City". I gave the old man a bit of toffee about spending the night at a friend's house and took the train down to Folkestone to see the show.

And what a show it was.

I managed to get right down the front and get up close and personal with Marc. I'm sure the gig only lasted about an hour but for that hour he completely spellbound me. Meeting your hero outside their office and seeing them on stage are two very different things. And when it was all over I slept on the beach with some other 'Bolanites' with one giving me my first toke on a joint which only added to the magic of the evening.

It wasn't just concerts that I was becoming a regular at because every week I was now getting a little 'Monday Night Fever' at the Tottenham Royal. And it was while dancing beneath the plastic palm trees to the rhythms of "South African Man" or "Jungle Music" in my wide lapelled brown denim jacket, slightly different shade of brown six button high waistband trousers, and a pair of brown platform boots, that I discovered that going to discos, clubs or whatever you wanna call them don't come cheap, because if you wanna start chatting up the birds in there via the avenue of buying them drinks well then you have to dig deep my son.

So it was just as well I was at the the height of my 'tea-leafing' exploits.

School, shops, youth clubs, in fact anywhere I could line my pockets with unpaid goods to sell on to my pals, and I got so good at it I started getting the odd 'grown up' taking me to one side asking me if there was any chance of me getting them any... You can fill in the blank. Which is why the old bill caught me trying to break in to a garage that belonged to my local off licence, attempting to get my hands on some boxes of Bovril crisps.

I'm sorry, that should have read bottles of whisky.

I tried to leg it, but they got me and bundled me into the back of the meat wagon. When they asked for my address I told them I lived in Rowley Gardens which turned out to be a bit of a mistake, because when we arrived there and they asked what block it was, I pointed a few hundred yards away towards my house and said, "No, I meant to say Green Lanes", which earned me a couple of quick hard digs to the head that I'll never forget.

I would usually spend at least a fiver in the Royal, but always saved enough dosh for a portion of chips on the way home. Which is why, when I received a letter from the head honcho at Woodberry Down, telling me that they wanted me back there to revise for my forthcoming exams, I was more than a bit annoyed because that fucked up the fiver I was getting every week at the Centre. My Monday Night Fiver.

And anyway, what's all this about exams?

I think they realised that I wasn't a violent troublemaker or anything like that, just a bit of a smart-arse who liked to see how far he could push things, and having me back to take these exams was a way of getting me to dip my toes back into the stream of normal society before maybe welcoming me back full time the next term hopefully as a model student.

Yeah right.

I told them I didn't think I was ready for any of this, and if I came back my behaviour might start going downhill, but they were getting wise to my fun and games and told me, in no uncertain terms, that it was going to happen, and if not it could be Borstal for me. So I went back and did the exams achieving some surprisingly good results...

I got 94% in Religious Studies.

God knows how.

And the next year I was back... and then I wasn't! I made sure I made good on my threat of worsening behaviour, and so they did a compromise deal with me of three days at the centre, and two days there, and life went on.

Just without the fiver.

Susan Cadogan	"Hurt So Good"
Shirley & Company	"Shame, Shame, Shame"
Judge Dread	"Je T'Aime"

The Lyceum in Wellington Street has always been one of my favourite venues in London, and I have seen many, many great gigs in this beautiful building. The Clash, Slade (supported by U2), and Joy Division quickly spring to mind but none were better than the one I saw on 18th February 1976, when T.Rex played there on their "Futuristic Dragon" tour. And even though Marc was a little overweight and was quite obviously a bit pissed as he pranced around in front of his dragon backdrop that looked like it had come last in a Blue Peter competition, it was still Marc. When the doors opened I ran as fast as I could into the ballroom to make sure that I got right to the front of the stage, and for the next three hours I held on to the crash barrier in front of me as if I was hanging on to a cliff-edge for my life. The set list was interesting: he played things like "Solid Gold Easy Action" and "Teenage Dream", which to my knowledge he'd never done, but the highlight had to be the acoustic set where he took requests from the fans.

It was heaven. A very sweaty heaven, but heaven all the same.

I really wanted to learn a musical instrument and I went for the bass guitar. My thinking was pretty simple, the bass only has four strings (not any more mate), which must mean that it's easier to play than his six-string relative, and as my birthday was on the horizon, I asked Dad if there was any chance of him getting me one.

His answer was a very firm NO.

I do have to say he was a man of his word though, because when I woke up on the morning of my big day there was no guitar shaped present at the end of my bed, just a card with some money in it, but to be fair it was a decent amount. I guess he thought if I was really serious about it, then I would put this cash away and start saving up to get one. Well, I've got news for you Dad, I was serious about it, very serious, but if you give a kid a lot of folding he will blow it as soon as he gets the first chance. Which of course is exactly what I did.

Oh, and before I go on to tell you how I actually managed to get hold of a bass without paying for one, I think I have to mention that I shared my birthday that year with the release of The Ramones' debut album, and if that wasn't good enough the day after The Baggies were promoted back up to the old first division after a three-year absence in the second division wilderness.

So, how did I acquire my instrument?

I'd like to be able to trot out some kind of Steve Jones type story that I stole it after a Bowie gig at the Hammersmith Odeon but the truth is, the dad of a friend of mine was the bassist in a band back in the 60s and as luck would have it had a couple of his old guitars just gathering dust underneath his bed, so he let me have one on loan until I managed to get my own. I was now the proud owner of a Futurama bass guitar.

Let's go back to the Ramones for a bit.

I'm proud to say that I bought their first album maybe a week or so after it came out. Not because I was the hippest cat in town, I'd simply seen their picture in the *NME* a few weeks before and thought they looked great but the real money shot was when I read they had a song called "Now I Wanna Sniff Some Glue."

"All the kids wanna sniff some glue"

And so I made my way down to Harlequin Records in Soho and grabbed myself a copy of the album and when I got it home it began receiving some heavy rotation much to the annoyance of big brother.

"Fucking hell man, take that shit off will ya!"

Their music was a gift from the heavens for me because even with my limited musical ability I could still work out how to play "Blitzkrieg Bop", "Beat On The Brat" and of course "Glue" on the bass with ease.

I was still hanging out at Marc's office a lot, and struck gold one hot July afternoon when he arrived with his girlfriend, Gloria, in their purple Mini (yes, that purple Mini). While he waited for her to park up, he told a small group of us that he was filming a TV show *Rollin' Bolan* the next day with Mike Mansfield in Wimbledon. Talk about a stroke of luck; and the best thing about it was I'd heard it from the great man himself.

I set off early to make sure I got there in time for Marc's soundcheck, and it was while I was hanging around outside the venue waiting for him to come out that the day turned into one of those double-bubble ones, because his support band were a little known Australian band called AC/DC, and they spent about an hour chatting to me; and let me tell you, when you're a young impressionable kid that really means a lot; and why (besides them being a brilliant band) I went to see them in concert at least twenty times over the next couple of years (mostly at The Marquee).

71

The lesson I learnt from artists like Marc and AC/DC was always treat the people who come to your gigs with the respect they deserve. It doesn't matter if your voice is a little bit sore, or you have a hangover from the night before, you should always make sure you make time for your audience.

Gil Scott Heron	**"Johannesburg"**
John Handy	**"Hard Work"**
Sex Pistols	**"Anarchy In The UK"**

The summer of 76 has gone down in history as one of the hottest that Britain has ever had, and the streets of London were burning, not with boredom but with the sight of extremely beautiful scantily-clad birds spending their lunch hours sunbathing in the park to a continuous MOR soundtrack of bearded men pouring their hearts out to the world on a Fender Rhodes.

Further out of town, this green and pleasant land was being invaded by swarms of ladybirds, and forest fires were destroying our trees and crops. I gained some first-hand experience of this because I spent some of that hot summer on a school camping trip in Wales, and even though the last time I'd been in a tent was probably not the best time that I'd ever had I still loved the whole tent experience.

The pitter-patter sound of rain on canvas is one of life's pure joys.

"Listen to the rhythm of the falling rain"

Do you remember I told you I had another 'noncing' story to tell you about? Well, this is where and when it happened, but because the instigator of unwanted attention this time was a bird, everyone who witnessed it seemed to think it was all right.

Bird = Teacher

And once again, the 'incident' happened just as I was getting ready to go to bed. She poked her face into the tent to say goodnight to me and the three boys I was sharing with when one of them thought it would be a good idea to tell her: "Hey Miss, Nick fancies you, he wants you to kiss him."

I was hoping she'd just laugh it off and go, but she came back with: "Oh, does he now, well, let's see if he really does like me."

And with that she pushed her mouth onto mine and stuck her tongue down my gob, all performed to the sound of cheering mates.

Now do you see what I mean?

Just because it was a woman who did it to me I was now seen as a hero in the eyes of my randy young friends, but fuck it I lived and anyway things were about to get a lot more exciting on this trip than a quick tonguing from a big-breasted teacher. It started off with me and two of my friends, Brian and Tony Smith, playing war games on a hillside and ended up with the mountain rescue being called out to save us from what we all thought was imminent death.

We were having such a good time fucking around that we didn't notice where we were going, and then in what seemed to be the blink of an eye it got dark, very dark, and because we weren't properly dressed to spend a night out in the Welsh hills we started to get cold, very cold.

The three of us tried putting on a brave face, but deep down we were all bricking it and just as we thought it couldn't get any worse, the heavens opened and it started to really piss down, and so we took shelter in a small cave we found with the plan of staying there until it eased off a bit.

All the time we were in the cave, making jokes and pretending to be brave, we could hear what sounded like helicopters all around us, but at no point did any of us think that maybe it would be a good idea to go outside and try to draw attention to ourselves by either shouting or waving our arms in the air, in fact anything to get us out of the shit we were in. No, I can say, without fear of contradiction, there was definitely no survival mentality amongst this trio of desperados (and to think, me an ex-scout, oh the shame): all we did was sit there like three little dummies.

When the rain eased off we decided that we should try and make our way back downhill to find our way home (good thinking boys, better late than never). Within a few minutes of reaching a road, the sight of a police car coming towards us made three soaked-to-the-bone children feel very happy and a lot safer. The officers put us in the back seat wrapped in thick woollen blankets and drove us back to the camp (which of course turned out to be not very far away from where we'd strayed) and after a few questions from our teachers and the old bill, we were allowed to go to bed.

It wasn't until morning that we found out the full strength of what had gone on after we'd gone missing. Not only had several search parties

73

been sent out with the old bill, but the helicopter noise I thought I'd heard was the mountain rescue unit. Of course, now I was back on safe ground my cockiness returned, so when one of the teachers told me all of this I replied: "It's nice to be wanted, isn't it Sir?"

He emptied a bowl of porridge over my head.

So, there you are, that was my near dice with death in Wales. It was a toss-up between either telling you that one, or about how I got caught pissing over a judge's chair on a trip we made to the law courts. On balance, I think I chose right.

When we got back from Wales, a friend of mine took me to a squat in Stoke Newington so he could buy a little bit of dope for himself and while we waiting there for the bird with the dirty barnet to 'bag it up' she also flogged him a bag of pills.

She called them 'Blues'.

"Baby you're built for speed"

We left the squat and went back to my pal's flat, so he could become extremely boring by smoking all his boring gear and forcing me to listen to some of his even more boring music. I repeatedly turned down his offers of a smoke, but when he swapped substances and handed me one of the pills he'd bought I necked it straight away, with a little help from a mouthful of warm, flat cider. There didn't seem to be any immediate effect, but an hour or so later and as we were making our way around Clissold Park for the third time talking absolute bollocks I knew this was my kind of drug. So, whenever I had a couple of quid spare, I'd head down to Filthy Towers and buy some, just like I did on 10th October 1976.

The day I went to see Kraftwerk at The Roundhouse.

I'd fallen in love with them after a friend played me their "Autobahn" album. I was hooked straight away; it was like having a magic musical telescope that could help you see into the future. Who needs *Tomorrow's World* when you've got Kraftwerk?

I don't know why I thought the best way to watch them would be with bulging pupils and saliva dripping out of my mouth, but that's the state I was in that night. I looked more fucked up than Jesus* did, but it was one hell of a show. Well, at least I think it was.

And how about this for a stroke of good luck…

74

The week I was finally pulled out of the Centre and told to go back to Woodberry Down full time coincided with the week the school decided to invest a shit-load of money in the music department, buying instruments and amplification and, most importantly, providing enough funds to employ musicians to come in twice a week to give instrument tuition to the kids. That's when I began getting bass lessons from a guy called Steve Beresford. Although I didn't know it at the time, Steve was a well-known avant-garde jazz musician, who later went on to make one of my favourite records ever, "Money" as part of the Flying Lizards, but you will hear more about him later on.

Lessons mostly consisted of Steve showing me where to put my fingers on the fretboard to learn all the bass lines from my favourite reggae records, and when I eventually mastered them, I would then teach them to any kid in the class who also wanted to learn them. At the time there were two essential ones you had to have in your locker: Tapper Zukie's "MPLA" and "Police & Thieves" by Junior Murvin.

One day, while showing a couple of my 'students' these lines, I decided to slip in one of my own just for fun and to my joy, they treated it with exactly the same respect they'd given the other two, and when they asked what the name of the tune was and I said that it was one of mine, the tiny music room erupted to the sound of loud finger snapping and random shouts of: "Wicked!" It was a moment I'll never forget, and from that day on I was treated like Woodberry Down's very own Robbie Shakespeare.

And now that I had access to equipment I decided it was time for me to start a band.

I'm gonna spare you all the boring details about finding the members, rehearsing, writing songs etc and tell that we were called Charisma and our first performance was on a cold November morning in school assembly.

That's right… C-H-A-R-I-S-M-A.

I know, it's a fucking awful name, but be honest, is it any worse than say Pilot or Racing Cars?

Who knows? Who cares?

We were a five piece for the show, playing a three-song set that got a good response, but I suppose for the kids anything was better than having to sing hymns accompanied by some old biddy banging away on an out-of-tune Joanna. It should have been a quartet but I insisted on having congas in our line up to make it sound more like T.Rex.

The songs were:

"Sunshine Of Your Love" - The Cream classic not really meant for fourteen-year-olds to play.

"Lost In A Dream" - A Welsh/Smith original vaguely reminiscent of The Byrds if you're tone deaf.

"Orgasm" - Another Welsh/Smith tune. A twelve-bar blues, with what we thought was an 'edgy' title.

On 1st December 1976, Charisma played a Christmas concert for the scout troop I used to be in (yeah, I'd outgrown out of all that by then man) which was great, but this was also to turn out to be a day that would go on to play a big part in the future of lots of kids just like me, all over the world.

I went home after school that day to pick up my bass and stage gear (Status Quo denim) and sat down with my spaghetti hoops on toast to watch a bit of pre-gig TV, and what did I see?

The Sex Pistols on the *Today* show, giving it plenty...

Plenty of "fucks", "shits" and "bastards".

I'd read about the band in the music press, but this was the first time I'd seen them 'in the flesh', if you know what I mean, and like any young kid would, I fucking loved it. I don't think I'd ever heard anything like it on TV before.

"What a fucking rotter"

Never mind the music, gimme the swearing.

I rushed out to meet the others to talk about it, but no one else had seen the show and in my excitement, I don't think I explained it that well to them: "Hold on, there was a sex show on TV and they were all swearing?"

As much as I wanted to (and I REALLY wanted to) I didn't let any of what I'd just seen creep into our show that night.

"Ok Scouts, this one's called 'Orgasm' it's all about fucking your gran up the arse."

Nope, I went about my business as if I was Bobby Crush playing to some old folks at a charity bingo night.

If my pals didn't know what I was talking about the night before, they certainly did when they woke up the next morning because the Sex Pistols were on the front page of every newspaper in the country and that, my friends, was how punk really kicked off in the UK. I'm sure a few of the bands from the scene would have eventually made something of themselves given time, but because of one slightly pissed-up guitarist acting no differently than he would on a night out with his mates in a pub, everything escalated to a new and exciting level overnight.

I went to two more gigs before the end of 1976. The first was when T.Rex were special guests at one of Gary Glitter's retirement concerts (or was it one of his comebacks?) and to be honest it wasn't one of the greatest performances I'd ever seen Marc give (dancing frogs etc.), but the second gig was a life changer.

I went to see The Damned with my best mate Brian at some small polytechnic in North London, which turned out to be a student only show and so we were turned away at the door; but as we were making our way out of the building we bumped into Rat Scabies who said something along the lines of: "Student cunts. I'll get you in on my guest list lads. Right, you're Steve and you're John."

This was a first for me. I'd chatted to bands outside of shows and stuff, but I'd never been put on the guest list by one of them. If this was punk then I liked it.

The gig was amazing, absolute fucking chaos; dare I say even a little anarchic. Rat set fire to his kit, the bass player was a nutter, they had a vampire singer and a Rolling Stones lookalike on guitar, who could seriously fucking play. I think it was the first time I'd ever left a gig in shock. But I tell you one thing, it wouldn't be the last.

*Jesus was a guy who was always at The Roundhouse, banging on a tambourine and generally being a dirty, annoying hippy.

I only wish I could remember it!

77

GIRL AT THE ROXY

Friday night and I'm ready to go,
On the 29, off to a show, so it's all right,
I heard that Menace are a band to see,
I think I read it in the NME, so it's all right.
I know it sounds strange but I just got to say,

Weren't you the girl I used to see upstairs at The Roxy?
Weren't you the one with the pink stripe in your hair?
Weren't you the girl I used to see upstairs at The Roxy?
Girl at The Roxy says she don't care.
I saw a girl who was out to flirt,
She had "No Future" written on her shirt,
So amazing.
I was young, with not a lot to say,
She said it didn't matter anyway,
So amazing.
I know it sounds strange but I just got to say,

Weren't you the girl I used to see upstairs at The Roxy?
Weren't you the one with the pink stripe in your hair?
Weren't you the girl I used to see upstairs at The Roxy?
Girl at The Roxy says she don't care.
Girl at The Roxy we were born to lose
Girl at The Roxy have you got any blues?

I'm always reading how 1977 was one of the most important years in the history of pop music.

There's not a month goes by without some hack going on about how this was the year the punks came to town, and kicked the shit out of all those 'dinosaur' bands, ELP, Yes and The Eagles, who apparently no longer had any relevance to 'the kids'; but the truth was those groups playing their long haired concept albums to their long haired fans, in their long haired (no that don't work) in huge stadiums, were now bigger than ever.

Top selling single of the year? "God Save The Queen" by the Sex Pistols? Try Wings' "Mull of Kintyre".

I do agree with them on one thing though, that, without doubt, 1977 was the most exciting musical year of my life. After the Pistols' now infamous TV 'performance', punk was definitely the buzz-word on my street and the musical shackles were well and truly off, and no longer would I have to listen to my old man trot out his usual party line: "If you cannae read music, you cannae be a musician laddie."

I was pretty sure that Paul Simenon or Dee Dee Ramone didn't possess that particular talent either, and they seemed to be doing okay so what could possibly stop me (besides not being in The Clash or The Ramones) from achieving my musical dreams? If punk achieved anything, it was that it stopped that kind of snobbery which allowed virtually no chancers like me the freedom to dream and express myself. I also believe it had to happen at that point in time, and not because of the usual 'boring supergroup' reasons that are normally trotted out. The country was in a right fucking mess; and I don't just mean the endless strikes or the sight of binbags with rats crawling all over them everywhere, I could handle that.

What I couldn't handle was the rise in popularity of a little firm called 'The National Front'.

Even though I'd seen 'NF' graffitied on lots of walls around my manor I had no idea what it meant, but that changed the day a message came over the school tannoy asking the kids to leave by the back entrance because an organisation called the National Front were waiting outside the front of the school to leaflet and recruit.

Ah, the pennies dropped... National Front = NF. Anyway, we asked the teacher who and what they were and her answer only succeeded in winding us right up, because, as I've already said, we were pretty much a tight knit group who didn't think about colour: your mates were your mates.

That's why, I'm proud to say, even though we were behind locked gates, a load of us went straight to the front of the school and started lobbing bricks and anything else we could grab hold of at the cunts and they soon had it on their toes. I was fucked if I was gonna let someone pick on a pal of mine just because he's got different coloured skin from them.

1977 was also the year I gave up on the idea of trying to become a professional footballer.

Even though the last couple of years had seen me start going to gigs where I'd have a couple of beers and occasionally experiment with the odd pharmaceutical I still never, ever failed to turn out for Parkside every Sunday; but as good as I was at that level I knew I didn't really have what it takes to make that huge step up in class to the big boys league, and to be honest I was losing interest in playing the game anyway because music was now taking over my life. So besides turning out in a few charity matches, including one very special game where I got to put on an Albion shirt in a testimonial game for former club legend Steve Hunt, my days of shouting "man on" to a team mate were now well and truly over.

The Damned were still top of my 'seen list' but there were now new entries from The Jam, Johnny Moped, and The Vibrators, who were all great, but what really excited me was the news of a forthcoming T.Rex tour of the UK, with support from The Damned. The London date was at The Rainbow on 18th March 1977. Before then, I had a few other dates at The Rainbow to see bands you definitely weren't going to read about in Sniffing Glue with the exception of Iggy Pop (with Bowie on keyboards), who had a tasty new album "The Idiot" under his belt. Iggy's show was great but I have to say, I can't ever remember going to a gig where you have a frontman as good as Iggy working his arse off, but most of the audience are looking the other way at the geezer sitting behind the Hammond! But the other artists I saw there were so far removed from what punk was about it was like watching an alien lifeforce from another planet.

Lynyrd Skynyrd for instance; they kindly invited me in to watch them soundcheck after seeing me hanging out by the stage door in the afternoon, but even that couldn't make me like them. They bored the fucking shit out of me, and why I went to see Canadian rocker Pat

Travers I'll never know; it must have been a bit of the old 'EBS'. Basically, we're talking about the kind of music I'd hear on the Nicky Horne show 'Your Mother Wouldn't Like It' on Capital, before religiously turning over at 10.00pm to listen to John Peel on Radio One where Captain Beefheart and Ivor Cutler would send me up the Wooden Hill to Bedfordshire, with their unique brand of bedtime stories.

A million miles away from the world of bands who could actually play their instruments, Charisma were due to play an NUS (National Union of Students) concert, that was being held in the assembly room at school.The band's line up and set had undergone a lot of changes from the previous year, and we were now a trio with the Cream and Hendrix covers swopped for songs of our own, all of which paid more than a little lip service to the new punk spirit. Unfortunately for us though, it wasn't just the musical side of punk we'd inherited, it was also the attitude, an attitude that led us to being dropped from the show, after we demanded we should headline the event because everyone else on the bill were 'boring old farts'.

Now besides being a bloody rude and stupid thing to do, it was also not true, because it was at this show my good friend Doug Trendle, (who would go on to find fame as 'Buster Bloodvessel', front man of Bad Manners) made his stage debut performing two songs, a cover of Bobby Pickett's "Monster Mash" and the one that absolutely stole the show that night, "Lend Me Two Pence". He was fucking brilliant.

I was really looking forward to seeing Marc again and hearing what the new band sounded like. The last original member of T.Rex, bassist Steve Currie, had gone, to be replaced by the brilliant Herbie Flowers, and Marc now had the rock solid Tony Newman on drums. I'd arranged to meet up with some of my fellow 'Bolanites' a few hours before the gig and they were more than a little surprised to see my beautiful flicks and denim dungarees had been replaced by spiky hair and ripped jeans, but the one thing that hadn't changed was that, just like them, I still had more than a little Marc in my heart.

Hand on heart the show was one of the best I've ever seen.

The Damned were brilliant and I wanted to know what my friends thought of them, but there was no time to ask because within a few minutes of The Damned leaving the stage, T.Rex circa '77 were on and sounding better than ever. The songs were shorter and punchier than in recent years, including a very fast 'punky' version of "Debora" that got me pogoing, much to the amusement of everyone around me. And I wasn't the only one with a new attitude, because the now slimline Marc was peppering some of his songs with a few expletives in "Jeepster" ("and I'm gonna fuck you babe"), and "New York City" ("fucking don't it show").

As I walked back home down the Seven Sisters Road that night, the only thing I had on my mind (besides what a great gig it had been) was that Charisma was a dead duck and I had to start a new band…

A PUNK BAND

"No more dreams of mystery chords"

Of course, I would be the bassist and Brian would still be on guitar, so all I needed was a singer and a drummer, oh yeah and some songs, a few of those would definitely come in handy. The singer proved quite easy to find. I'd known Paul Forsyth for a few years, and although he was my brother's age we used to hang out at Parkside together playing snooker and generally upsetting as many people as we could. He was also the owner of a great Burns Bison bass, which he said I could use if I let him join the band, so the decision for him to be the frontman was, as they say, a 'no brainer'.

To this day, I don't know where the drummer came from, all I can tell you is his name was Steve and he had a twin brother and a car, the latter being a big plus in my book, and so with our line up complete and with a strict 'No Cover' policy we began rehearsing and writing.

The first song we came up with, "Sod The Monarchy", was a joyous punk celebration of our glorious Queen's silver jubilee year.

**"Sod the Monarchy,
Sod the Monarchy,
Tell you what it means to me,
The Queens a whore, a royal bore,
Sod the Monarchy"**

I think we knew it was no 'God Save The Queen', but at least it was our own.

"We're the future, your future"

Paul came up with the band's name. He was really into shock rock; now, for those of you too young to remember it was rock theatre: mostly American groups with lots of stage props and even more make-up. Kiss, The Tubes and the godfather of it all, Paul's idol, Alice Cooper, which is why he so desperately wanted to call us The Dead after his song "I Love the Dead". I didn't really like the name, but as I was using his bass I didn't bother to question it.

Sex Pistols	**"God Save The Queen"**
The Heartbreakers	**"Chinese Rocks"**
The Damned	**"Neat, Neat, Neat"**

We rehearsed in Paul's kitchen for about a month, and by the middle of May we had a set completely made up of original material, which in our eyes was good enough for us to take our rightful place next to The Pistols, The Clash and the rest of punk's top boys.

"I Wanna See Her Corpse"
"She's So Stiff"
"Schoolgirl Obsession"
"Police Informer"

Our next move was to ring around all the pubs and clubs in London that put on live music, to get ourselves some gigs; but most of the time, as soon as the promoter heard that four letter word P-U-N-K, the phone was put down before you could say "safety-pin". And if they did decide to engage with us for a little longer, they'd usually tell us why we were on their unwanted list. It went something like this: "I don't want a load of dirty punks, who can't fucking play, flobbing in my venue."

Well bollocks to you too.

About three times a week I would go to gigs to check out what other bass players did on stage. I fucking hated the 'bass player looking bored at the back' look, you know the kind of thing, Bill Wyman was the absolute king of it. Every time I saw him on stage I thought: "If you don't wanna be there mate, why don't you just fuck off?"

At least John Entwistle wore a skeleton suit.

I suppose the person I tried to copy was Captain Sensible because he was a man who knew how to entertain, and although I wasn't prepared to go stark bollock naked, like he'd done at his birthday party at The

Roundhouse (The Damned, Motorhead and The Adverts, what a fucking show), I did shamefully nick some of his moves and shapes to incorporate into my stage performance.

There was one show I went to though where I didn't get a chance to study the bass player and that was at The Marquee on 4th June 1977. The date's easy for me to remember, because it was the same day Scotland beat England 2-1 at Wembley, and all the Scots fans invaded the pitch and nicked the fucking goalposts - and by the time I arrived for the gig they had invaded that as well. The Marquee was banged out with pissed up Jocks, carrying little bits of white wood in their sporrans, and in their eyes they were the main attraction; and so the band who thought they were headlining Chelsea had to be content with being a side show to all the drunken antics of the Scots fans that night.

"The right to work? Fuck that pal, all we want is the right to drink!"

One of the things that meant so much to me back then was that the bands would make themselves very accessible to the punter. Now, I know you could argue that none of the groups were in the tax exile bracket yet, and so it was in their best interests to be friendly, but you have to remember that to me the Pistols, Clash and Damned were my Beatles, Kinks and Stones.

Moving away from punk for just a moment, 1977 was also the year I first became acquainted with the term 'banged up'. Do you remember when I told you our school had invested quite heavily in their music department? Well, I decided, in my new self-appointed role of school security officer, that things in that department really weren't up to scratch, and I decided the best way to demonstrate this to the teachers was by breaking in and stealing some of their newly acquired equipment with another light fingered little bastard called Tony Smith. And so, armed with just a couple of torches and a house brick, we broke in at night and grabbed a couple of tenor saxophones the school had only just taken delivery of, and, don't ask me why, a fucking xylophone. Just for the record, I think it was totally unnecessary for us to piss all over the floor before we left but we did and we got away with it ...

For a while.

Question: Where does a thieving little bastard go to sell a hot saxophone in his area?

Answer: Berry's in Harringay.

I let Tony take control of the negotiating side of things, while I passed the time playing one of the many pianos in there, much to the annoyance of everyone in the shop. After a few minutes, he came back and said: "Sorted, they're giving us £40 for it, but we gotta come back in twenty minutes to get it."

But when I returned to get the dosh, instead of green backs we were greeted by blue bottles.

Tony had forgotten to tell me a couple of things:

1. That he knew the guy who worked in there, but still decided to give a false name, "Tony Tosh", (he was a big fan of the 'Legalize It' album) which the geezer knew was fanny.

2. That he told them that the ILEA (Inner London Education Authority) stamp on the side of the instrument was the name of our band!

Well done mate.

And so off we went to St Ann's, where I got my first taste of a police cell. It had taken me a while to reach this pivotal moment in my life; sure, I'd been punched in the face by a copper and dragged into a paddy wagon by one for a quick smack at football, but this was a real step up, I now had a cell all of my own.

They split us up so we couldn't rehearse our story, you know, to make sure we weren't on the same wavelength, but they needn't have bothered, because I had absolutely no idea what fucking wavelength, or even galaxy, my good friend Mr Tosh was on.

After a few hours, they let us out and questioned us, before eventually letting us go home with just a caution. My old man came to pick me up and I have to admit that I was shit-scared of what he was gonna do, but his attitude was surprisingly more piss-take than admonishing. It goes without saying that I learnt a very important lesson that day: make sure that this is the first, and last time, you ever do a 'blag' with Tony.

The Dead's first gig was on 9th July 1977 at a 'Women's Right to Choose' benefit show in Waterloo, which came to us courtesy of Steve Beresford. I think he'd invited us along because he felt bad that a couple of months before me and Brian had been thrown out of a show he'd invited us to at the ICA. We'd been asked to leave by virtuoso guitarist Derek Bailey for the unforgivable act of 'eating crisps too loudly' during one of his long and very boring solos, but Steve was one of the good guys, and bless him had found it very funny.

I mean he didn't even have a go at me when I went to his flat while he was out and put talcum powder in his trombone.

How did the gig go?

Well, all right really, and I can say that because forty years later, I'm sitting listening to the show on a cassette tape (Orange Agfa), and we don't sound too bad at all. Midway through our set you can hear my teenage voice taking centre stage with a question for the audience:

"What's red and slides down a tree?"

"A monkey's miscarriage."

Cue drum roll.

How punk was that?

But instead of getting slated by the audience, which was obviously what I was looking for, the brown-ricers lapped it up in a 'fuck the system' sort of way. I didn't give a fuck what they thought either way though, because I was fifteen, out to shock, and loving every fucking minute of it. On the tube home after the gig, we talked excitedly about how bright our future looked, before ending the evening in perfect punk fashion by jumping the barriers at Manor House station and legging-it up the stairs, leaving the ticket collector for dust.

I'd like to see you try that now mate.

Four days later was the big one. We'd secured an Audition Night slot at the home of all things punk... The Roxy.

Well, it had been six months earlier, but six months was a long time in year zero, and since then it had since changed hands from the original owner, Andy Czezowski, into the paws of an evil monster, Kevin St John. I don't want to waste too much time on him, but I will say he was, without doubt, one of the most odious creatures I've ever met in my life; just thinking about him makes my skin crawl. Over the years, I've met many old Punks who've told me stories of how this cunt tried to fuck them up the arse, or offer them a couple of free drinks for a blowjob (which way I don't know), and this wanker really took a shine to one member of The Dead.

Have a wild guess who.

The only thing about him that can bring even half a smile to my face is that The Roxy is now a Speedo shop, which is probably the closest you can get to describing this horrible fucker.

"Well I'm spending all my money and it's going up my nose"

The Roxy may not have been attracting the calibre of artists it had done when it first opened its doors, but it had only been three months since the venue had hosted the launch party for Bolan's "Dandy in the

Underworld" album, and now I was playing there and boy did that excite me! And what's more, I knew it was gonna be packed out, mostly with our school friends, but hey, a crowd's a crowd.

A seasoned pro musician once told me: "When you're on stage, always make sure that your eye-line is just above the punter's head." Which is good advice, but he didn't have to play a show with my brother and his sort of a girlfriend standing in front of me wearing matching 'Starsky' cardigans which to this young punk was a little off-putting to say the least; but you know the old showbiz saying, the show must go on, and that night our show did.

We were down to play for forty five minutes, but we somehow managed to stretch that out to nearly two hours to an audience reaction good enough to get us invited back two weeks later, FOR A PAID GIG! With two bands, Cock Sparrer and Dead Fingers Talk, who, get this, both had major record deals and, have some of this, on the week of the gig, *Melody Maker* ran a picture of me and Brian (more him than me), standing at the front of the stage at that Chelsea gig I mentioned earlier, underneath a headline reading: "TEDS V PUNKS".

Big time or what?

Well, it must have been, because we even managed to get a roadie to come along and help us carry our equipment. I say roadie, but our new employee, Bobby, was the school bully who'd basically forced me into giving him the job. I suppose I only had myself to blame. He'd been quizzing me for weeks about the punk scene, asking me, "Is the punk scene really full of birds, out of their nuts on glue, getting their tits out?"

I didn't want to disappoint him, so I lied, "Yes mate, of course it's true, the papers don't lie do they?"

And so, when he found out my band were playing The Roxy, in his psychotic mind I went from being class weirdo to new best mate; he was telling everyone, "If anyone gives my mate trouble, I'll do them."

That's rock 'n' roll for you. I hadn't even done the gig, but I now had my very own punk rock Terry McCann minding me and his favourite band was Eddie And The Hot Rods.

On the day of the gig I was waiting at the bus stop with Paul for the 29 to come and take us to our first professional (paid) gig, (Brian took the 73, Steve went in his car). As the Route Master approached, so did two friends of ours, Doug Trendle and his partner in crime Eric Delaney, both of whom were coming to the show, but as they got closer to me I could see they both had a very mischievous look in their eyes. We all

87

made our way upstairs to the top deck and sat down but within seconds, an all too familiar and repulsive smell began rearing its ugly head. I immediately recognized it, having been a major player in the 'Woodberry Down Stink Bomb Craze' of 1975, which, long story short, involves a pupil crawling on their hands and knees along the floor of the corridor, opening a classroom door, rolling a Stink Bomb into the lesson, and then running like hell away from the scene of the crime, which is why I got up a bit sharpish and legged it down the stairs so I could hold on to the exit pole and get as much of the passing air as possible.

The other passengers were not as quick off the mark as me though, and pretty soon the bus was filled with the sound of OAPs coughing and gagging. The conductor (remember them?) rang the bell, the bus pulled over, and everyone was told to get off and on to the next bus that came along.

While we waited, I got some very nasty stares and angry words from my fellow passengers: "I suppose you're happy now are you? Johnny Rotten?"

Presumably, they were directing their anger towards me because I was the most 'punk-looking' of the four of us: Doug and Eric had long hair, Paul more of a 'Steve Perryman' type cut. Even though it wasn't me I was fucking glad I was there to see it.

"Something's happening and it's happening right now"

Cock Sparrer were soundchecking when we arrived at The Roxy and so while Paul went for a much-needed wash I sat in the dressing room chatting with Dead Fingers Talk. I'd already met their singer Bo Bo Phoenix (yeah that's right, Bo Bo) at that squat in Stoke Newington where I used to buy my blues, because it also doubled up as a rehearsal studio.

Bo Bo had an extremely camp voice, the kind of voice fifteen-year-old boys find really funny, but I didn't take the piss out of him, because he and the rest of the band were all really nice guys, offering to lend us equipment, as did Cock Sparrer, who were just as friendly but more importantly let us share their lager while Sparrer's guitarist, Garry Lammin, got changed out of one slogan ridden boiler suit into another almost identical one for stage.

It raised a few eyebrows in the room, but I didn't find it strange at all, because coming from a 'showbiz' background, that's exactly what I'd been used to seeing all my life, and even though it wasn't the Palladium, this was still showbiz, just our generation's twisted version of it; and that's exactly what we gave the crowd that night.

Our version of the recent Bay City Rollers hit "I Only Wanna Be With You" (yes after just two gigs, the covers ban had been lifted), which was now called "I Never Wanna Sleep With You", went down a fucking storm, especially with DJ Don Letts.

"I don't know what it is that makes me hate you so,
 I only know I never wanna see you though,
 'Cos, you started something, can't you see,
 Ever since I slept with you I've had VD,
 It happens to be true, I never wanna sleep with you"

It went down so well we played it twice!

After the gig, a tasty little Punkette gave me a couple of blues, bought me a drink and started flirting with me, but it soon stopped after she asked me if I was in the band full time, and like a mug I told her, "Well, I am during the school holidays."

When she realised that maybe I was a bit too young for her, she went from a 'Siouxie' type vamp into a motherly "you're so cute'" type of bird and so within a couple of minutes a potential bang went... bang.

Note to self: next time, just keep your fucking mouth shut Nick.

To be honest, the thought of getting my youthful leg-over didn't even come close to the excitement I felt when I discovered Joe Strummer and Mick Jones had been watching us, and it got even better when they came over and said some really positive things about the band to me, but let's have it right, I know they were just a couple of good guys being kind to a member of a very young group, who were not, and would never ever be, of any threat to them... ever. I tell you what though, I wish I had a photo of that night.

The Damned	**"Damned, Damned, Damned"**
Sex Pistols	**"Never Mind The Bollocks"**
The Clash	**"The Clash"**

In the weeks that followed, we did a lot more gigs around the capital. One was at a youth club in Holloway called The Roundhouse, that ended with us being chased across nearby Highbury Fields by about thirty lads who hadn't taken kindly to the band "chatting up their birds". My diary also shows me we played two shows in Covent Garden on 19th August 1977. The first was at a great little club in Shelton Street called The Basement that had a proper 60s mod vibe to it and so it came as no surprise to me when a couple of years later I saw they'd shot scenes in there for the film *Quadrophenia*. After the show, we carried our equipment (with the help of Bobby) around the corner into Neal Street, because we were back at The Roxy this time with Eater, a band who had a drummer, Dee Generate, who was even younger than me!

The band earned £20 from those two shows, which worked out at about a fiver a man, and let me tell you, in 1977 that wasn't a bad bit of wedge and a long way from the fucking 'pay to play' deals some young bands still have to suffer today; and if that isn't bad enough, they also miss out on the joy of pre-internet shagging, when you could pull a bird at a gig, have a bit of fun and never see them again, whereas nowadays you can be found within minutes on social media and you're bang to rights mate. Back then, safe sex was not giving your number out afterwards.

Let's talk gigs.

I was very keen on Ultravox! I saw them every Thursday at their month long residency at The Marquee that summer. Of course, I'm talking about the John Foxx version of the band, not the latter-day Midge Ure "it means nothing to me" incarnation. I was completely in love with Chris Cross's bass playing, fuck me did he used to rock that thing. Out of all the punk/new wave albums released that year I think I play their debut more than any other.

This was a period when promoters had the idea of putting punk and reggae bands on the same bill, so you might get Sham 69 or Generation X sharing a stage with Black Slate and Steel Pulse. It really was the best of both worlds.

The difference between gigs then and now is in those days people went to a show and just had a good time, whereas today, all I see are people standing around filming the band on their camera phones. I'll tell you what though, I'm glad they weren't around back then because I'd hate to have my memories shattered by finding out that maybe The Lurkers or The Cortinas weren't as brilliant as I thought and still think they were. And let me tell you this, nothing will ever replace the feeling I got from buying all those wonderful slices of seven-inch amphetamine madness that looked so beautiful in their picture sleeves.

The Clash	**"Complete Control"**
Ultravox	**"Young Savage"**
The Users	**"Sick Of You"**

Right, let's forget about all those great bands and get back to The Dead.

On 15th September 1977, we played The Rochester Castle in Stoke Newington to a sprinkling of punks carefully pogoing around a woman in her 80s who was a regular in there. If you saw her in the day she looked just like any other old biddy, sitting in the corner, reading her paper and sipping on a Double Diamond, but when they had a band on at night you'd find her at the front of the stage dancing with her knickers around her ankles while her husband (well I think he was) spent the whole evening trying to drag her off the dancefloor and back to the safety of a dark corner. I have to say having her old grey pubes staring me in the face while I was trying to do backing vocals made my job a lot harder and who knows, maybe that's why drummer Steve mumbled his resignation speech into my ear after the gig. It took me about five minutes to work out what he was trying to tell me!

This now meant we had to find a new drummer which was a bit of a blow, but not as big as the blow I received when I woke up the next morning (no I didn't have a bird there), when my old man knocked on my bedroom door and told me Marc was dead. It took me a few minutes to take it in, mainly because I was still a bit pissed from the night before (pissed on a school night eh? That's punk) but when I finally got it together, my mind started racing.

How can Marc be dead?

He's only fucking twenty nine.

It seemed so cruel; he seemed to be on his way back up after a few lean years, he was looking great and had a hot new band, and even though his TV show *Marc* was a bit pants, it was still a chance to see our main man every week on the box.

NICK'S TOP FIVE T.REX SONGS.

1. **"Metal Guru"**
2. **"Woodland Rock"**
3. **"Telegram Sam"**
4. **"Raw Ramp"**
5. **"Jeepster"**

I walked to school in a state of shock.

Everyone there knew I was a big time Bolan fan and offered their sympathies, except for one kid, who'd always been a bit of a wanker, who made some piss-take comment to me, and my reply was to smash him in the face as hard as I could. He was still on the deck while I was making my way to the Headmaster's office, to be handed another in a long line of suspensions, but that was ok, because it now meant I had the time to find a drummer, and when I did, man, was he a strange one.

I don't exactly know how The Dead ended up with Ivor Drumstick, maybe someone gave him my number, because I do remember him ringing me up and going on about how he'd seen us play at The Roxy and loved it, and so I arranged to meet him for a beer and a chat at The Music Machine. He turned up in a really flash car and took me back to his big drum (no pun intended) in Hendon. I wonder if it was because I was only fifteen that he tried to pass himself off to me as only twenty-three?

"Anything goes where no one knows your name"

Because beside the fact that he looked like he was in his mid-thirties maybe he should have hidden the photograph that stood proudly on his mantelpiece showing him at the opening of Apple, with a fucking great big beard, taking a picture of John Lennon (no beard), in 1968.

If my maths were correct, that would've made him a very hairy thirteen year old, with access to the most famous band in the world! After ten minutes of me interrogating him 'Jack Regan' style, he broke down and admitted that he was a little older than he'd said and had only done it because he really wanted to be in the band.

I didn't really give two fucks about his age, because he was actually a good drummer, (well he would be, wouldn't he? He probably started playing in the 40s) but what was of much more importance to me was I now had my own personal chauffeur, prepared to drive me around London whenever and wherever I wanted to go and so… Ivor was on the firm.

He surprised everyone by turning up at our first rehearsal with a song he'd written. A song writing drummer, that's a novelty. Unfortunately, it was called "Jailbait".

Do you want a sample of the lyric?

"Put your high heeled shoes on and make up on your face,
Your mother should see ya, you're such a disgrace,
With rouge on your cheeks and mascara on your eyes,
When the cops find out your age, they'll get a surprise,
Because you're... "(wait for it here comes the 'rapey' chorus)
"Jailbait, Jailbait,
The kind of girl men love to hate,
Jailbait, Jailbait,
You'd better stay home tonight and..."

I'm only typing out the lyrics, and I'm starting to feel scared.

I'd only been back at school a week after my last suspension when I finally managed to get myself expelled. That gave me all the time in the world to do whatever the fuck I wanted.

Dad had other ideas though. He started to get pissed off at me lying in bed until midday, wanking myself off to 'Our Tune', and so he arranged a job interview for me in Denmark Street with an old pal of his who owned a very successful publishing company, Campbell Connelly.

Check this out.

The job would earn me £40 a week (plus LV's) and all I had to do was listen with my 'young ears', to all the demos the company received from what they classified as new bands, and put the good ones to one side for them to check out.

Easy or what?

Well, it was until the boss told me I'd need to wear a suit, which I didn't quite understand because he said that I was going to be stuck in a room on my own surrounded by loads of cassette tapes, so why the fuck did I need to wear a whistle? I told him I didn't own one, but Dad came up with a solution to that: "Your brother's got a spare suit that you can wear."

"No way! It's fucking flared!"

"What's that got to do with anything?"

"Joe Strummer wouldn't wear a flared suit."

"White people go to school where they teach you how to be thick"

We walked back down Tin Pan Alley in total silence, and I think it would be right to say he had the band needle with me, but he obviously just didn't understand some of punk's ground rules. I suppose I could've met him halfway and ripped the whistle up a bit and stuck a few safety-pins in it.

Ivor's first and last gig with The Dead was at The Roxy's '48-Hour Non-Stop Party' that started on Christmas Day and ran right through until midnight on Boxing Day. We were originally booked to play on Christmas Day, but I moved it forward. I might have been a Punk, but there was no way I was gonna miss *The Morecambe and Wise Christmas Show*, and that year it was a cracker.

The Stranglers	**"Peaches"**
999	**"Nasty Nasty"**
The Boys	**"I Don't Care"**

When we arrived to play, we were greeted by the sight (and smell) of a couple of hundred punks lying on the floor, nursing amphetamine comedowns and drinking bottles of cheap cider, and this was at 2.00pm in the afternoon!

We opened our set with Ivor's thinly veiled message/threat of sexual violence towards young females and it went down like, now how can I put this?

Like a reggae band at a KKK meeting.

Now, I don't know if this was because the audience were all totally fucked up, or we just sucked (a little bit of both probably), but we cut our forty-minute set down to a cosy fifteen and fucked off to Camden Town to see Siouxsie and The Banshees at The Music Machine. We blagged our way in by giving it large to the doorman about how we'd just come offstage at the world-famous Roxy and wanted to hook up with our music-biz friend Siouxsie and luckily for us he bought it, and even escorted us up to the 'celeb bar' at the side of the stage, where I got talking to Steve Jones and Paul Cook about the forthcoming Pistols tour of America, and then in a starstruck moment I asked for (and got) Johnny Thunders' autograph, which I still have in a frame on my front room wall.

It reads… LAMF. Johnny Thunders. Oh, and Phil Lynott bought me a pint.

But all that pales into insigfuckingnificance, when put up against the kiss I got from Siouxsie after the show, which seriously made my legs turn to jelly.

The year ended with a night I will never forget. On 31st December 1977, I went to see The Ramones at The Rainbow with Generation X and

The Rezillos supporting them. Now tell me, can you get a better line up than that?

The only downer was, I had to go with Ivor, because he'd bought my ticket and was also picking me up in his motor to take me to and from the show, but I managed to give him the slip as soon as we got into the venue (after he'd bought me a pint), which just goes to show what an old slag I am. Even though I had more than my fair share of lager that night I definitely know I was there because a few years ago the show was released on DVD, "I'm Alive", and all the way through it I can clearly see the fifteen-year-old me (with a huge Beatles badge on my lapel) the whole way through the concert.

After the show, I got talking to some gorgeous bird at the bar, who after a couple of drinks invited me to go to a warehouse party with her down by the Thames. She was definitely giving me the impression my evening would end with me depositing some of my fluids inside of her and so as I didn't want some ageing, leather clad gooseberry fucking up the evening for me, I gave Ivor the slip.

We took a night bus to the party, and as were making our way in, a well pissed Peter Cook, with a bird on his arm, was making his way out.

Me: "Alright Peter, how's it going?"

Peter: "Not bad. A little bit of advice though, you can fuck my wife, but don't wipe your cock on the curtains."

And that's how 1977 ended for me, on a high, thinking that this was how life was always gonna be for me.

The never-ending stupidity of youth.

But I will always have a safety-pin stuck in my heart for all the music that was given to me by all those year zero heroes, and yes Bobby, that does include Eddie And The Hot Rods.

Ramones - It's Alive The Rainbow Full Concert (1977)
Staring like a psycho killer

95

GOODBYE PICCADILLY

It was a rainy Monday when I stepped off the train,
A bag of blues, jam shoes and I ain't going back again,
I ain't going back again.

Well here I am in London, just a wide-eyed teen,
And in my sights, the Soho lights, and touch everything I've seen,
Touch everything I've seen.

Hello Piccadilly, hello happiness,
I used to dream about you at night, but now I'm here in the flesh,
Now I'm here in the flesh.

Another cup of coffee in the Golden Egg,
Hoping someone will notice me, a smile or a nod of the head,
A smile or a nod of the head.

Sometimes I go out dancing, with my money made,
Or spend the night under neon light, down in the penny arcade,
Down in the penny arcade.

Hello Piccadilly, hello happiness,
I used to dream about you at night, but now I'm here in the flesh,
Now I'm here in the flesh.

But nothing lasts forever and nothing's like as it seems,
But when you're young, it's said and done, a boy's got to follow his
dreams,
A boy's got to follow his dreams.

Goodbye Piccadilly, hello happiness
I used to dream about you at night, but now I couldn't care less,
Now I couldn't care less.

I suppose 1978 was always gonna be bit of an anti-climax after all the excitement of the previous year because even today, I still think 1977 was the best year of my life; but as a four-chapter book isn't really an option here I'd better continue!

Without having the distraction of going to school, my life was now just one big green-light to do whatever the fuck I wanted to, which basically meant taking loads of blues at gigs.

Other band's gigs.

It had to be because Paul had decided to leave The Dead and join a power pop band (remember that?), which fucked us up a bit, because most of the band's equipment belonged to him, although when he told us he was moving on, I can't remember the rest of us putting up too much of a fight to get him to stay. What I do remember though is coming up with the idea of telling the music press he'd died in a hit and run accident outside a club we were playing in Paris.

Clever eh?

We made sure that it happened abroad so it was harder for them to check up on, although we didn't really have to bother because in those days you could just tell them any old bollocks without ever having to show them any evidence or proof to back it up, and they would put it in the next week's edition of their paper.

I remember going down to the *NME* office in Carnaby Street, where I was taken over to some young scribe's desk so he could take down all of my sad news. He clocked the Bolan badge on my lapel and said: "Hold on, I've got something in here that will interest you."

He pulled a small brown envelope out of one of his drawers and handed it to me. I saw 'Marc Bolan's last remains' written on the front of it, which apparently contained a small blood-stained fragment of windscreen with some of Marc's hair attached. He offered it to me as a gift, but I passed, and handed it back unopened.

Cunt.

For a couple of weeks, we did make the effort to look for a new singer. Ivor The Bear even made a request for one, from the stage of the 100 Club at an Alternative TV show that you can hear on their classic album "The Image Has Cracked". It was also the same night that I received an unexpected gift from some punk bird, who'd recognised me while I was enjoying a nice underage pint at the bar. She told me how she'd read all about our singer dying and how horrible it must have been for me.

I played the part of the friend in distress perfectly. The gift? She let me suck her tits in the ladies' bogs.

Class… pure punk class.

The Clash	**"White Man In Hammersmith Palais"**
Rich Kids	**"Rich Kids"**
PIL	**"Public Image"**

I didn't think being in The Dead was gonna get any better than that, and so I also handed in my notice, even though I'd caught the gig bug and wanted a lot more of it, and so I did what everyone did in those days, checked the 'Musicians Wanted' ads in the *Melody Maker* Classifieds.

You know the sort of thing, they usually read like this:

BAND SEEKS GOOD LOOKING BASSIST FOR GIGS, RECORDING ETC. MUST HAVE GOOD POP SENSIBILITY, TRANSPORT NOT ESSENTIAL, NO BREADHEADS. PLEASE RING…

One stuck out for me. It had all the usual fanny, but with the addition of: "Influences: Generation X and The Buzzcocks."

Which was right up my street.

I rang the number, only to find I knew the bloke at the end of the line. Well, not him exactly, but his sister, who I used to knock about with the previous summer. His band were called The Clique and they were holding auditions the following week underneath a paint shop in Islington, about half a mile from where I live now, and on the day I went dressed to impress in my best new wave gear and Steve Marriot barnet. I must have either come across well, or there was no other cunt up for the gig, because at the end of an hour's jamming with them, they told me the gig was mine if I wanted it.

The answer had to be yes, because it was certainly a step up from my last band.

Why?

1. They could actually play their instruments and had some really good songs.

2. The band owned all their own equipment

3. They had a drummer who looked like a young Terry Scott.

We started gigging straight away, mostly in London and the South East, with one of our shows sticking out like the proverbial sore cock. The venue was a youth club in Dagenham and we were second on a four-band-bill with The Purple Hearts, who part of the new mod revival, headlining. I was standing outside the venue after soundcheck, chatting to Terry Scott, when our conversation was interrupted by a couple of skins asking us what time the show kicked off, which actually turned out to be a very appropriate choice of words.

I could see one of them was wearing a t-shirt that read 'Hitler On Tour' that was very popular with 'fronters' at the time but although it made me think the geezer was a complete cunt, I wasn't really in the mood for a ruck that night, so I thought: "Just let it ride mate."

But our stupid cunt of a fuckwit drummer just couldn't keep his sheltered middle-class mouth shut: "I take it you'll be taking your offensive shirt off before coming into our show?"

And the reply: "I'll see you later mate."

And off they walked, with those five little words hanging in the air like an impending prison sentence.

"You stupid cunt! What the fuck have you done?"

"What do you mean?"

"Those two are obviously gonna come back, firm handed, to do us. Maybe I should just smack you now and save them the bother."

These were rough times, as anyone who was there could tell you.

"Somebody's gonna get their head kicked in tonight"

I'd had some right tear ups at Sham 69 gigs and don't get me started on The Clash's RAR show in Victoria Park. That was a right naughty turn-out, at what was also one the best shows I ever saw the band do, and I went to over sixty of them. In those days violence was part and parcel of a night out; if you managed to get away from seeing a band without getting a back-hander, you'd had a result.

Anyway, back to the hiding we were soon going to be receiving.

When I told the rest of the band the SP they absolutely shit themselves, but I came up with an idea that might help us to get out of Dodge. We'd tell the promoter our singer had just received a bit of bad news from home and had to get back there ASAP, and then ask if we could go on first and let the opening band take our slot.

He and the band both agreed without any argument.

Wasn't I a clever little bugger?

You see, all bands wanna be as high up on a bill as possible, so if you offer them something that's a bit like getting an upgrade on a plane, they ain't gonna turn it down, and so we went on first and played our set like we were The Ramones if they'd just taken some really blinding whizz, and then pissed off a bit fucking sharpish. I didn't give a toss the next day when I heard around fifty skins had come down after we'd fucked off and smashed the place up but now I'm a little older and wiser (?), I have to admit, the thought of some musician getting his gear smashed because of my cunning plan does give me more than just a little twinge of shame. But hey, don't blame me, blame the drummer.

On a more positive note, it was during my time with The Clique that I recorded "My Desire", my first self-written track, at Fairdeal Studios in Uxbridge. I thought it sounded like The Buzzcocks meeting The Rich Kids in a club owned by XTC. I say "thought it sounded like", because after recording it in the summer of 78, I lost the cassette the studio gave me of it. However, in 2015, through the wonder of the internet, I managed to get in touch with the band's singer Terry Faulkner for the first time in nearly forty years, and the little diamond sent me a copy of it on CD. Of course, when I listened to it, it sounds nothing like my description, but what I will say is, for a first effort it's not too bad at all and maybe one day I might even get round to putting it out.

I only spent six months in The Clique, because, well you know how it is when you're young, you want the world and you want it now. When I'd joined them, there was all the usual 'record company interest' talk from the band's manager who promised everything but delivered fuck all, except for a contract he tried to get me to sign that would have made me his musical slave in perpetuity. I handed in my notice.

It had now been over a year since I'd been thrown out of school, and in that time I had made absolutely no effort to find any work, which pretty much left me a skint boat. I was picking up a few quid from the odd bit of petty here and there, but if I wanted to buy some decent equipment and go out to gigs three or four nights a week, it was now time for me to make the ultimate sacrifice... I had to put being a musician on hold and get myself a 'proper' job, which in the late 70s, I have to say, was a piece of piss.

It really was.

You could walk into any Job Centre in the morning, pick a card, and by the afternoon you could be starting a brand new life of misery and boredom in EC1 working as a Trainee Lithe Printer or a Warehouseman for sixty quid a week. It seemed like every job on offer there was for sixty-fucking-quid a week. I knew that because all my mates had told me, but now it was my time to pick a card and take it up to the geezer behind the desk who looked like his life had fucking ended in 1958.

Man: "How do you fancy working for a newspaper in their post room?"

Me: "Sounds alright."

Man: "Go along to their offices in Covent Garden tomorrow at 2.00pm, for an interview."

And so I did, and it turned out that I'd picked an ace.

I knew that if I was to stand a chance of getting any job, I'd better make a bit of an effort in the image department. My outfit? Purple drape jacket and black leather trousers; which turned out to be the perfect clobber to wear for the interview because when I got there I found the job was at *Sounds*, which I suppose was a newspaper of sorts, just one where you were more likely to see a picture of Joe Strummer on page three, rather than a bird with a big pair of tits.

I sailed through the interview by using the same technique I used with girls: tell them exactly what they want to hear.

They asked me to start the following Monday, which suited me down to the ground because the next four nights of my life were going to be spent in the company of The Clash at the Music Machine, and that was going to involve drinking a lot of alcohol while jumping around to the best rock 'n' roll band in town. It was also going to be the place where I would have my first ever line of coke. I arrived for the first show already buzzing from a handful of blues I'd taken earlier, and was getting stuck into my second pint of the evening when I started to find myself paying more than just a passing interest to the first of the night's two support bands...

The Specials

Who, I'm sure I don't need to tell you, was an early incantation of what would go on to become one of Britain's greatest bands ever...

They didn't sound like any other group on the circuit at that time. They even managed to get my speeding arse on the dance floor when they delivered a great version of the Harry J classic "Liquidator".

The next band, Suicide, didn't really do it for me, and I think most of the audience felt the same because they began lobbing bottles and glasses at them, and that's when I decided that maybe this was the perfect time to go for a piss. I pushed the only cubicle door that didn't look like it as being used only to find a large, bearded man hoovering up some white powder off the top of the cistern.

Me. "Sorry mate, I thought it was empty."

BM: "No problem, do you fancy a line?"

Me: "What is it? Speed?"

BM: "No it's coke, and it's really good."

And so, for the first time, I found myself in the confines of a very small toilet with a man I didn't know handing me a bank note to stick in my hooter and snort a little class A.

"I've got cocaine running around my brain"

But his generosity didn't end there, because straight after giving me a bump he offered to buy me a drink and so without a second thought for the mates I'd come to the gig with, I fucked off to the bar with my new friend.

I was used to the sight of middle-aged men in The Roxy or The Vortex, trying to pick up young punks; mates of mine would often stand chatting and flirting with them at the bar just to get a few free drinks, or even better a couple of quid, but this guy didn't come across like that, to me he seemed, for want of a better word, straight. Anyway, he bought me a pint and while we stood there watching Suicide become a human bottle bank, I began thinking: "Why do people go on about how great coke is?"

And *then* it hit me, and I mean, hit me.

I don't know if it was the blues I already had in my system that slowed down the effect, but fuck me did I start to feel good, waffling away like a good 'un, and boy did I have some front: "Give us another one then mate."

And so it was all back to the bogs, but this time he gave me two lines.

I was just about to buy him a drink as a thank you for his kindness when the lights went down, followed by a huge roar, which could mean only one thing...

IT WAS TIME FOR THE CLASH.

"Sorry mate, I've gotta go."

And with that I legged it down to the front of the stage, pushing aside any men, women, OAPs, kids in wheelchairs, anyone who dared to get in my way, to make sure I was in the best possible position to see the punk fab four.

It was the same for the next three nights as well. No, not taking coke with strangers in toilets, but watching The Clash who were, at that time, in my opinion, the greatest live band in the world.

I'd like to take this opportunity to thank that bearded man for introducing me to a life of excess. You bastard.

When my first day on Respectability Street arrived, I felt bright, breezy, and ready for a hard day's work.

I'm sorry, that's a total lie.

The truth was, I turned up absolutely fucked after a mad weekend on the piss, but somehow, I managed to get through that first day, with a lot of front and a couple of blues. Besides working in the post room, I also had to do a little bit of menial around the building like emptying the coffee machines, which turned out to be a job that would usually top my wages up by at least a tenner a week. Other perks were: instead of taking all the new album releases upstairs for the journalists to review, I'd grab a box for myself and head straight down to Cheapo Cheapo's in Rupert Street to flog them, with the ackers received going towards a good night out in The White Lion, a great little drinker just around the corner from the office.

The White Lion was the kind of boozer where you could either find yourself having a cuff with the singer of a well-known heavy metal band or, like I did one lunchtime, standing shoulder-to-shoulder at the bar next to the late, great Leonard Rossiter. I thought about trying to impress him with my Rigsby impersonation, but thankfully I had a rare moment of common sense and just went for the 'I'm a big fan' routine instead.

One person who seemed to live in there was Garry Bushell, who at this time was bringing a breath of fresh air to an otherwise stale music press, writing about and championing bands who otherwise would have never got a look in.

The problem with a lunch hour is exactly that: you have just sixty minutes to get as much alcohol down your neck as possible. I would usually have maybe three pints with a ham roll chaser to soak it up, but on this day, I saw Garry in there getting pissed up with The Damned and thought it would be rude not to go over and join them.

My three pints quickly became six or seven, by which time I'd forgotten all about my afternoon's postal duties, and when the band invited me to come and watch them rehearse in a little studio just around the corner from the pub at closing time it signalled the end for me and my cushy little job. It was P45 time. I know I could have said no and gone back to work, and pretended that I wasn't totally mullered, but the opportunity to watch The Damned rehearse, well, it was all bets off.

So, for the next three hours I sat in the corner of some shitty little room, with a couple of cans of lager, watching them construct a song they called "Melody Lee", which for me was a lot more fun than sticking envelopes into pigeon holes.

I got in to work early the next day to get stuck into the morning post and when I made it to midday without anyone saying anything to me, well, I thought I'd had a touch, but then I got a message to go and see the boss and by 1.00pm I was out the door. They obviously wanted to make sure that I did all my jobs before giving me the elbow, but they still managed to put a smile on my face by giving me a £600 pay off.

I'd only been there for four months!

I managed to spunk my double carpet windfall in less than a month with most of it going on essentials… Records, drink, amphetamine, gigs, more records, more drink, more amphetamine.

And then there was heartbreak.

Early one morning I got a call from University College Hospital telling me Mum had been involved in a car accident, and although they couldn't tell me how serious her injuries were they did ask me to come up to the hospital straight away, which of course I did.

I was trying to find out from a nurse if she knew where she was, when a trolley came past with a woman on it who I didn't know from Adam…

It was Mum.

Her face was completely unrecognisable. It was like something from a fucking horror film. I was only sixteen, and I'd never seen anything like that before.

She was on her way home at 6.00am after working on her hot dog stall she ran outside the Global Village and was involved in a serious car crash on the Warren Street underpass, with the poor cow going through the windscreen, ending up on the kerb.

Now you don't have to be Sherlock Holmes to work out she was a right little grafter. Mum used to open her shop every morning at 7.00am and work there all day until she closed up at 7.00pm, and that's when she started serving hot dogs to all the Charing Cross piss heads until the early hours.

She spent the next three months in UCH, before moving to a rehabilitation centre in Clacton where she basically had to learn how to live again. It's the worst feeling in the world, seeing your Mum like that and all you wanna do is wave a magic wand and make everything better, but of course life isn't like that and of course I knew that just like I knew that she was never, ever gonna be the same again.

After the accident, she lost her shop and her partner but she never lost me.

I think I'd better get back to the music.

Now I was footloose and broke again I set about trying to find some like-minded musicians with the aim of forming a band that played original songs. Ok, what I mean is play MY original songs! The problem for me was all the musicians I knew who were in or around my age group didn't want to play punk rock anymore. They'd either moved on to the more socially acceptable sound of new wave, after seeing the Boomtown Rats on *TOTP,* or were jumping aboard the new mod movement that was on the rise in the UK.

But this time, instead of doing my usual of fucking off an idea before it even has a chance to fly, I carried on hoping that eventually I would meet someone who was on the same wavelength as me, and then one Saturday afternoon I did.

I was half way down the Kings Road, on my way to The Chelsea Potter where I'd arranged to meet a guitarist, when I saw an old friend from the Bolan days, Steve Treatment, coming towards me with a guitar in his hand and a feather boa round his neck. I was so happy to see him that I forgot all about the guitarist, who cited Television and Talking Heads as his musical influences, and fucked off with Steve down The Drugstore for a whizzy afternoon of 'do you remembers?' that carried on into the night after discovering a shared love of all night cinemas.

At least once a month, I would go down with a couple of friends to Leicester Square or Warren Street and spend the night speeding and watching biker or soft porn films in cinemas that smelt of sweat, piss and you've guessed it… spunk. It was also a great place for junkies and the homeless to get their heads down for a couple of hours, which was fine by me, even though sometimes you couldn't hear the film over their fucking snoring!

While we are on the subject of films, let's have a list:

NICK'S TOP TEN FILMS (In no order)

1. 'Brief Encounter'
2. 'Ice Cold In Alex'
3. 'A Hard Day's Night'
4. 'The Wild Geese'
5. 'Sapphire'
6. 'Yesterday's Hero'
7. 'Home Before Midnight'
8. 'Dracula AD 72'
9. 'The Long Good Friday'
10. 'The Dambusters'

Anyway, during the course of the day, the subject of music raised its head many times. Steve told me he had a lot of songs but needed help arranging them and because he knew that the old man had arranged some of his favourite Cilla Black records he wanted me to sprinkle a little Welsh magic over his material.

He always did have a very vivid imagination.

"It was just my imagination running away with me"

I was happy. Even though it wasn't going to be my songs I'd be working on, at least I'd found someone who I wanted to work with, and so I began listening to all his material suggesting changes to both words and music here and there until eventually we chose what we considered to be the best ones for us to record at his next studio session.

Steve had already released a five-track EP that had received some great reviews in the music press. I'd heard it on the Peel show, but hadn't realised it was the same Steve I used to knock about with a few years before. I don't know if it was because our friendship had originally blossomed through the Bolan connection but the songs lined up for this release were a lot more T.Rex influenced than the ones on his debut EP.

I booked a day at Fairdeal Studios in Uxbridge, the same place where I'd recorded with The Clique, and decided that with just eight hours studio time available to us it would be for the best to focus on just finishing two tracks: "Heaven Knows" and "Step Inside A Worn Out Shoe".

I'm glad to say that we managed to achieve that, even after the drummer I'd booked for the session got up from behind his kit after recording the first song "Heaven Knows" and announced: "Sorry, I gotta go now, I've got to go and meet my bird."

And dashed out of the door.

This really wound me up, but not Steve, he didn't seem to think this was a problem at all, because in his wonderful world of misplaced faith in me, it was simple: I would play the drums on the next track! Because I didn't want to burst his bubble, I went into the drum booth and for the next three minutes of my life I was a Rat Scabies tribute. Seriously, if you ever get a chance to listen to "Step Inside A Worn Out Shoe", you will hear a very bad impersonation of the The Damned's "I Feel Alright".

With both tracks completed, Steve went about sorting out the artwork for the cover, while I began looking around town for musicians for our new band, The Zodiac Fashions. The double-A-side single was released in February 1979 and sold well, getting good reviews mainly due to us spending many hours walking the streets of London looking for any record shop we thought might take a few copies off us, and when it was time for a break we visited all the pubs we knew where the music journos drank, to slip them a freebie disc with the pint we'd just bought them.

It was DIY indie payola!

Although I didn't have much luck finding musicians for the band, after the relative success of the single Steve wanted to go straight back into the studio to record a follow up, only this time he wanted it to be a five-track EP and it had to be recorded in a day!

I was now beginning to understand Steve a little better: the more chaotic everything was, the happier he was, and with that in mind I booked a studio in Tooting that looked like a house bombed in the Blitz and asked Richard to play drums, even though he'd never been near a drum kit in his life. My instincts were right, because he loved it, and unbelievably we did manage to record and mix five tracks in one day that to my ears sound a lot more in line with his first EP than the "Heaven Knows" single, which for me was a good thing.

Once again, the record sold and was received well.

If you look online you can sometimes see both records on sale for nearly £40 a pop. All I can say is that I wish I had a couple of boxes of those little fuckers now!

Over the next few months, I recorded with Steve a lot, on his own music and sometimes with other bands, like when we did backing vocals on the Cuddly Toys single "Madman", but we never did manage to get a band together. And apart from the occasional trip to an all-night cinema, or one very funny time at a gay roller disco in the Global Village (Heaven) where I was shown how to skate by two huge leather bound 'clones', we drifted apart.

He would ring me from time to time, sounding a little worse for wear, and I would spend most of our conversation telling him how he should be looking after himself (I've always been good at giving other people advice) and then in 2015, I received a call from Chuck Warner, boss of the American record label Messthetics, telling me of their plan to release all the tracks we'd recorded together on a vinyl-only compilation album.

These were his words: "How do you fancy ruining your career by helping Steve put a band together, to help promote the album?"

After much laughter, I agreed, thinking it might be a bit of a hoot to hook up with my old friend but unfortunately, before we could make it happen, Steve was found dead in his flat.

The guy was the type of character I don't seem to meet anymore and I was chuffed to see he received a Guardian obituary after his passing. He would have creamed himself over that! Sleep well mate. You were one in a million x.

My mind just drifted back to that night skating at Heaven, reminding me that I spent a lot of time back then going to gay clubs and pubs because I'd made a lot of gay and bisexual friends on the punk scene and hanging out with them was always a laugh.

Once again, it was time for me to put music to one side and get myself a proper job, to make a few quid, and I landed a good 'un. I started working as a messenger at The Film Editors in Lexington Street. I had all the best intentions of just getting my nut down, doing the work, and not going for lots of lunch time piss-ups that would ultimately end in my dismissal, and for a while I did just that. My day was spent delivering or picking up cans of film from all over London, either on foot or on my trusty bike. But after a couple of months, a lot of the pick-ups I started to make were definitely not film related, and were usually done in a taxi in the Ladbroke Grove area. I would be sitting in reception, and one of the editors would poke their head around the door, and beckon me to the privacy of their editing suite:

Editor: "Nick, do you fancy going and picking up a little parcel for me?"

Me: "Yeah, fine. Usual runnings?"

Editor: "Of course, here's the taxi money and a tenner for yourself."

And so, off I would go, on the moonlight for an hour or so, down to some big gaff in 'The Bella', to sort out an editor's entertainment for that night.

I was a teenage drug mule!

Another thing I helped them out with was to hold the 'rushes' for them as they ran through a machine that looked not unlike a submarine's periscope. This was most definitely the pre-digital age. For my help, I would often be slipped an extra little bit of poke, which was always most welcome, but to be honest I really enjoyed doing it. It made me feel like I was making a contribution, however small, to some of the wonderful art the company were working on at the time which had a roll-on effect of me getting to meet some of the real masters of the film world, like Ridley Scott, who I had the privilege of spending a little time with one afternoon, debating the merits of which was the best British 'kitchen sink' drama ever made.

How cool is that?

I loved working in the West End.

My first delivery of the day was usually to De Lane Lee in Dean Street, which was a studio specialising in voiceovers for films and adverts. They had a right tasty blonde bird on reception who I tried dropping all my best lyrics on with absolutely no success. She probably got the same patter from all the hunky actors who came through there (although the only one I used to see regularly in there was Richard Briers), so it's understandable why she always brushed off my awkward teenage advances.

I'd always take a short-cut through Meard Street on my way there, which is where all the brasses used to hang out, and because I'd do it so many times a day the working girls got to know me and sometimes when I was on my way through would call out: "Hey Nick, wanna come in for a freebie?" I never did though, because I only had eyes for the receptionist.

As jobs go, it was a good one. There was even talk about training me up to become an editor, but I knew I was only ever gonna work anywhere for a couple of months, just to get a few quid in front before going back to chasing my musical dream. So, after a few months I handed in my notice and picked up my guitar again, only this time I boxed clever by getting myself a job on a record stall in Soho market for three days a week, which meant I could earn a few bob and be in a place where I could meet other musicians.

My instincts proved right, because I met quite a few musicians there, in between annoying all the stall holders around me by playing lots of Sham 69 really loudly, and chatting up the endless stream of rockabilly birds that came down to the market to buy all their 50s gear from a stall next to mine which sold everything from brothel-creepers and second hand 501s to headscarves and hair gel.

Chas & Dave	**"Gertcha"**
Nick Lowe	**"Cruel To Be Kind"**
Sparks	**"Beat The Clock"**

If I'd spent as much time flogging records as I did trying to slip into some of these girls, we'd have made a fortune, but I've always been a sucker for that look on a woman.

Because I thought the geezer I was working for was a right wanker, and because back then I was a dishonest little fucker, I used to invite my mates up to help themselves to whatever they wanted, offering them a very generous discount, which always went straight into my bin. Well, how else was I gonna fund a good night out with one of those sweet rockabilly rebels?

Anyway, back to the musicians.

It always seemed to be the same story with them: we'd meet and they would talk a good gig, giving it all the usual 'who's your influences then?' guff, before swiftly moving on to tell me how great their band was and ending with an invite to come down to their rehearsal room to see if I was indeed the missing piece in their world domination jigsaw.

Now, I might not be the best songwriter/musician/performer in the world, but these people were fucking deluded if they thought there were gonna be the next big thing. Even though I was only seventeen, I could see they were absolute shit. And to make it worse, that scenario must have happened to me at least six times.

On most Sundays during the summer of 79 you would find me in another market, this time in Camden Town. This was nothing new for me, because I'd been going there since 1975, mainly to scour all the record stalls in search of bootleg albums, which in the 70s were a big and serious business. And by serious, I mean illegal. You had to really get to know the stall owner before they might invite you behind the counter to have a butchers in one of their 'special boxes', where maybe you would find one of those holy grail albums you'd been searching for. There was always a good chance that while you were bent down, salivating over some new Bowie bootleg, the stall could be raided by the old bill, which was something that happened a lot back then.

The price of one of these badly pressed albums, in a white cardboard sleeve with a photocopied bit of paper stuck on the front, was about £10 a pop. Now compare that with the £3 you'd lay out in a record shop for an official release, with its glossy cover and readable sleeve notes, well that's a nice little mark-up for the dealers. They knew that no serious record collector will buy "Wings Over America" if they can have "Wings Over America... The Soundchecks" instead!

After walking around the markets for a couple of hours, I would make my way to one of the many Irish owned pubs in the area for a well-earned midday pint.

"And the beer I had for breakfast wasn't bad, so I had one more for dessert"

I would sit at the bar, watching the world go by through dusty windows and velvet curtains, while Patsy Cline or Frankie McBride would pour their hearts out for ten pence a go on the jukebox. Sometimes, if I was feeling brave, I would take on one of their traditional Irish roast dinners, which even with my huge appetite would rarely ever be finished. The grub would come on two plates, meat and veg on one, and all kinds of potatoes on the other! Along with three or four pints, it was the perfect thing to set you up for a little afternoon kip on the sofa, before a relaxing Sunday night session.

It wasn't long, though, before one by one these wonderful places began to disappear, to be replaced by (and you couldn't make this up) fucking Irish theme pubs! Boozers decorated with green wallpaper and four leaf clovers, bar staff putting shamrocks in your Guinness, and the occasional leprechaun stripper on stage (alright, I made that one up.)

So, let me take this opportunity to raise a glass or two to the Camden Town I knew. The one that had great little drinkers on every street, full of characters and atmosphere. Not the soulless, generic coffee shop type pubs of today. Staying in Camden, I'd like to say a big fuck you to all the cunts running stalls selling Ramones t-shirts to mugs, who probably think they're the stars of a new Reality Family TV show on MTV.

Before we leave this chapter, and the subject of drinking and pubs, here's another quick list:

NICK'S TOP THREE PUBS THAT ARE NO MORE.

1.   The Manor House, Manor House
2.   The George Robey, Finsbury Park
3.   The Intrepid Fox, Soho

Goodbye old friends, you served me well.

A 'Grade A' gig

SHE'S MAD ABOUT THE 80'S

She's mad about the 80's,
Cocktails and cocaine,
Once she heard the Thompson Twins,
She never was the same.
She's mad about the 80's,
She just loves that gated snare,
She's mad about the 80's,
And that's why she don't care.

She had a kid, a very nice kid, twenty-five years ago,
They didn't have too much of anything, only a radio,
And so sad, with no Dad, to help them on their way,
Just the fun of Radio One, and that is why today,

She's mad about the 80's,
Cocktails and cocaine,
Once she'd heard the Thompson Twins,
She never was the same
She's mad about the 80's
She just loves that gated snare,
She's mad about the 80's,
And that's why she don't care.

These are the days of different ways,
Ain't that the truth,
Some girls wear their Ra-Ra skirts to reclaim their youth,
And now the kid has got her own kid, Heaven's at the NEC,
Seven bands for thirty-five pounds and one of them's OMD!

She's mad about the 80's,
Cocktails and cocaine,
Once she'd heard the Thompson Twins,
She never was the same.
She's mad about the 80's
She just loves that gated snare,
She's mad about the 80's,
And that's why she don't care.

113

I was still checking the classifieds every week, hoping that I would find that one in a million ad that catered for all my tastes, but there was now a new dance craze in town getting the kids onto the dancefloor, and of all places, it originated in Coventry.

The music was called 2-Tone, the brainchild of Jerry Dammers, keyboard player in The Specials. Remember that group who'd caught my eye a year or so earlier supporting The Clash? Well now it was their turn to be the headline band.

I'd seen them whipping up a storm one very hot night down The Nashville, playing their glorious punk, ska and reggae hybrid. I'd also caught an early Madness show at the Hope and Anchor and they seemed to have a shared love of all things offbeat. What I didn't realise at the time was I was witnessing the birth of a musical movement that would go on to take the UK by storm.

More and more people were wearing newly acquired pork pie hats, Crombies and Doc Martins at shows I went to, but it really sank in on a night out with Bad Manners.

I hadn't seen the band for a little while, because I'd been too busy chasing birds with headscarves and wasting my time in rehearsal studios, so I was well pleased when I ran into Doug and he told me that they were playing a show that night at Chats Palace, a sort of hippie venue in Hackney, and invited me along.

It had only been a couple of months since I'd seen them play, but now they had an almost entirely different image and set list. Out went the comedy songs I loved so much and in came covers of "Double Barrel" and "Elizabethan Reggae", with Doug in boots and braces shouting "Skinhead!" a lot over the top of them. It was like coming back home after working away for a few months, to find your punk missus was now listening to ELP and Yes! You could say that it was bit of a shock for me, not unlike the first time I saw my dad wearing jeans.

After the show, I asked Louis what the deal was. He told me he thought the band had a much better chance of getting a record deal by playing more ska and reggae in their set, which I totally understood, although it did make me a little sad to think the band I'd had so many good nights out with was never gonna be the same again; but as you know it paid off because within a few months they were signed by Magnet Records.

Fuck knows why they went with them.

I was there the night the band went to see Roger Ames from EMI at his tasty London drum and he really wanted to sign the band, but for some reason they went with Magnet instead. Maybe the chance of being on the same label as Alvin Stardust was too hard to resist!

Lene Lovich	**"Lucky Number"**
Prince	**"I Wanna Be Your Lover"**
The Clash	**"London Calling"**

Britain was now in the grip of 2-Tone fever, with The Selecter, The Beat and Bad Manners joining The Specials and Madness in one big, glorious black-and-white party.

Although I really liked the whole vibe, I didn't want to play that kind of music. Not until one night when I was at a party and someone introduced me to a well-pissed A and R man from Phonograph, who was desperate to sign something 2-Tone related, and by the end of the evening I'd convinced him The Charlton Brothers were exactly what he needed.

"Who the fuck are The Charlton Brothers?" I can hear you ask.

Well, they were a duo (Jimmy and Billy) who magically sprang into existence after about my sixth pint that night. They allegedly had a huge following in North London, but only played secret or private gigs, with a set list including such sure-fire future hits as "Non Shrewd", "Not Many Benny" and "Do Me A Lemon" (all big Woodberry Down speak circa 1975).

I must've really impressed the record company man with all my old fanny, because at the end of the evening he gave me his number and told me to ring him the next day, and when I did, and reminded him of the offer he'd made the night before (he hadn't) of paying to put The Charlton Brothers into a studio to demo a couple of tracks, he just swallowed it and invited me up to his office to pick up a kite for £200, along with the words: "Do the best you can."

Well, I'd already done pretty well, because the studio I was gonna book was only gonna cost me £80, so I was already a long 'un to the good, and when he said to me: "Go and help yourself to any records you fancy from the stockroom" I knew I was onto a touch, and so I grabbed about fifty or sixty albums, which certainly wouldn't be going anywhere near any turntable of mine: their new home would be 'Steve's Sounds',

115

a record shop in Soho, owned by a good friend of mine whose name was... Steve (it must be some kind of record shop owner thing).

Now, although this may not have been up to the standard of Malcolm McLaren's record company scamming, in just under an hour I'd managed to get a couple of hundred quid out of a major label, to go into a studio and record tracks for an act that didn't actually exist.

All I needed now was to find another Charlton Brother.

To be honest I knew I wouldn't have to look too far, because as soon as I got home and told Richard what I'd been up to, he was well up for a bit of it, and we got straight down to writing a couple of songs we thought might be the kind of thing that our future record company might want to hear.

The only thing in the whole of The Charlton Brothers story that was anywhere near truthful was that on the two songs we recorded, "The Bounce" and "(Living On A) Tightrope", the only musicians who played on them were actual brothers. I wouldn't say that this was a good thing though, because if you listen to "The Bounce" (which fortunately for you, you can't, because it's not available) it goes in and out of time the whole way through. I suppose this was because Richard played drums on it, and in his defence, it was only his second time behind a kit (the first time was with Steve Treatment).

Before I took the tracks to Phonograph, I dropped into *Sounds* to play them to Garry Bushell who liked the scam enough to start writing about us regularly in his Jaws column, which was great promo for us, but not enough to sway my man at Phonograph, who told me he was "A little underwhelmed by what I'm hearing".

And he quickly decided that maybe the £200 he'd given to me was best put down to a drunken misadventure, and told me it wasn't really what he was looking for, before foolishly adding: "But if you've got any other songs you think I might be interested in, drop in and see me."

This was my green-light to pop into his office once a week, over the next month, to play him my latest masterpiece. Each received the thumbs-down, with only one of them, "Non Shrewd", given a second hearing. Of course, I knew he wouldn't be interested, but it gave me an opportunity to end our meetings with: "Is it ok if I grab a few albums for myself mate?"

I suppose if I was going to be honest with him I should have added: "So I can go and flog them to give myself a bit of extra drinking money."

After my third or fourth visit, he pre-empted my request with: "Yes, you can go and help yourself to some records, and then please don't come back."

And that's where The Charlton Brothers' brief flirtation with the big-league ended.

"I don't feel you anymore you darken my door"

It wasn't too long after this that 2-Tone handed the flavour-of-the-month-baton over to the new romantics, who were basically working class Bowie fans from council estates, playing watered down disco to supermodels on yachts. Although I could have handled the lifestyle, there was no way my legs would've looked good in a kilt, so all that bollocks passed me by. I was still a punk rocker at heart, and the only thing that came anywhere near to that vibe was Gary Bushell's vision of a new musical utopia described to me as: "The Clash, fronted by Sid James, singing songs about strippers, lager and pie and mash."

Oi!

This all sounded great to me, but unfortunately as the Oi! movement began gathering momentum, it also started attracting some tossers who seemed determined to replace Garry's vision of good times and fun with hatred and racist stupidity. I knew these nut-jobs were in the minority, and that the majority of punters were good decent people, but even one of those cunts at a gig of mine is one too many. The bottom line is, I don't want to stand on stage playing to people with that kind of hate in their head. Which is why I turned down the chance to sing in a mate's band, even though I thought it might be good fun to jump around on stage singing my pal's songs, which had titles like: "Who Killed Mrs Slocomb's Pussy?", "I'm Gonna Put My Toad In Your Hole", and my own personal favourite "Let's Kill My Mum (And Shag Her)".

The idea of being stuck in somewhere like The Bridge House in Canning Town on a rainy Monday night trying to escape the attentions of a few mental right-wingers (just like I had to do a few years before in Dagenham) didn't really provide a worthwhile payoff for me.

My last word on Oi! is, and you probably won't remember this Garry, you once turned down a track of mine for inclusion on one of your Oi! compilation albums. You obviously didn't think "The Yorkshire Ripper" by The Armchair Beast was suitable listening for young impressionable skinheads.

117

Staying at *Sounds*, here's a story that has nothing to do with Mr Bushell…

I'm sure by now you've worked out that in my youth, I was always on the lookout for an easy earner, to keep me in a lifestyle I wanted to become accustomed to, so when a guy I knew who ran a music and film memorabilia shop asked me if I could get my hands on any photographs of rock stars, one place immediately sprung to my thieving little mind: *Sounds*.

When I worked there, I would often be asked by some hack to a pull a file on this or that artist (a bit like the old bill really) so he could choose a picture to go with the article he was writing, and they had a lot to choose from because each file held about three hundred black and white 10 x 8's, so my flash little 'erbert answer was: "Yeah, easy mate, just write down a list of the people you want."

The truth was, it wasn't that easy, because the gaff had security cameras on the entrance that clocked you as you entered the building, and then you had to sign in with a security guard in the reception area, before you could take the lift up to the *Sounds* office on the third floor. When you're young though, you don't let little things like that stand in your way of earning a nice few bob and in my mind, I was now a North London Richard Harris, masterminding a big heist in some awful late 70s waste of film.

I decided it had to be a three-man job. Two of us would go up to the office and fill three blue laundry bags with the files, while the third man's job was to get us into the place without any suspicion.

And how were you gonna do that then?

Easy mate.

"Easy like Sunday morning"

I got a pal of mine, who worked in the post office, to ring on the bell in full uniform, to fanny to the guard that he had a delivery for one of the reviewers.

Now, who would think that was dodgy?

Genius.

It all worked like a dream: we followed him in, took the stairs up to *Sounds* and filled our bags before making our getaway on the Piccadilly Line back to Manor House.

If I had those pictures today they would be worth a lot fucking more than the £400 that greedy cunt gave us. All the names on his 'want' list were the big boys and still are: Bolan, Bowie, Beatles, Stones, Clash, Sex Pistols. All artists that sell, and sell quickly.

Of course, you always think the grass is greener in someone else's garden, so I did a bit of asking around and found another shop who were more than a little interested in taking a slice of rock history from me. And even though I didn't really take to this geezer, he was offering me £700, which was quite a jump in the moolah stakes. So, the greedy little cunt in me decided to ignore all the old 'never return to the scene of the crime' bollocks and go back for a second visit (using exactly the same method of entry) and I had another touch.

Do you remember when I said that I wasn't that taken with my new buyer? (I hope so! It was only a couple of lines ago!) Well, my instincts were proved to be right when it came for the time to settle up with me. I took the photos down to his shop and the first thing he tried to do was to knock the price down to a monkey, which I wasn't having any of, and so we danced around for a bit before agreeing on £600. Then to piss me off even more he said he didn't have the cash on him and asked if I could come back in an hour while he went to the bank, so I went for a couple of pints in The Cambridge.

When I returned I was greeted, not by the sight of folding, but by two longish-haired, moustached coppers wearing silk bombers, offering to take me along to Bow Street for a little chat. I will say one thing about them, they did have a sense of humour, because they both laughed when my reply to their "Have you got anything to say?" was: "Am I being arrested by two members of The Eagles?"

My next eight hours were spent banged up in a cell, next to some pissed-up Glaswegian shouting: "Jailer, jailer, let me 'oot. I promise I won't hit her again."

I knew I was in trouble, but to be honest the only thing on my mind was getting out of the cell in time to go and see Slade at The Music Machine. Which is why, when they did finally get around to questioning me, I just stuck my hands up and signed a statement saying that it was all down to me, before legging it as fast as I could out the door and up to Camden Town for a crazee night out with Noddy and the boyz.

A few weeks later I was up before a geezer in a wig at Bow Street.

There was some talk about me maybe having to do a little bit of bird, but with no previous I never thought that was really on the cards and in the end all I got was a year's probation and a verbal slap on the wrist; but I still gave it large to my pals on my "acquittal drink up" in the West End that afternoon. With each passing lager, my pathetic life of crime grew and grew. I think it ended with me telling anyone who'd listen that I'd had an officer at West End Central 'straightened' (don't blame me guv, blame Euston Films) with a few quid to get me off.

I've just remembered something else...

The night before my hearing, I had a going away piss-up with Doug and Louis, so perhaps, in the back of my mind I did think that maybe I was gonna have to spend a few months inside.

I never did find out why that cunt grassed me up to the old bill, and although a lot of payback thoughts entered my mind frequently, I never carried them out because I'm not a violent person, and in the end I decided to just 'chalk it up' on the lesson learnt board.

Stacy Lattisaw	**"Jump To The Beat"**
Dennis Waterman	**"I Could Be So Good for You"**
David Bowie	**"Fashion"**

There was one good thing that came out of the whole affair though. While I was checking out all the other music/film based shops in London to try and sell the photos, I came across a great couple who ran a record shop next door to mate Steve's (no names here so let's call them Harry and Sally). Although they weren't interested in what I had to offer that day, we got on really well and so every time I was in the area (which was a lot) I'd pop in to see them for a chat. After a few weeks (without boring you and incriminating me) I acquired an "interest" in their shop, which gave me a welcome safety-net of a few quid a week, and also enabled me, on my days off, to jump onto what seemed like a never-ending merry-go-round of looking for other musicians to help kick start my musical career.

I was still playing the odd show with various bands here and there, some I can remember and some I can't. Recently, online, I stumbled upon one of the can'ts. Apparently, I played lead guitar with a band called London PX for two gigs. All I can say is, it must have been bad, because I can't play lead now, so fuck knows what I was like forty years ago!

In the summer of 1981 violence erupted on the streets of Britain, to the soundtrack of The Specials' "Ghost Town". Although in my mind, if you're gonna smash a few shop windows and loot the gaff, it would be more fun doing it to the "Can Can", which was also riding high in the charts at the time.

Now, some people would like to have you believe that these "riots" were a demonstration against unemployment and all that bollocks. I'm sorry if I sound a bit fucking cynical here, because if you wanna do a bit of thieving that's fine by me, but please don't do it in the name of people who are actually looking for work to try and put food on the table.

Anyway, let me tell you about my experience of the "riot".

I'd been on the piss with Doug all day in Stoke Newington, which was something that used to happen quite a lot, and sometimes it didn't always end well. He once took a kicking for me outside a pub in Albion Road, when some regulars took offence to having a punk rocker drinking in their boozer and made it clear I was gonna get a spanking. Doug told me to leg it, while he and a pal stood toe-to-toe with them. On another occasion, he stepped in for me when I was out of my nut on downers and getting a little bit lemon. Thankfully this time there was no one wanting to give me a spanking.

Anyway, we'd just finished a goodbye pint in our favourite boozer The Brownswood and were making our way out of the door to go home and sleep it off, when we bumped into a regular coming in who grabbed my arm and said: "You're not going up to Manor House are you?"

"Yeah, why, what's up?"

"It's fucking kicking off up there mate, bottles, bricks. There's fucking claret everywhere."

It didn't matter to Doug because he lived opposite the pub, but I was going that way. I looked towards Manor House and it felt like any other warm peaceful summer night. I thought he was either a bit pissed, or on the wind up, so I laughingly told him that I'd better get up there sharpish and join in. As I began walking up Green Lanes I started to hear noises that got louder and louder with every step I took but it wasn't until I turned the corner by the boys' club that I saw the full strength of it. To misquote Sly Stone...

"There was a fucking riot going on."

I couldn't believe my eyes.

There were sirens wailing and lots of little teams, throwing anything they could find at the old bill, who were quite rightly shitting-it behind their riot shields. I saw someone lob a petrol bomb at a motor and it went up in flames, but (and I don't know if this was because I was pissed) I just continued walking through it all, dodging the odd brick here and bottle there, and made my way on down into Harringay.

It really was one of those moments when you have to stop and think to yourself: "Did that really happen? Did I really see that?"

Because of the trouble there were no buses or tubes running, so I had to do the whole four mile journey back to my flat in Palmers Green on foot. For a while it was pretty quiet, but when I reached Wood Green it was kicking off fucking big time again, not with people holding banners with "WE WANT TO WORK" or "JOBS NOT DOLE" written on them, it was just kids (and some not so young) on a jolly of theft and destruction.

"We gonna be burning and a looting tonight"

What the fuck has nicking a pair of trainers out of a sports shop got to with finding work? I'm sure they didn't take a break on the Jarrow march to go and turn over a tobacconist's.

The electrical shops must have got off easy though. Nowadays, you would see loads of hooded men running down the road with brand new Sony iPads under their arms, but I can't imagine that back then anyone would've wasted their time and energy carrying an Amstrad music system back home, only to find out that the door would fall off within a week and your favourite records would sound like a piece of shit on it.

What makes you think I sound like a man who was mugged up into buying one of them back in the day?

Kim Carnes	**"Bette Davis Eyes"**
Stray Cats	**"Rock This Town"**
Rolling Stones	**"Start Me Up"**

For the next few years music took a back seat for me, while I focussed on earning money to keep myself alive. That's why on most days you'd find me either in the record shop helping collectors to find a new piece of vinyl to take home and knock one out to, or in in the company of the two Micks in The Porcupine next to Leicester Square tube station.

There was Irish Mick, who you won't be surprised to find hailed from the Emerald Isle. He stood six-foot-seven in his stocking feet, and fuck me did that geezer love a row. Then again so did his best mate Mickey Teflon, who earned his name from the old bill's inability to make anything stick on him. He was also as game as they come, and never ever let his diminutive five-foot-two frame stand in the way of giving someone a nasty back hander.

In between downing pints, the two of them would be on the dog, trying to knock out their latest line of bent gear, which could be anything from a brand-new VHS recorder to individual packets of hotel shampoo. But what you have to remember is, this was pre-mobile days, and so they did all their business on the payphone in the saloon bar. They always had huge piles of 10p's in front of them on the bar, and God forbid if anyone tried to squeeze in between them to get anything as simple as a drink and knock their coins over, which was something I saw happen a few times. I always thought it was a bit over the top when they gave that person a dig for what was basically an accident, and on one occasion, I said as much. Irish Mick's answer to me? "I know they don't mean to do it, but the truth is, I just don't like people who wear suits."

Thank fuck he never saw me on a night out down The Wag!

Although I didn't really like the psycho side of their nature, I put up with it because:

1. If I'd said anything, pals or not, I might have been the one to get a back hander.

2. They put a lot of goods my way, which I sold on, putting much needed money in my bin.

They weren't the only characters on the manor. At least once a day without fail someone would come into the shop with a boat looking like it had been on last week's *Police 5* (for younger readers that's my era's *Crimewatch*) offering me this or that for a couple of quid. And let's not forget all the shoplifters who thought they could come in and turn me over, and maybe some of them did, but if I had a pound for every time I caught someone trying to fill their bag with goods various and I had to kick them out the place, I'd have about £67!

There was one time when I had a couple of customers in the shop and one of them asked me to show them a single that was on the wall behind me. While I had my back turned to take it out of its plastic sleeve, I heard a noise and looked round to see someone legging it out the door (not the person I was dealing with). I instinctively dropped what I was doing and ran after him. I chased the cunt right up Charing Cross Road, eventually bringing him down with a rugby tackle that Eddie Waring would have creamed himself over just outside Foyles.

I went through his bag and found about £70 worth of stock. His response tickled me: "I was gonna pay for them later."

The geezer had quite long hair, so I grabbed it and marched him back down the road giving it all the "Let's see what the old bill have to say about this then eh?"

Of course, I was never gonna bring them into it, and by the time we reached Cambridge Circus I got bored with his whinging, so I gave him a boot up the arse and told him never to show his face in my gaff again. The funny thing was though, all the time I was out playing *Dirty Harry*, I'd left the shop unattended. But in one of those all too rare faith-in-human-nature moments, when I got back there the guy I'd been serving was still waiting to buy his record! I rewarded his good behaviour by giving it to him free (it was only £6), but let me tell you something, that guy would come in at least once a week after that and would always buy something. Does that mean honesty really IS the best policy?

And the reason I'd never call the boys-in-blue in for something like that is simple: what's the fucking point? It's not like he's a murderer or a nonce is it? He's just someone trying to get by, I just don't want him to get by out of my pocket!

Let's face it we are all at it in some way, aren't we? I know I was, and I was just about to find out that the couple who ran the shop definitely were.

Shalamar   **"A Night To Remember"**
Marvin Gaye   **"Sexual Healing"**
Carly Simon   **"Why"**

It had been just over two years since I'd first got involved with Harry and Sally. Two fun and enjoyable years, that had flown by. And in that time, they both always seemed to have some kind of dodgy deal going on. I would often see hands being shaken at the poker evenings Harry used to host after shop closing time, or clock mucho folding being slipped into well-tailored pockets over a few drinks at the bar of what was one of my favourite places in the whole world, Walthamstow Dog Track (R.I.P.).

I never thought it was anything too heavy, mainly because Harry was a complete coward, but everything changed the day Steve came back from one of his many holidays abroad after leaving Harry in charge of his place. I got the feeling everything was far from hunky-dory when he

124

took me to one side over a few cocktails in The Tea Rooms (R.I.P.) and asked me how business had been for me. I told him it had been a good fortnight, and suggested it must have been the same for him because his gaff had been rammed for most of the time he'd been away. But he shook his head and said: "No mate, in fact my takings were well down. Listen, you don't think Harry's at it, do ya?"

I said no straight away, because I couldn't believe anyone would do that to him, especially someone who was supposed to be his mate, because Steve was the type of guy who would never turn you away if you ever had to put your hand on him for a few quid, and on the flip side of the coin, he definitely wasn't the kind of person to let anyone take the piss out of him.

And so, he set a trap to see if his suspicions were right, and I'm afraid to say they were. When it all came on top, instead of Harry coming clean and trying to work something out, he just fucked off and went on the hoof. It turned out that Harry had some very large gambling debts (thank fuck that's one vice I've never embraced) and I guess he just saw a chance of making a little extra cash to help him pay off some of what he owed, but you know what…

RULE ONE. Never stripe your friends up.

As for his other half, Sally; just a couple of days after the dust had settled on Harry's stupidity, she also went on the "missing list" to avoid what I later understood was a much more substantial debt to some very nasty drug dealers. I've always liked to think of myself as a pretty streetwise type of guy, but I swear I never saw that one coming. Yeah, from time to time she'd ask me if I fancied a line and would rack 'em out, but you know, we are talking about the 80s here, a time when the world and his wife were steaming it into the bugle, big time. But apparently this bird was in the hole, and it was getting bigger all the time.

"There I was, digging this hole"

I was tipped off about what was going on from a mutual friend, who told me to expect a visit at the shop from some very wicked people, who were wanting to collect what they were owed. On hearing this, it didn't take me long to come to the conclusion that as it had fuck all to do with me, and as I didn't really fancy explaining my innocence to her creditors, maybe it was time for me to leave Soho pronto, and so that's what I did.

Robert Wyatt	"Shipbuilding"
The Smiths	"This Charming Man"
David Bowie	"Let's Dance"

I was back to square one, chasing a living wherever I could.

Luckily, a few tickles came my way, courtesy of some of the record shop connections I'd made in the previous couple of years telling me about shops about to close down who were wanting to sell off their stock quickly and cheaply. One of them, R & B Records, was just around the corner from where I was living in Stamford Hill, and I'm telling you, this place had a serious history.

The R & B in the name stood for Rita & Benny (King), a lovely Jewish couple who, besides owning the shop, also started their own record label in the 60s, releasing a lot of classic ska and reggae music. I first visited R & B in the early 70s, and immediately fell in love with the place. This was mainly down to the fact that you could still listen to all the new releases in the comfort of your own private booth, which by this time was something that had all but disappeared in record shops.

Now, I don't want to sound like the owner of one of those secondhand furniture shops who scour the obituary columns of local rags looking for vulnerable people to take to the cleaners, but when I heard Benny was selling up because he wanted to retire due to having a dodgy raspberry, I was, as they say, 'in there like swimwear'. In my defence, I wasn't just looking to make a quick killing buying and selling on, I was a collector too. The chance of picking up a few good ones for myself was just too good to pass up.

Anyone who collects reggae on vinyl will tell you, to find anything that's remotely near to mint condition, you'd have to send out Anika Rice to find it. So, please forgive me when I tell you that I started to get a semi as each pile of unplayed singles, still in their original sleeves, were placed in front of me. I walked away from there with well over a thousand singles, and yes, I made a good few quid in the process, but it was the love of music I really got off on.

And when I got friendly with the owner of Paul For Music in the Cambridge Heath Road, who allowed me access to the shop's basement, which was home to more vinyl than I've ever seen in one place in my whole life, I was in fucking heaven. And, even though there was a horrible smell of damp down there, it just seemed to add to the excitement of searching through hundreds of boxes, to pick up records that today would go for an absolute fortune.

When I wasn't rummaging in basements, I suppose life was pretty ordinary for me. Yeah, I was still going out on the piss and indulging in the odd pharmaceutical now and again, but this was a time when, if I wasn't visiting my mum or going to see WBA lose somewhere, I was happy just sitting indoors making up songs which, if I was in record shop mode, I would file under the Comedy/Novelty section.

As far as being inspired by other bands to help me write and record music of my own, well, nothing much had changed. The only contemporary music I really enjoyed listening to was soul, but one thing I am is a realist, and I know I ain't ever going to be the next Marvin Gaye. I had the idea that maybe I could tread the same musical path as say Half Man Half Biscuit. I mean, I'd grown up listening to comedy records on the radio, so what if I mixed humour with the music I liked?

I could be an 80s punk rock Stanley Holloway!

"With a little bit of bloomin' luck"

It was a phone call from Louis, inviting me to his house to fuck about on his new porta-studio that was to kick start my next musical project, and it certainly had a healthy dose of humour involved in it.

For some strange reason, we decided that the best time for us to do this would be straight after our weekly 'Let's Get Hammered' night held every Thursday in a little lesbian boozer just off the Balls Pond Road, and on the evening in question your honour, we were joined by our old pals, Brian Smith, Paul Hyman and Alan Perry.

It was basically a school reunion, only with people you like.

I still have a cassette recorded on a ghetto-blaster after closing-time that night and it's very funny indeed. Turn on the tape and you will hear five extremely pissed school mates, trying to make music on Louis's new machine. I think it would be fair to say he hadn't quite got to grips with it yet, but drunks don't let things like that stand in their way, because after a few lagers they all turn into George Martin!

You can hear me telling everyone about this new song "Ice Pole" I'd just written, an ode to that artificially coloured stick of iced water that I would buy every day, without fail, in my school lunchbreak. Of course, after opening-up and serving my friends this barrel of eight-pint nostalgia, they now all wanted to hear this masterpiece.

127

When the laughter finally died down at the end of my 'performance', Louis stood up (well sort of) and, with his handlebar-moustache making him resemble an alcoholic First World War General, announced to his troops that he had come to a decision: that was it was time for the five of us to leave the safety of our trench and form a band.

I was more than a little surprised when Louis rang me the next day and started chatting away enthusiastically about the idea of us putting a band together.

First of all, I didn't have a phone... sorry, I love that joke. Seriously though, I'd had it down as just a bit of pissed-up banter, but he told me that he'd already spoken to the others who were all up for it, so what about me?

Well of course I was.

It was a chance for me to make some music with a few of my best friends as a casual arrangement with no pressure attached. After all, Louis and Paul had their Manners commitments and I was under no illusion that any group who were going to write all their songs AFTER having their weekly jolly were ever going to be anything more than a giggle.

And so the Love Squad was born.

We all met up the following Thursday, when something really weird happened: our 'liquid get together' was uncharacteristically cut short because, and get this one, everyone suggested that we should drink up and go back to Louis's and start writing songs. Don't get me wrong, of course we dropped in at the off-licence for some supplies before putting pen to paper, but I was really taken aback by everyone's enthusiasm for our new project, and it was an enthusiasm that seemed to grow as each week went by, as did the band's material, some of it good, some of it bad and a lot of it fucking awful, but as I said before, to me the whole thing was just a bit of a bubble between mates.

Then Louis surprised me again; not once, twice, but three times!

He told me he wanted us to start gigging, suggesting we should add a bassist and drummer and when we had a few shows under our belt go into the studio to record some of our songs. All of a sudden, the bubble was starting to get a little more serious. Now this was ok with me as long as it still remained a laugh. We drafted in another old Woodberry Down lag, the man with the totally unpronounceable name, Bolaslavi Usaveski, who by the way was the same guy who got me arrested in Berry's just a few years before, which I suppose shows I don't hold a grudge!

The drummer was not from the old school though. Tara Gordon was a pretty boy from Golders Green with an ultra-camp voice sounding like Larry Grayson surrounded by a gang of sexually frustrated bikers on a desert island. But a voice can be deceiving because anytime we ever met he always had a pretty bird on his arm. Tara was the drummer who fucked off early from that Steve Treatment session a few years earlier, leaving me to make a complete cunt of myself behind the kit, but I suppose that shows I don't hold a grudge! (Fuck me Nick, you're getting old mate, you just said that a couple of lines ago.)

We were now a seven-piece, so we moved rehearsals from Louis's cosy front room to the slightly more spacious smelly basement in my house in Stamford Hill, to the obvious annoyance of my mainly orthodox Jewish neighbours, as we thrashed out our unique brand of folk/ska until we considered it to be palatable for the rest of the human race. So, just a few months on from that first pissed up night where the band was conceived, we were now ALMOST a 'proper' band.

Smiley Culture	**"Police Officer"**
Womack & Womack	**"Love Wars"**
ZZ Top	**"Sharp Dressed Man"**

We decided to end 1984 by showcasing our talents at Louis's NYE party, with Love Squad becoming an eight-piece just two days before the show when the wonderful Jimmy Scott joined us on congas.

Jimmy was, at this time, playing percussion in Bad Manners, but he'd been a face around the London club scene since the 60s, performing with Georgie Fame and giving Paul McCartney the inspiration for his song "Ob La Di Ob La Da", which was one of Jimmy's many sayings.

"Ob-La-Di, Ob-La-Da life goes on bra"

Of course, there was a lot of alcohol consumed before the entertainment began.

The band's theory was that if you drink X amount before a rehearsal, then that amount should be at least doubled for a show, which makes some kind of sense... doesn't it?

Just before we were about to play, there was a fucking huge banging on the front door. You know the type, the one you hear just before the old bill smash your gaff up and cart you off for questioning. The good

129

news is when the door opened it wasn't the boys in blue coming to feel a few New Year's Eve collars (but I tell you what, if it had been they would've got a nice result) it was only Fatty, a pissed-as-a-fart Fatty bringing even better news with him because as he stumbled into the party, I could see he'd got a new mate with him:

THE MAN THEY CALL "THE UPSETTER"... MR LEE 'SCRATCH' PERRY!!

I'm telling you, I couldn't believe my fucking eyes!

I ran straight up to Doug and gave him a big drunken hug. He then introduced me to Scratch and for some reason I began shouting "I Am the Vampire" at the top of my voice (in my defence, besides being well Brahms, someone had just stuck some poppers under my hooter). He didn't seem to mind anyway, and we gave him a nice big VIP armchair right in front of an open fire to watch the band.

Our set was made up of 100% new material, of which I'd say maybe 70% would mean absolutely nothing to anyone who hadn't gone to school with us!

There were songs about former girlfriends and teachers, and tales of playground bullies and nicking from the local sweet shop. Our one non-school related song, "Stampede", went down an absolute storm; the track was a semi-instrumental wild west influenced slice of ska that invited the audience to stomp as hard and fast as they could on the floor every time we shouted out: "S-T-A-M-P-E-D-E!"

Yeah, I know all the people there were friends of the band, but everyone seemed to really love what we did, including my long time musical hero Lee 'Scratch' Perry, with whom, twenty years later, I would win a Grammy award for my work on his 'Jamaican ET' album as well as being employed in the role of musical director in his band.

Alexander O' Neal	"If You Were Here Tonight"
Bobby Womack	"I Wish He Didn't Trust Me So Much"
Scritti Politti	"The Word Girl"

Although the original plan was to do a few gigs before trying to record anything, in a complete turnaround we found ourselves in a little eight-track studio in East London just two weeks after our first show, putting down four of our new songs.

Personally, I thought it was all a bit too much too soon, but the session turned out ok, maybe even a little better than ok, and that's probably why the whole ethos of things changed almost overnight and by the end of 1985 we'd recorded twenty-two tracks, but only played four gigs.

NICK'S TOP FIVE LOVE SQUAD SONGS

1. "Stampede"
2. "Theme From Love Squad"
3. "Love Makes The World Go Round In Circles"
4. "Let Your Conscience Be Your Guide"
5. "Junkie Christmas"

There were a few reasons that contributed to this, with the biggest obviously being that Louis and Paul were out and about with Manners quite a lot of the time and the rhythm section had fucked off after only a couple of months, and so the Love Squad just kind of wound itself down. The following year we tried again to get something together, this time under the moniker of Cabbage and Bollocks, with the emphasis more on the comedy side of things.

We played a couple of university shows and one at The Town and Country Club in Kentish Town at a benefit concert for the family of Jimmy Scott who tragically passed away at the end of a Bad Manners USA tour.

What both those stabs at 'getting something together' did was give me the taste of being in a band again, because although today I really enjoy being a solo performer, back then I very much wanted to be part of a gang, crew, band whatever you wanna call it, and I was soon going to be very much back in that role.

R & B RECORDS

IT'S ALL HAPPENING AT R. & B.---
With Reggae and Soul plus Tapes
10 per cent DISCOUNT OFF ALL RECORDS and TAPES (EXCEPT IMPORTS)

WE SPECIALISE IN JAMAICAN and U.S. IMPORTS
BEST SELLING LP ON IMPORT---BILLY DE VAUGHAN

THAT'S R. & B. RECORDS
260 STAMFORD HILL, N16 TEL: 800 2988

Offbeat heaven

SKAVILLE UK

This ain't downtown JA,
This is Skaville UK!

Can you dig the rhythm?
Are you hip to the beat?
Do you row your body?
When you move your feet.
Let's rock to the music,
It's ska so sweet.

Let's rock to the music,
That's been away,
Now it's back to hit you,
Like Sugar Ray,
It's a UK party,
Let the organ play.
This ain't downtown JA,
This is Skaville UK!

In early 1986, I got a call from Doug Trendle asking me if I wanted to come down and play on his solo album. It was a call that was to shape the rest of my musical life.

"What fucking solo album is this then mate?"

He told me to get myself down to this little studio down by the River Lea, conveniently next to The Anchor and Hope, a dodgy drinker he liked to frequent, and all would be revealed.

The studio was owned by a guy called Pete Ker, who I'd met a few times before with Doug in The Anchor. Pete had a very impressive CV, including co-writing the classic Arthur Brown hit "Fire" and producing the single "Airport" for The Motors.

I sat down to listen to the first track, expecting to hear some ska or reggae, but I couldn't have been more wrong. It was a thing called "Hawaiian War Chant", which I have to say I couldn't get my head round at first, but I'm always up for a challenge and after a couple of run throughs I put down some bass, guitar, and keyboards on it. Pretty soon it began growing on me, and I started to see why Doug thought this was a good choice of song for him because the more I listened to it, the more I could picture him in some silly outfit, miming to it on an afternoon kids' TV show.

When the session was over we all retired to the pub to get legless.

"But the rhythm of the glass is stronger than the rhythm of the night"

It was always a laugh hanging out with Doug, even though he did seem to attract some of life's, shall we say weirdos, as his mates. I asked him why he was doing a solo album and he told me that the band wasn't working enough for his liking, and that the last album they'd done "Mental Notes" wasn't really ska enough for him, to which I replied: "Well, if you ever wanna record any of that kind of stuff let me know, because I'd be well into doing it."

Less than a week later he called me again, but this time with a completely different proposition: "Oi Nick, Manners have a gig in Scarborough next week and we need a keyboard player, how do you fancy doing it?"

Well, it took me by surprise but after a little persuading I agreed to do it. I had to learn the whole set in just under a week, without having a full band rehearsal, just me and some cassettes of their recent live shows for

133

research, but as I was already familiar with most of their material it wasn't really that hard.

The day before the show, I asked Doug if there was any dress code for stage and he told me just to wear whatever I wanted, and so I chose a really nice whistle I'd bought a couple of weeks before. It was perfect for a night out trying to pull birds in a West End club, but apparently not suitable for playing onstage with Manners! As I put on my made-to-measure whistle in the dressing room Fatty laughed and said: "Fuck me, you look like Bob Grant."

Maybe I should've worn the question mark suit Louis had offered to lend me. It didn't really matter anyway, because there were only about twenty people in the place and they didn't seem to be that interested in "Tossing In My Sleep" and "Tie Me Up". They only came to life when we played "Lip Up Fatty", "Special Brew" or "Can Can".

I was a bit taken aback by the whole day, because it seemed to me that no one in the band had much interest in it anymore, which was kind of rubber-stamped when Paul Hyman told me: "We just meet up once a month now to do a gig and reminisce about Woodberry Down."

And there was no bigger fan of the band than Paul.

I think the recent death of Jimmy Scott from pneumonia, at the end of their last USA tour, had knocked the stuffing out of everyone a little more than they cared to admit.

Madonna	**"Papa Don't Preach"**
Cameo	**"Word Up"**
Run DMC & Aerosmith	**"Walk This Way"**

I thought the show would just be a one-off, but in the months that followed I played a few more gigs with the band. My services were required because the keyboard player, Martin Stewart, had started a full-time job selling insurance and didn't want to take any time off from his new lucrative income to play shows that were basically paying fuck all. I didn't mind stepping into his shoes, but I have to admit they were quite big ones to fill. The man has a unique, individual style of playing, that I consider essential to the band's sound.

As we moved into 1987, I found myself not only covering for Martin, but also on occasion standing in on bass, down to Dave Farren's sudden interest in the Hare Krishna!

And it was while I was sitting in the back row of some dodgy hired mini bus, at 3.00am after one of these shows, dreaming of my bed, that Trendle leaned over and said to me: "How about me and you starting a band up together? Nothing too big, just to play a few local pub gigs."

I got the impression, from the level of his voice, that maybe he didn't want the rest of the band to hear what he was saying. If the idea was just to play a few drinkers for a bit of fun, I didn't think it was anything he had to be secretive about so I said: "Yeah alright mate, as long as it's nothing too serious."

At that point, I didn't really want to commit myself to anything that would take up too much of my time, because I had plans of my own. I'd been writing a lot of new songs that had a kind of modern reggae vibe to them. In fact, I'd just recorded three of them at Chrysalis's basement studio in Stratford Place that very week, with ex-Polecat and future Morrissey sideman Boz Boorer engineering.

Doug took me for an afternoon breakfast the next day at a little cafe in Springfield Park that did a blinding full English. He took out the big brown leather diary he used to take everywhere with him to scribble down all his illegible lists and began his sell to me: "The band's gonna be called Buster's All Stars, and here's a list of songs I wanna do."

He then went on to tell me what my role would be: "I want you to find the musicians. Now, they must all have bald heads, with John Lennon national health glasses, oh, and I want them to wear Crombies that don't fit."

I agreed that the image sounded interesting, but maybe we'd be better served just trying to find people who could play their instruments! And if they did happen to have all those other, very special, physical attributes then we'd had a result. Luckily for me, it didn't prove that difficult to find good players who were interested in jumping aboard (none who fitted Doug's description), even though many of them were already playing regularly on the London pub/club circuit, in bands like The Trojans, The Forest Hillbillies and The James Taylor Quartet.

Now, as far as I can remember, there weren't too many rehearsals before we played our first BAS show at Gaz Mayell's Rockin' Blues. We thought it would be a nice low-key show for BAS to kick off with, in front of a few ska loving punters on a Thursday night in Soho. Well, fuck me, the advertising might have been low-key, but there was nothing low-key about the turnout. There must have been about three times as many punters as I'd ever seen in that sweaty basement. The place was absolutely heaving, which I suppose was good for us to perform in front of, but not so good for my dad, who I'd invited along to see us.

I'd arranged to meet him and my brother a couple of hours before kick-off in The Tottenham pub in Oxford Street for a few pre-match drinks. He turned up his usual dapper, sporting his trademark well-groomed greying beard, looking just like James Robertson Justice after a crash diet. We had a few cuffs before making our way down to the club, but after just a couple of minutes in there the old man said: "I'm tired son, sorry I'm away to my bed."

I remember thinking: "Fuck me, Dad's getting old."

He was only fifty-eight, just a couple of years older than I am now.

I walked him around the corner to the mini-cab office in Rupert Street to make sure he got his sherbet ok but even though it was only a two-hundred-yard stroll, he still managed to cause an incident on the way. After being approached by some brass asking if he wanted 'business', he said something to her to fuck her off and she started digging him out, which was the signal for two huge pimps to come out of the shadows and get involved. Long story short, we managed to calm it all down and poured the old man into a taxi and I made my way back to play BAS' first gig, with a set consisting of a mixture of old classics "Big 5", "Mafia" and "Bonanza Ska", alongside a couple of Manners hits. There was even a reworking of the Love Squad's "Stampede".

The dark Soho basement was so hot, and my boat was red raw from rubbing it with some rancid old bar towel between songs, but it was a fucking brilliant night and gave us the shot in the arm that we needed to go and book some more shows.

Marrs	"Pump Up The Volume"
LL Cool J	"I Need Love"
The Fatback Band	"I Found Lovin'"

We began ringing around all the usual suspects, The Dublin Castle, Sir George Robey, The Pegasus and The Rock Garden, who were all more than willing to put us on, but let's be honest, it wasn't much of a risk for them because we were going out for fuck all; although that's the norm for a new band, we did have the advantage of being fronted by Buster Bloodvessel, who was still very much a face.

And I have to hand it to him, because there he was, sweating his bollocks off for jack shit in some of the same old dives he'd played in nearly ten years before when Manners were first starting out. His ego must have been taking a bit of a hiding but he never showed it, he just mucked in with the rest us. I admired him for it so much; it showed me that my mate still had fire in his big belly.

At every show we did the crowds grew and grew. There were skinheads, punks, mods and a new movement that had begun to show its unwashed face on the streets of London... CRUSTIES!

Word spread around the capital that BAS was a great night out.

So, I was now playing in two bands, no hold on, wait a minute, we'd better make that three! I'm forgetting I was also (along with Louis, Dave, Chris, and Paul) providing the support at Manners shows under the banner of Tony Casino and Vegas, performing such crowd pleasers as "Sweet Caroline", "You've Lost That Loving Feeling" and "Kung Fu Fighting", for which we would receive the princely sum of £30 a man.

And for desperate complete-ists of my music, let me inform you that from time to time we would also slip in the odd Nick Welsh original, little gems like "Too Fat To Fuck" and "The Aids Song", which, when played at a Manchester University Freshers' Ball Pyjama Party, drove the students into a glass throwing frenzy... at us. I don't know if it was the content of the song, or my awful Morrissey impersonation, but whatever it was, it definitely cut short Mr Casino's performance that night!

Any money I made from shows went straight towards recording my new songs. One of them, "Skaville UK", was conceived on a sunny Hackney morning as I walked along Mare Street. I was thinking of Dave & Ansel's "Double Barrel", when out of the blue I shouted: "This ain't downtown JA, this is Skaville UK."

Because I didn't want to forget it, I kept on shouting it as I made my journey home. No one bothered me though, because in those days it was completely the norm to see nut-jobs on the streets of Hackney shouting out random rubbish. You'd just put your head down and walk off the other way in case you made eye contact. I ran into the front room, picked up my old battered acoustic guitar and began singing it into my beloved ghetto blaster, and within ten minutes I had the whole thing down.

Chords, lyrics, riff. Everything!

And it didn't stop there, because almost immediately I began singing another melody based around the same chord sequence I'd just used, and this went on to become "King Hammond Shuffle". Not bad eh? Two songs written in about half an hour, and when I listened back to them the next day they still sounded good, which made me think that maybe this could be the start of something that could form the backbone of an album for myself.

I knew I had to try and write another while I was on a roll, so I took out my cheap-as-fuck Woolworths organ (complete with broken keys) and began vamping a two-chord, bluebeat style rhythm, that led me to start singing the line "Well I might take a train if I ever see you again" over and over, mantra style, in a false(tto) Jamaican accent. I reached over to my ever-present exercise book and wrote down the words "Memory Train" as a possible title.

With the help of high-speed-dubbing on my twin-deck tape machine, I put "Memory Train" onto the same cassette as my previous day's efforts. To my ears they all sounded very fresh and exciting, because nobody else was doing this kind of stuff at the time.

At this point, I'd like to give a big up to my friend Tim Wells.

Because it was over many a liquid lunch with the future bard of Stoke Newington, bending his shell-like about my idea of recording an album, and selling it as a long lost forgotten classic from back in the day, that he gave me no end of help with my future project with a few inspired directional pointers.

We talked about how the genre had always been filled with artists calling themselves King-this or Prince-that, so maybe I could be Lord-something, but Lord what?

I picked up a newspaper and on the back page was an article about Manchester United.

Fuck me, that's it: I'm Lord Manchester!

Everything was falling nicely into place. I had the songs (well only three but I wasn't gonna let that stand in my way) and now, after playing them to a mate of mine who really liked what he'd heard, an offer to record them for fuck all on his porta-studio. I accepted gratefully, even though he and his studio were both from South London (that old North/South divide!).

The exciting news coming out of the BAS camp was that we were also heading off for a couple of days to a studio, but this one was in Coventry and owned by Roger Lomas, and because Roger's a top geezer, he not only gave us the studio and his time for nothing, he also found us a drummer to play on the sessions; because, when I say BAS, it was only me, Doug, and Alan Perry. We recorded four tracks on the first day: "Return Of The Ugly", "Skinhead Love Affair" and covers of The Three

Degrees' "When Will I See You Again" and Symarip's "These Boots Are Made For Stomping".

Roger was quite taken with "Skinhead Love Affair", telling us that he thought it had a very good commercial melody, before adding: "But don't you think the subject matter is a little bit limited?"

The second day was taken up with mixing, so I took the opportunity of leaving Roger to it and made the short journey from Coventry up to the Black Country to see my beloved Baggies, and waste another few hours of my life. When I got back, not only was all the mixing done, but I was surprised to find out that "Skinhead Love Affair" had now become "Christmas Time (Again)".

Talk about limited!

The song I'd written, hoping skinheads all over the world would relate to it, had been turned into a Christmas song, and what kind of life span do they have? About three weeks if you're fucking lucky, unless you're Slade or Wizzard.

Still, on the positive side, we had five tracks in the can and Manners' old manager Andy Cowan Martin had offered his services to shop them around to help us place.

Just like Roger, when Andy heard "Christmas Time (Again)", he told us he thought we had a potential monster hit on our hands. Mind you, it has to be said that most things are monster to Andy, as he only stands about four feet tall in his built-up shoes!

Only joking mate x.

Andy was working for PWL at the time. For those of you who don't know, they were at this point the biggest record label around, ruling the airwaves and much more importantly the charts, with artists like Kylie Minogue, Jason Donovan, Rick Astley and Sinitta. Andy's first bit of advice to us was, because Doug was very much a visual artist, we should make a promo video for "Christmas Time (Again)", to give it a bigger sell to any possible companies who may have an interest in it.

I'd like to say I had some creative input in making the video, but I'd be lying: it was totally Doug's baby. Somehow, he'd managed to find a mini Fatty, a rather overweight child whose father had been persuaded (after a drunken night in the Anchor and Hope) by Fatty to let him shave his kid's head so he could appear in his new celluloid masterpiece. His powers of persuasion didn't stop there though, because he also got permission (well I think he did) to film it all in a local hospital ward. The whole thing was done and dusted in one night, and the end result was perversely brilliant, in a sort of Pink Flamingos kind of way.

I heard that when Andy showed it to PWL boss Pete Waterman, he laughed so much his fucking ribs nearly fell out. But even though it apparently appealed to his sense of humour, he never offered us a deal. Doug put this down to Manners turning him down to be the band's producer back in the old Magnet days. I'm not so sure so about that, I think it had more to do with the band's image not being compatible with label mates Kylie and Jason.

The following year, me and Doug shared a table with Pete at some boozy record company Christmas party in Brighton. "Christmas Time (Again)" was never mentioned, but I found Pete to be very entertaining company, although I was much more interested in chatting to a couple of other people who were also at our table: Noddy Holder and Jimmy Lea from Slade.

Some of the stories they told me that night were absolute gold dust.

I'm not sure how hard Andy had looked for a deal, but he got us fuck all, which was a bit of a downer for us but I think it was the kick up the arse that gave Doug the idea of starting up his own label. He asked me if I'd be interested in coming in on it, but I thought "No, it's your baby you rock it", but that didn't stop us from sitting together in his front room making lists of possible names for it. Some were good and some were awful, but then out of the blue something happened to make him put all the names into a great big 'who-gives-a-fuck' pile.

The phone rings and it's Doug: "Nick, how do you fancy a drive in the country? There's someone I've gotta meet."

He wouldn't tell me who it was but I was intrigued enough to tag along, and a couple of hours later we were standing outside a tasty looking drum at the bottom of a beautiful country lane.

"You're gonna find me out in the country"

Fatty knocked the shit out of the big old brass knocker on the front door, shouting out: "Open up in the name of the King!"

Well, you could have blown me over when a couple of seconds later some geezer, looking exactly like Richard III, opened it and greeted us with: "My dear boys, do come on in."

I was introduced and discovered that this royal lookalike was none other than Siggy Jackson, owner of Bluebeat Records and a name I'd seen many times on loads of dusty old 45s I'd owned as a kid. After a couple of large 'getting to know you' brandies, Siggy began talking to Doug about the possibility of allowing him to use the Bluebeat name and logo to release his new music. As I sat there listening to them bunny, I thought to myself: "Fuck me mate, you've had a right touch here."

And it wasn't long before they shook hands on a deal and Doug walked out as the new owner (even if it was in name only) of one of the most iconic record labels ever.

Something's just crossed my mind: there must have been someone else with us that day because neither me or Doug can drive. Maybe we went down there in Doug's latest acquisition... A big black hearse.

I remember him saying to me: "You know what Nick, you get more looks in this thing than you would get if you were in a Roller."

Well that's probably because 'this thing' was on its last legs, extremely noisy and had no fucking windows, which allowed a famous popstar to poke out his head and stick his tongue out at passers-by!

But before the Bluebeat wheels could be set in motion, BAS (the whole band this time) had a commitment to record two tracks for a forthcoming Link Records ska compilation album: "Licensed to Ska". The songs we chose to do were "Skinhead Love Affair" and "Pipeline" and it was at those sessions that I made a mistake I would regret for the rest of my life...

I'd written "Skinhead Love Affair" and "Rosemary" on my own (I still have my original demos) but Doug said to me: "Look, why don't we credit these songs to 'Welsh/Trendle' and try and get a publishing deal for ourselves. I'm sure my profile will get a bigger one than you'd be able to get on your own and we can split everything 50/50." And like a mug, I said yes.

Which is the reason why, for the last thirty years I've only ever received half of what I should really be getting. But do you know what? Fuck the money, it's the songwriting credit I'm more annoyed about, and every time someone comes up to me and says "I really like your version of that song" it fucking winds me up, but what can I do? Carry the cassette tape of me making it up everywhere with me? What's done is done, and I suppose that's why these days I'm so precious and much more protective about the songs I write.

I see them as my children.

Bad Manners were still doing the odd gig here and there, while BAS continued their adventures around London's toilet circuit. I watched a

DVD of us at The Rock Garden recently; although it was a bit rough around the edges, it did have a great spirit to it and we certainly looked like we were having a good time on stage. What really springs to mind about that night though was not the songs, or the band's performance, it was the morning after the show when one of Doug's pals turned up at The Anchor with a box full of Rock Garden sweatshirts that he'd "acquired" the night before. I bet you can't guess what the fashion item of choice was for all the regulars for the next few months.

As I thought, things eventually came to a head about the two-band situation.

Doug called a meeting, and invited all the disgruntled Manners members to air their feelings on the situation. It was agreed it would be for the best if the Manners members who didn't feel they could give 100% to the band anymore left and in return, Doug would stop going out as BAS and merge the two bands to form a bigger, and better (?) version of Bad Manners. To be honest, I wasn't that happy about it, because I thought there was room for both bands to exist, and it also meant that I would be saying goodbye to playing with some old and treasured friends.

Two weeks later the 'new and improved' Bad Manners did their first show in the back room of a little pub in Palmers Green called The Fox. It was originally booked as a BAS gig, and was advertised as such, but word soon got out about the change. It made for a stupid amount of people trying to get into a very small room as we took to the stage that night. It also quickly became obvious to me that a lot of this stupid amount of people were… stupid!

Or should that read: a bunch of fucking Nazi wankers!

From the first note we played those cunts caused trouble, banging into punters who were just trying to have a good time, and throwing their pint glasses up in the air, which of course smashed over everyone on their way back down. Worst of all, when it came to Johnny T's solo spot, at least thirty of those slags began 'sieg heiling' at the poor sod. I could never understand why those mugs came to our shows. To make things even worse, they were back again two weeks later at our next gig, this time at a South London venue, the imaginatively named Tunnel Club situated just by the entrance to the Blackwall Tunnel.

Why was it even worse? Well, because we were sharing the bill with Desmond Dekker, and although I saw a few of them throwing Nazi salutes during our set, there were a hell of a lot more of them doing it during his. I even heard a couple of lads talking at the bar saying something along the lines of: "Shall we go now? You don't wanna stay and watch this coon do ya?"

Stomach turning or what?

Let me tell you something I heard once that really shocked me.

I was chatting to this bloke I knew who was a company director and someone I considered to be a bit of a smart bod about all things ska and reggae, when he came out with this: "Oh, I always thought Manners were racist. You know, Bad Manners = BM = British Movement."

Well, if that's what he thought, what the fuck would someone a little further down the smart tree have in their nut?

I tell you what they should've all done. Taken some of the brilliant Ecstasy that was flooding the streets of London at the time, and then maybe they would have gone to gigs with their hearts full of love instead of hate.

In my 'Greatest Inventions Of All Time' book, E's are right up there with TV and blu tac. I had some great nights out on it (Public Enemy, PIL and De La Soul spring to mind), completely off my tits having an absolute ball in my sweat-stained t-shirt. Ah, good times!

I'd love to go into more detail, but it's now time for you to put on your sombrero and tight-fitting Union Jack shorts, because I'm taking you off to Spain for the "El Vino Collapso" tour, and we've got Laurel Aitken coming along for the ride as our very special guest.

"Oh this year I'm off to sunny Spain"

I'd shared a couple of bills with the great man before, but this was to be the first time I'd have the honour of performing on stage with him.

As the band's MD (musical director) I sent 'The Godfather' a list of songs I thought would be suitable for us to play, mostly his skinhead reggae cuts like "Skinhead Train", "Jesse James" and "It's Too Late", and went to work rehearsing the band. What I didn't know then, but got to learn in later years, was that Laurel was a man of many surprises, and here was his first one…

When he turned up for rehearsals the day before the tour was due to start, he'd brought along a set list that had absolutely no resemblance to the one we'd been learning for the previous few weeks.

There were none of his 'Spirit of 69' classics because Laurel had now decided he wanted his music to take a more soulful direction, so in came "Spanish Eyes", "Spanish Harlem" and "Stand By Me". Agreed, they are

143

all great songs, but maybe not the kind of material most of the audience would want to hear from Laurel. But as we were all good lads, who just wanted to do our best for him, we faithfully (and quickly) learned all the songs he wanted to do, in what I would call a 'cabaret rocksteady' style. We did eventually manage to get him to do a few of his crowd pleasers, so when we wrapped up rehearsals at the end of the day everyone felt happy and confident with the set.

And me?

Well I was extremely happy! I was going home with a signed copy of Laurel's classic "Scandal In Brixton Market" in my bin.

The good vibes continued the next morning, with everyone getting very loud on lager on the train to Gatwick. So loud, that we managed to make fellow passenger Richard Branson move carriage. I can only assume that was down to our never-ending requests for big money, solo record deals. But happiness can be a fickle mistress, and on this day, she was working at passport control.

I still don't know exactly why Laurel got turned away and told he couldn't fly with us, but I think it was down to some sort of passport discrepancy. We tried to argue his case, but you know the score at airports, it doesn't matter whether it's a lost ticket or a little bit of overweight luggage, you just can't argue with them. So sadly, we had to wave goodbye to him and fly out to Spain Laurel-less, where there was another shock waiting for us when we touched down to meet our promoter at Bilbao airport, who had the unpleasant job of telling us that the nine shows in ten days we were expecting was now just three in ten.

The "El Vino Collapso" tour had done exactly that… collapsed!

I might as well tell you how the tour got its dubious name.

A couple of months before, me and Doug were getting pissed in some wine bar in the city when we were introduced to a couple of odious music biz suits who over a few drinks tried to sell us a song which, in their words, would "suit Manners perfectly". Now, I could be wrong here, but I think these geezers wrote for Black Lace and the song they were touting to us, "El Vino Collapso", was very much in their style. For the next month, they took us out at least once a week to get pissed with them, and at some point, they would always try to sell us one of their songs. We did actually record "El Vino Collapso" but thank fuck it never saw the light of day and for that the British public should be very thankful.

Right, let's get back to sunny Spain.

144

Having most of our gigs knocked on the head was a bit of a blow, but by way of an apology the promoter booked us into a five-star hotel, picking up all our food and drink bills. We all immediately went from being beer and cider drinkers to brandy and champagne and of course it had to be steak for breakfast, lunch, and tea. It must have cost him a fucking fortune, and maybe that's why he got us on to a prime-time TV show, just to keep us away from the comforts of the hotel bar and restaurant!

The show was a right laugh and of course we caused quite a bit of chaos on set. I got made-up next to Sinitta, who I totally pissed off with my constant David Essex impersonations (I think I'd read he'd been her fella for a while), although her dancers seemed to find it very funny. The band got fucking hammered before our slot so I can't even remember what songs we did that day.

Even though there had only been three shows for us to do, the disappointment was lifted more than a little when I found out that two them were festivals with Dr Feelgood. I'd fallen in love with them from the moment I saw them performing "Roxette" on the *OGWT* in the mid 70s, looking every bit like a bunch of blaggers on *The Sweeney*.

Whereas most people had Wilko Johnson down as the star of the band, my eyes were always firmly fixed on the man in the sweat stained suit: Mr Lee Brilleaux, and even though he was now the only original member of the band, they were still the absolute dog's. We had to be right on top of our game for those two nights. I got to have a drink and a chat with him and he turned out to be a lovely man, or maybe that should be a diamond geezer.

Neneh Cherry	**"Buffalo Stance"**
Ziggy Marley	**"Tomorrow People"**
Public Enemy	**"Night Of The Living Baseheads"**

When we got back from our holiday in the sun, I began meeting up with Doug every morning in his front room at 33 Spring Hill, to try and bang out some suitable new material on his delightfully out of tune grand piano, for a potential release on his new Bluebeat label. I can't actually remember any of the songs we wrote together seeing the light of day, although there were some that were very funny like "Give Us A Cuddle", a song we wrote for Rod Hull, or the anthemic "Millwall", that correctly predicted the destruction of that area.

What was hard for me to get my head around was, although BAS had ceased to exist as a gigging band, Doug still talked about recording a BAS album. It all got very confusing for me, especially when he came up to me one morning with a big smile on his face and said: "Guess what? I've got a seven-date tour of California for us."

Which of course put a big smile on my face.

"The west coast has the sunshine and the girls all get so tanned"

I thought by 'us' he meant Manners, but I was wrong because what Fatty had arranged was for me, him and drummer Andy Bruton to go over to America as BAS with the rest of the band made up of members from the LA based group Donkey Show; although I have to admit, I really didn't give a flying fuck who went, as long as I did.

A couple of nights before we were due to fly out, Doug nearly fucked the whole thing up.

We were on a night out to go and see the Motown legend Junior Walker perform at Dingwalls. Now, I just wanted to hear him blow, but Fatty had got the idea into his head that he should try and sign him up for Bluebeat. On route, we decided to drop in at The Dublin Castle for a couple of swift halves, which of course turned into about eight pints each.

By the time we arrived at Dingwalls we were well and truly slaughtered, but that didn't matter because we knew all the bouncers there and they were always more than happy to let us in free of charge, pissed or not. Doug had a different idea though, insisting that they form a human wall, and he would charge through them to get in! They could see he was plastered and humoured him, by letting him get past and into the venue.

At the end of a really good show we made our way to the great man's dressing room, which was probably not the best plan of action considering how pissed we were. Once we were in, all the big ideas about him becoming a future name on the Bluebeat roster went out the window. Instead, Mr Walker had to suffer the two of us giving it a load of: "I love you mate. I fucking love you!"

With no real harm done, we decided that maybe it was time to head home to sleep the night off, but before we did, once again Doug thought it would be a good idea to challenge the bouncers to another battle of manhood. However, it was now about 2.00am and they also just wanted to fuck off home to their beds for a well-earned kip, not wrestle with some pissed up pop star, but Fatty insisted and made another drunken attempt to get past them. This time one of them stuck a leg out, and Doug fell over, letting out a very loud and painful sounding scream as he landed on the cold Camden cobbles.

So, here's the news: two days before our US tour, the singer has a broken arm and is laid up in hospital with the doctor saying he needed at least a couple of weeks complete rest; but Doug ain't having any of it. He discharged himself and we jumped on a plane to the Sunshine State.

Up to this point, BAS had only gigged in tiny London pubs and clubs to, at most, a couple of hundred people, and so our first show in California was going to be a bit of a step up to say the least. The venue was the 2500 capacity Variety Arts Center in LA, and as we drove in from the airport we started hearing radio adverts for the show: "Come and see big old Buster Bloodvessel from Bad Manners this Friday night, with his new band Buster's All Stars."

We couldn't stop laughing.

The last show we'd done was at some dingy boozer in King's Cross, where the advertising was a couple of flyers on the pub windows. We plotted up in an area called Whittier, which to me looked like a nice sleepy suburb, but I was quickly and reliably informed by Donkey Show's singer Ray that looks can be deceiving and sometimes it could get a little bit naughty there.

Donkey Show threw a party to welcome us, which was really nice of them, but just as things were getting into full swing there was a loud bang on the door and we were greeted by the sight of two cops telling everyone in no uncertain terms that the party was over. I couldn't believe it when the music was immediately turned off and everyone put their coats on and fucked off! Can you imagine that happening in England?

The next morning our drummer Andy was woken up with an early morning cock in his face, courtesy of my new mate Ray, who I'd bonded with the night before over a bottle of brandy.

My first day in LA was spent in a sweaty little rehearsal room, teaching American musicians how to play our songs while Doug fucked off on the lash, arriving back for the last hour, when thankfully his pissed-up attempts to sing couldn't ruin anything, because everyone had learned their parts perfectly and it sounded bang on.

It wasn't ideal that the LA show was the first and biggest one of the tour, but I suppose there's nothing like being thrown in at the deep end.

On the night we were joined by three other bands, the stand out one for me being No Doubt. No, not because they had the gorgeous Gwen out front, because if I remember rightly she was one of the backing singers. The reason is, they came into our dressing room to say hello and they were all dressed in suits that looked like they'd been made with material that had been nicked from a deck chair!

I have a few good memories from my first US show, and here's two of them… After soundcheck, we were taken by the promoter to a Chinese restaurant where all the employees were ex-cons out on parole who had been given jobs there in an attempt to get them back on the straight and narrow. I got served my special-fried-rice by a geezer who had topped his wife! Then, just before I was about to go on stage, some cute, blonde, Californian bird came into the dressing room, pulled out a bag of white and said to me: "Hi, do you wanna get high with me?"

What a great introduction to life on the other side of the pond.

Murderers and blonde sorts with gear!

There are a couple of other things from that night I think are worthy of a mention, for instance, it was the first time I ever performed 'Skaville UK' live. Doug always took a break in the middle of the set and let the band play a couple of instrumentals, so I thought this would be the perfect opportunity for me to try the song out in front of an audience to see if it was as good as I thought it was. As Doug made his way off stage I shouted into the microphone: "This ain't downtown JA, this is Skaville LA!"

The crowd went fucking mental, and I knew there and then that I was on to a winner.

I'd arranged to meet a couple of people outside the venue after the show, but when I tried to leave the place I was stopped by a copper putting his arm across my chest and saying: "You can't go out sir, there are some Ku Klux Klan skinheads causing trouble in the street."

I thought he was taking the piss and tried to make my way past him, but once again he put his arm in front of me, and this time he was a little more serious: "Get the fuck out of here."

At which point I asked him (and I can only assume that my newfound braveness was down to the gear I'd just had): "How do you know they are skinheads if they have pillow cases on their heads?"

Which I have to say didn't seem as funny to him as it did to me.

He then told me, in no uncertain terms: "Get the fuck out of here or I will take care of you."

And so, because I didn't think he meant take me home and give me some homemade soup with a warm toasty roll, I made my way back to the safety of the dressing room and the bird that seemed to have a never-ending bag of flake.

I fell in love with the States on that trip. Like a lot of English kids, I grew up listening to American music, but on my first visit there I have to say how I was surprised at how little they knew about their own music. Anywhere I went I would make my way to all the local record shops, to spend as long as I could rummaging through boxes of old 45s, which was my idea of heaven.

And the people... they were so nice to me. "Oh my God, you're from England! Do you know the Queen?"

I would go to 50s diners, and put quarters into my own personal juke box, while stuffing my face with burgers, or turkey and mashed potato. It was real kid-in-a-candy-store stuff.

Getting the chance to perform in places like San Diego, Santa Cruz and San Francisco was a dream come true for me and I got the chance to cross the border into Mexico and spend a wild night in Tijuana. This was a place like nowhere I'd ever been before. As we made our way towards what Donkey Show described as a lawless town, they gave me the lowdown on its history. They'd named the band after a show you could see there (come on it doesn't take much working out), and all you had to do to enter this palace of sin was push your way through a turnstile just like I'd done many, many times before at football

The idea of being in a town with no rules excited me.

We pulled up outside the venue, to be given a big hello from the guy standing at the door. He showed us inside to what we thought was the gig, but was in fact a strip club, and because we were new in town and didn't want to appear rude to the locals, we went in and ordered ourselves a couple of cold ones.

Now I've been to a lot of strip clubs in my life, but this one was well and truly off the fucking scale.

It was strictly a den of iniquity for low life losers. I stayed and had a few beers, just so I didn't look like too much of a killjoy, before making my excuses and heading out onto the street for what I thought might be a little bit of sanity, but outside the club was even worse than inside, there was unbelievable poverty all around me and it brought tears to my eyes.

While I was looking in a shop window, I felt something or someone pulling at my trousers. I looked down to see a young kid no more than

149

five years old putting his hand in my pocket to try and grab whatever I had in there. I felt so sad that I gave him all the shrapnel I had on me.

Just before we were due on stage, I made my way back to the bar to pick up Doug. He was absolutely wankered, which of course I was no stranger to, but it put our new American friends into a state of shock seeing their idol in this condition. I knew his performance would now basically consist of him singing in a language from another planet, dropping the microphone constantly, and blaming the soundman for everything that's wrong in the world. Oh and of course, we'd be playing "Lorraine" at least three times, if not more; and Doug didn't let us down on any of those things, although his performance on stage was nothing compared to the one off.

After the show, he went straight back to the strip club and started doing tequila slammers like there was no tomorrow, and in my role as loyal mate I tried to keep up with him but failed miserably. When I suggested maybe it was time for us to make our way back to the safety of California, his reply was to pour another drink down his gob and fucking leg it out of the club.

I couldn't be fucked to go after him, so I went back to the van where Donkey Show were and waited for him to come back. We waited and waited and...

He eventually turned up an hour or so later, and was totally fucked up.

After about thirty minutes of me trying to persuade him that he didn't really want to live in Tijuana for the rest of his life, we made our way back to the border, which now had a totally different vibe from when we were there just a few hours before. There was old bill everywhere and they made us get out of the van so they could search it, at which point Doug jumped out of the vehicle shouting: "I love your country, I love your culture, I love your hot dogs!"

Now, this declaration of love seemed to upset the old bill more than just a little bit, but after an hour or so of us crawling to them, they eventually let us through and we lived to fight another day. That little hiccup didn't change my mind though, my love affair with the place was already cemented and I couldn't wait to get back there again.

Things started to pick up for us when we returned to the UK. We began getting offers to do shows from all over Europe, but before we could do anything like that, we had a thirty-date tour of the UK to undertake, ending with us headlining the first ever London Ska Festival at The Fridge in Brixton. The shows were booked to help us sell our first Bluebeat release "Eat The Beat", an album that has possibly the worst cover ever: it looks like an invitation to a wedding you wouldn't want to go to. What really mattered though were the songs inside this 12" world of cardboard tackiness. I thought they were great, and they would be well represented on our forthcoming tour of the UK.

Although our setlist was great the routing was fucking mental. How many musicians out there fancy Plymouth to Aberdeen, back to Glasgow and then on to the Isle of Wight? Luckily, I was young and could handle all the travelling and gigs you could throw at me.

What I couldn't handle was that a week before it was due to start my dad died.

I can tell you where I was when I got the news: at a rehearsal studio in East London, going over some new songs for my King Hammond project, and I know this because I have it on tape although you'll understand it's not something that gets the play button pressed on it ever. We were taking a little break, when one of the guys who owned the place knocked on the door, came into the room and said: "There's a phone call for you Nick."

My brother broke the news that Dad had passed away from heart failure.

I felt numb and went home to lie down on my bed and cry. But after about half an hour of sobbing, I got up and played some of his records and the tears stopped. I just felt very proud of this talented man.

Having to go and view his body was not one of the greatest experiences I'd had up to that point in my life, but it wasn't the first time I'd seen a dead body: about six years before a man I knew had a heart attack and pegged it right in front of me, which of course freaked me right out, but with all due respect to him, he wasn't my dad.

My old man was lying there, with white lace across his face and for the first time in my life saying nothing to me. I leaned over and kissed him on his cold forehead. I was half hoping he'd open his eyes and smile at me, but as any sane person will know that was never going to happen.

His funeral was held a week later, the day before I was due to start the tour in Cork, which understandably I now didn't really fancy doing, but I kept on hearing the old man's voice whispering in my ear: "The show must go on son".

And of course, it does.

In Dad's honour, I got really pissed with Doug in the van on our way to Swansea to catch the ferry over and the drinking continued over some very choppy waters, until we finally reached the Emerald Isle and it was time for us to get back into the van and off the boat. We were halfway down the ramp when a drunk and emotional Louis started shouting: "Stop the van! I've left the fucking float money on the ferry!"

He jumped out the vehicle and ran back up the ramp and on to the ferry. Naturally, we all thought that would be the last we'd ever see of the money, but a few minutes later he came back with all of it still in its unopened envelope.

I don't think I ever really got time to grieve about Dad's passing, because I was constantly on the road gigging. Maybe this was a good thing, because although I didn't see him a lot in the last few years of his life, he was still my main inspiration to make music, and although I knew I'd never get anywhere near to his standard of musicianship, I still wanted to make him proud of what I might achieve.

He still lives on through my memories and the music that he made.

Sleep well big Nick I owe everything to you xxx.

I could tell you a lot of funny things that happened on that tour, but I think I will just focus on the Brixton show.

The first thing I saw when I arrived backstage was the wondrous sight of Prince Buster chatting to Laurel Aitken. Let me tell you, if you're a ska fan, seeing those two together shooting the shit gives you more than a little tingle mate. Obviously, I'd met Laurel a few times by then, but I'd only been lucky enough to meet Buster once about a year before, when Gaz Mayell introduced me to him at The Dublin Castle.

It's weird ain't it? Here's a man whose records I'd salivated over since I was a boy and for years didn't think was a real person - I had him down as some kind of cartoon character from a far-off island - and there I was in a small boozer in Camden Town breaking bread with him! At first, I thought Gaz was on the wind-up, because the man looked far too young to be the Prince, but as soon as he shook my hand and said "Nice to meet you Nick" I knew it was him: there was no mistaking that voice.

I remember someone at school telling me that all the music he'd played me, that I loved so much, came from Jamaica. So I went to find it on a globe I had, which took pride of place in my bedroom on top of a chest of drawers. I couldn't even find the place at first, it was so small on there.

152

I went over and said hello to Laurel and reintroduced myself to Buster. I can't remember what we chatted about, but I came away thinking: "I have to make sure I impress them tonight."

I mean, without those guys, I think I'm right in saying there would have been no 2-Tone.

Even though we were sharing the bill with Laurel, I knew we'd be the highlight of the evening. I hate to say something like that, because I adore Laurel, but we had the songs and a band as tight as can be (well after playing thirty odd gigs on the trot you should be!) plus we had the bonus of having the Can Can girls with us for some added titillation. And I wasn't wrong, because we rocked that night, and I think both legends were suitably impressed with both myself the band; and so 1988 ended on a real high.

But I tell you what, 1989 would prove to be an even bigger one.

ALL ACCESS
BAD MANNERS

SEPTEMBER 20, 1988
THE DNA LOUNGE
SAN FRANCISCO

Backstage pass US tour 1988

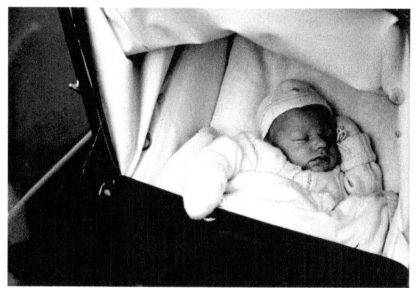

Fair of face?

Mum

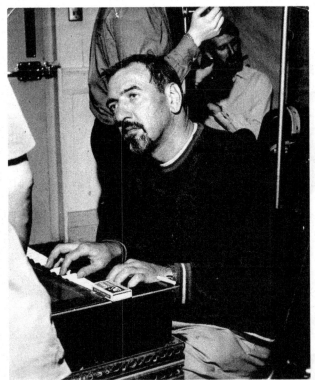
Dad

With Mum and big brother at the seaside

Ahead of the pack at Butlins

Oink Oink

Can you guess which one is me

I wanna be Jeff Astle when I grow up

157

You look nothing like David Cassidy

Look at the state of those fingernails!

Highbury Roundhouse
71A Ronalds Road
LONDON N5

(seafort)   01 226 6070
            01 226 5095
            01 359 5416
(Tony)   01 359 7727
            01 609 0143

August 1st

Dear Nick + Brian + the Dead,

This is to confirm that you will be
playing at the Highbury Roundhouse
on Thursday August 4th.

Bands usually go on about 9-15 - 930p.
but could you be set up before 8 pm

Guarantee of £10 to you for
playing the gig

See you there (about 7.25 pm — or
a little earlier.
        Regards Stefan α

I don't think we got that tenner

THE ROXY CLUB

41/43 NEAL ST.,
COVENT GARDEN, WC2

Wednesday July 6th
Audition Night
30p before 10 pm
50p after 10 pm

MODEL MANIA
+ ZERO

Thursday July 7th

SKINFLICKS
+ NEW HEARTS

Friday July 8th

SKREWDRIVER
+ RENOIR

Saturday July 9th

MEAN STREET
+ SWORDS

Wednesday July 13th
Audition Night
30p before 10 pm
50p after 10 pm

OUTPATIENTS
+ THE DEAD

THE ROXY CLUB

41/43 NEAL ST.
COVENT GARDEN. WC2

Wednesday 17th August
Audition Night   Adm 50p

DOLE QUEUE
RABIES &
COOL THRUST

Thursday 18th August

LONDON
JOHNNY CURIOUS
& STRANGERS

Friday 19th August

EATER
THE DEAD

Saturday 20th August

SHAM 69
MENACE

Tuesday 23rd August
Audition Night   Adm 50p

SPEEDOMETERS
TAX EXILES

Adverts for The Roxy

160

Backstage at The Roxy

Dead and gone

THE DEAD, a london punk band whose lead singer Tone Deaf was killed in a hit-and-run accident in Paris recently, are to disband.

However, bassist Nicky Walsh has a single released shortly on Angry Records called 'Mystery Girl'. The other members of the band are expected to find new bands shortly.

Sounds 1978

The Clique 1978

Steve Treatment single 1979

The gig is a benefit for hard-working albeit underpaid Music Machine DJ **Peter Fox** and already **Buster Bloodvessel, Charlie Harper, Captain Sensible** and **Max Splodge** are amongst the sensitive artistes who have agreed to appear *naked* with the Brothers. A stripper by name of the **Lovely Doreen** will also be taking part.

For obvious reasons details of the venue are being kept quiet for now although ticket prices are believed to be around the five blue ones mark.

Meantimes after jamming with **Max Splodge** at the MM recently **Jimmy Charlton** slaughtered fat-guts **Dougie Trendle** in that **Richard O'Sullivan** impersonating competition. Incidentally, word reaches us from attractive North London skinhead **Mary** of a recent incident when **Bad Manners** played Sheffield. Apparently she was alone in the dressing room with Dougie and the fat fraud started absent-mindedly singing Genesis's 'Lamb Lies Down On Broadway' so confirming recent rumours about his hopeless hippy past.

Finally Jimmy Charlton signs off for this week, with a new challenge. He challenges **Spandau Ballet** to a ruck outside Blitz at 1pm this Saturday.

Sounds 1980

unwaged.

SATURDAY, JULY 12 – 6.00pm
IN LOVING MEMORY OF JIMMY SCOTT. PYRAMID ARTS present PYRAMID DRUMMERS, ONE STYLE, KARESS, DOOBIE WAH, VISUAL THINKING, CABBAGE AND BOLLOX, JAH GLOBE and more. £3/£1.50 **unwaged.**

Gig advert 1986

Bad Manners 1987

Busters All Stars 1987

Gig flyer 1989

CONTENDERS

LONGSY D & BUSTER BLOODVESSEL: This Is Ska (Remixes) *(Big One)*

This is - it aint somethin' else, as Bob De Niro so astutely pointed out. Never mind Ska, never mind House never mind 'that' Revival. This is a *Scooby Doo* theme for the (better) late (than never) '80s. I'm telling you whay you already know because deal that contains a B-side bursting to be an A. Buster Bloodvessel has revamped, reduced and *reclaimed* Longsy's original (so soon!). Away with the Acidic refrain; on with bust-a-gut vocals and new (old) bass by Bad Manners' Nicky Welsh. The result will ska your bot for life.

"This Is Ska" NME review 1989

THE SELECTER

The Selecter promo pic

Big 5 promo pic

presents this certificate to

Nick Welsh

in recognition of your participation as a

Musician

on the GRAMMY®Award-winning album

"Jamaican E.T."
(Lee "Scratch" Perry)

in the category

Best Reggae Album

45th GRAMMY® Awards Year 2002

Working with 'Scratch'

The Godfather

The Prince

Original cover for the Skaville UK album "1973"

The King (Thanks JC)

170

MEMORY TRAIN

Well I might take a train if I ever see you again,
Well I might take a train if I ever see you again,
I might live for tomorrow, but my eyes fill with sorrow,

All I'm asking from you is to tell me what shall I do,
All I'm asking from you is to tell me what shall I do,
I might live for tomorrow, but my eyes fill with sorrow.

And I'll keep getting away from you on that memory train,
And I'll keep getting away from you on that memory train.

Well I might take a train if you say my love is in vain,
Well I might take a train if you say my love is in vain,
I might try to forget you, but I don't think I want to.

And I'll keep getting away from you on that memory train,
And I'll keep getting away from you on that memory train.

For the first time in ages I had some time to myself, to pay some attention to my solo venture. So, let me bring you up to speed on where I was with that…

First of all, I ditched the idea of the Lord Manchester bluebeat sound and replaced it with a full blown 70s skinhead reggae experience. Fuck being a Lord. I was gonna be a King…

KING HAMMOND!

While I'd been putting in the miles on tour with Manners, I hadn't been wasting my time. I would sit on the bus, putting pen to paper, making lists of possible song titles and ideas that all had very 70s themes: "Enter The Dragon", "King Hammond Vs The Exorcist" and "Confessions of An Organist".

I kept the idea of my pseudonym being a small-time, struggling artist from the past: a man who would jump onto any new craze that came along, but always with the same result... Failure! He could be an early dub pioneer with a badly received album: "King Hammond on the Buses", or a band-wagon-climbing glam rocker, camping it up on *Magpie* in 1974, to his latest single, "Skinhead Revolution" (chart position 277).

The King could be whoever I wanted him to be, and the story started to grow and grow.

I claimed I'd found and bought the original King Hammond master tapes from a market stall in Dalston for £2 and to be honest, that wasn't too far from the truth, because the 2" tape I actually ended up recording those first two albums on (I can't be fucked to go through all the technical bollocks on how we managed it) were bought for that price off a stall in Brick Lane. The little Jewish guy who flogged them to me told me it was film tape, but I knew better. They were fucking filthy, and it took me ages to clean them up, but in the end I managed it. You wouldn't believe the shit that came off them!

And so, this is how "Revolution 70" was done and dusted. All the drums and keyboards on the album were recorded on that mate of mine's four-track porta studio in his south London council flat, just off the Elephant & Castle. At the time, I thought I'd captured the spirit of those early skinhead reggae tracks, but listening to it today it sounds fuck all like that. What I will say though is, it does have a unique sound like I've never heard before.

I then took the tracks down to Pete Ker, who as luck would have it had just opened a brand new studio, Scarf, in Bow. We bounced everything onto the Brick Lane tapes, before adding bass, guitar, and vocals to it.

Bob's yer Uncle. I had a very special, if a little strange, album in my pocket.

The whole thing was done within the first two months of the year, while Manners were off the road. I didn't even have to tout the record around either, because as soon as Doug heard it he wanted to release it on his Bluebeat label, which I was more than happy to let him do.

None of the first batch of King Hammond songs I'd written actually made it on to "Revolution 70", simply because they just didn't seem to fit the vibe of the album. I thought I could maybe license them to one of the many labels that were releasing ska compilations at the time, and within a few weeks, Link Records had taken "King Hammond Shuffle" and "Right On King Hammond" for their "Ska For Ska's Sake" and "The 15 Commandments Of Ska" albums. They had tried to get "Skaville UK" but I had to say no, because I knew that Doug wanted to record it and release it as a Manners single to launch the Bluebeat label. I wasn't that keen on the idea, because I thought it was the best of the three, and might do a bit of good for me further down the road; but if the single got the push I was told it was gonna get, then the money I'd receive from the publishing would be sweet, so I gave it the thumbs up.

And that's why the next time I was back at Scarf, it wasn't to record songs about Kung Fu or exorcism, it was to put down what I considered to be my UK ska anthem.

We put it to bed quite quickly and that's when Doug started talking about what should be on the B-side of the single, and how he had to have a songwriting credit on the record. He mentioned he'd always liked my song "One Dollar Hotel" (which was going to be the opening track on "Revolution 70") and suggested that if he put a vocal over the top of it we'd have our flip-side and we could share the writing credit. The result was "Rocksteady Breakfast", which in my mind is a load of old shit, but at least Fatty was happy, and back then I thought "Fuck it, he's my mate and it's just a song".

"Skaville UK" was released in April 1989 and was accompanied by a promo-video of us poncing around the streets of London in an open-topped double-decker bus, which was a bit of a giggle to do. On our way around the capital we bumped into Radio One DJ Simon Bates as we drove past the BBC building. We tried to get him to jump aboard and join in the fun, but he made his excuses and pissed off down Regent

Street like Linford Christie on fire. To his credit, Mr Bates was the first person to play our single, even though he did play the wrong fucking side, which we used as an excuse as to why the single only achieved a low chart placing.

It was a bit of a let-down for everyone involved.

I can remember a lot of excitement in the Bluebeat offices when the midweeks came through and "Skaville UK" was somewhere in the 40s, but the truth of the matter is simple, there just wasn't enough money to pump into the promotion of the record; but I still see it as the beginning of the revival in the band's fortunes though, picking up good reviews in the music press, and gigs were rolling in a lot faster than they had done in a long time.

In 1989 we were definitely the student band of choice, playing every Fresher/Valentine/ Christmas Ball they could throw at us and those gigs were great, I loved them. In one week alone we did eight gigs in Cambridge and Oxford. You didn't have the worry about getting paid, or how many people were gonna turn up. You got great food and drink, and most of the time you'd be surrounded by shit-loads of pretty, posh crumpet, who were usually up for a bit of rough.

One that sticks out for me was at Cirencester College on 25th May 1989.

There are two reasons why I can remember the date so well: the first is because it was the day Arsenal won the championship at Liverpool, in one of the most exciting games I'd ever seen, with an ending you couldn't write. The second is, Bad Manners had a match of their own that afternoon on the campus playing fields, against the Bay City Rollers!

What a fucking laugh it was.

"It's a game, a game, a game that we're playing"

It was a very hot day, so running around, slightly pissed, on a full-size pitch was probably the reason I eventually collapsed in a heap on the floor, gasping for breath. I finally had to admit to myself, and my team mates, that maybe I was no longer the player to man-mark Eric, or keep Woody in my pocket. But it was a great giggle, and almost as funny as the bomb scare...

I was sitting backstage at Guildford University, chatting to some of the other bands on the bill, when the Ents Officer walked in: "I'm sorry everyone, we've just had an anonymous phone call tipping us off about a possible IRA bomb somewhere in the building, so would you please all go and stand outside in the field."

(Oh yeah, I forgot to mention that the gig was being held in a tent.)

We all trundled off into a dark and very cold field, to wait for the bomb squad to come and do their stuff, just like I'd seen them do a million times on *The Sweeney* and *The Professionals*. Luckily for us it turned out to be a false alarm, but thanks to that hoax-caller, I now have a memory that will stay with me forever: seeing members of Bad Manners, Mud, The Glitter Band and Geno Washington, in full stage gear, standing around in a field, shitting themselves.

We also used to play quite a few hospital balls, where the ticket price could be as much as £100 a pop, which was a lot of fucking money then (still is now). It would always cross my mind that maybe the money they spent on hiring fairground rides and booking artists like The Darts, Alan Price or ourselves could have been better spent on things like employing more staff, or getting some new beds for the wards, but then I suppose doctors and nurses need to let their hair down too.

One night we were playing St Bart's, and Brian Connolly, lead singer of The Sweet, shuffled up to me asking if I knew any of their songs and whether I would be into joining him on stage, because his band hadn't turned up.

And so, for the next hour, I was the new Steve Priest.

Unfortunately, as I sat working out the basslines for "Hellraiser" and "Teenage Rampage", his boys turned up and I was relegated to the glam subs bench.

At another one of these events I was chatting to Les Gray from Mud - yeah, that's right, 'Mr Tiger Feet' himself - when out of the blue he gave me his phone number and asked if I would be interested in writing some songs with him. Before I could say yes, a member of his road crew interrupted our conversation, wanting to know if he could have the fiver back he'd lent him the previous week on the ferry coming back from Belgium. In a flash, my childhood memories of seeing him miming to "Rocket" on *TOTP* were smashed against the wall like a bottle of cream soda.

I never did get around to ringing him, but I did carry his number around for a while in my pocket and when I was pissed, I'd show it to mates I knew would be suitably impressed. "Yeah, me and my mate Les are working on some new things together, and I tell you what, it will fucking knock "Lonely This Christmas" out of the water."

175

The pissed-up lies of a glam rock wannabe.

DIARY ENTRY; 7/7/1989... Met Viv Stanshall at the Screamin' Jay Hawkins gig tonight. We got well pissed, had a dodgy kebab and then played snooker in Archway until the early hours.

In between bomb scares and hanging out with glam legends, we undertook a couple of European tours and I'm pleased to say we finally managed to get Laurel on board, which, besides giving me the opportunity to play with him on stage, also gave me the chance to spend some quality time with him off it. I loved listening to all his stories about the early days, his bluebeat experiences, and the musicians he'd worked with. Some funny, some sad, and a lot that I will always keep to myself. Not because they were nasty, or libellous, but simply because it was a confidence shared.

Laurel was a keen photographer, and always brought his camera out with him. One day, we were spending the afternoon walking around Hamburg, with him snapping away while we chatted. He really loved the place. I asked if he fancied going to the Reeperbahn, so I could show him around some of Europe's most naughty streets, with the advice: "Best not to take any pictures though mate, the girls working in the area don't like it."

So, like the gentleman he was, he kept his camera around his neck, but that didn't stop one very large lady screaming at us as we walked past her. I don't know what the fuck she was saying, but I could tell it wasn't anything complimentary. I can only assume that she'd seen the large Nikon around Laurel's Gregory, and presumed he was gonna start snapping away. Laurel looked at me and said: "What's her bloody problem?"

At that moment, I felt the best plan of action was for me to front it out, so I shouted: "Fuck off you big fat tart!" and walked away, giving her the wanker sign, thinking she was never gonna leave her window. How wrong could I be? She came steaming out and gave us both a dig. Had you been there on that sunny afternoon, ska fans, you would've witnessed the sight of your writer and Laurel, pegging it down the road together laughing.

Then there was the time we tried to run to the top of the Notre Dame Cathedral, nearly killing ourselves, and when I had to carry him out of a venue in Marseille after some Nazis had set off CS gas.

So many memories, so little time.

The Beatmasters	**"Ska Train"**
Shelly Thunder	**"Teenager In Love"**
A Tribe Called Quest	**"I Left My Wallet In El Segundo"**

The follow up to "Skaville UK" was the dreadful "Gonna Get Along Without You Now". Doug got it into his head that this song was a hit, and to be fair he was right, although it was ten years earlier for Viola Wills. But he called the shots so I faithfully went into the studio and did the best I could for him, by playing bass, guitar, and keyboards on it.

And since it is nearly thirty years later, I will come clean and admit that the backing vocals I did on the record were a direct lift from John Lennon's "Woman".

When the backing track was completed and it was time for Doug to put his vocal down, I handed him the lyric sheet but he handed it back to me and said: "No, I'm not gonna be singing it, Verona from The Deltones is."

After getting over the initial shock that he wouldn't be the singer on a Bad Manners single, I came to the conclusion that maybe this was quite a smart move on his behalf, because I certainly couldn't see him fucking singing it. Verona came in, did her part in about three takes, and was a real pleasure to work with.

The B-side of our platter, sports fans, was the fucking awful "Oh Jamaica". The song was written by Doug, and was even worse than the A-side. If it wasn't bad enough that the melody was a straight rip of Eddie Grant's "Gimmie Hope Joanna", the lyrics were cringeworthy, and I think he knew that, because he fucked off and left me on my own to teach it to Verona. I don't know how I managed to persuade her not to walk out, but I did, and thankfully it was all over within a few hours. Worse still, when the 12-inch version of the single was released it had reggae and ska mixes of "Oh Jamaica" on it, which were just the track slowed down (reggae) and sped up (ska).

We made a promo video to help push the single. This time we filmed it in the beautiful surroundings of Cambridge (or was it Oxford?), and just like our previous effort it had a very cheap kitsch feel, but it was a laugh to do. Even when the boat we were in sank, and the icy water nearly froze my bollocks off.

The single flopped.

Maybe the fans didn't like the idea of a Manners single without Doug on it?

No sooner had the record sunk without trace (just like that boat), Bluebeat (Doug) decided to release another single and surprise, surprise, "Sally Brown" was an even bigger disaster than the previous two, only this time it had nothing to do with a disinterested public. Long story short, Bluebeat printed shit-loads of 7" and 12" records in full colour sleeves, placed adverts in all the trades and then... decided they didn't want to release it after all!

I feel it's also worth mentioning that Doug found both the label's accountant, and the A & R man, from the pages of *Loot*, a magazine where you'd maybe look to buy a secondhand pram, but certainly not to hire important, record-company-machine cogs.

Bluebeat then decided it should pour all its time, effort, and money into the release of the "Return Of The Ugly" album, which everyone felt would push the band, and label, onto a different level. I wholeheartedly agreed, even though quite a few of the tracks on it had already appeared on the limited edition "Eat The Beat" release the previous year.

I was on my way to see my old mate George 'Porky' Peckham to master the album at his studio in Shaftesbury Avenue, when Doug rang telling me to put it off for a couple of weeks. The reason I had to hang fire was because he'd received a phone call from the producer Longsy D, who'd just released a track called "This Is Ska" that was receiving a lot of good press interest, and he wanted to see if Doug had any ideas on making the track 'a little more ska' and said he'd send a tape over straight away for him to check out.

On first hearing, I thought it was great, but needed a totally different bassline, you know, a proper ska one, to make it palatable to a ska audience. Also, there were no offbeat guitar or piano chops on it. After a few more listens, Doug turned off the tape machine and came out with the classic line:"Come on Nick, let's go and put some magic on it!"

And so, a couple of days later, we met up with Longsy in an East End studio and I went to work giving "This Is Ska" a new lease of life. I explained my thoughts about changing his acid computer bassline for a live one to him, and he looked suitably impressed when I nailed the fucker in just one take. My next move was to add some guitar and keyboards giving the track an 'old but new' feel. I guided the horn section through the track's main lick, and then it was down to Doug to put a few vocal ad-libs on it, and that was it.

I could see that Longsy and his manager were well pleased with all my work, which made it a lot easier for me to sort out a decent financial deal for myself.

Fatty also struck up a deal with Longsy: they could use our version on his new remix 12-inch, and in return the track would appear on "Return Of The Ugly", and so, with everyone getting what they wanted, I finally got to go down to Porky's, and master the album, with the addition of "This Is Ska".

When Longsy's 12-inch remix came out, it did well. I can't remember what chart position it got to, but I do know that it got a very positive review in the *NME*, even mentioning my bass-playing. I was well chuffed with that, but it didn't go down so well with the hard-core ska fans, who considered it too dance orientated and thought we were selling out to 'skacid', the name the press had given this ska/dance hybrid. But we liked it, and put it straight into our live set, with Longsy joining us onstage quite a few times to perform it.

Nearly thirty years on "This is Ska" is considered to be a bit of a classic. It gets spun regularly by DJs at scooter rallies, and mullered by cover bands all over the world. That seems to be what happens when you dip your toes into new and uncharted musical waters: it takes people a little bit of time to accept what you're trying to do.

The only thing that left a bad taste in my mouth about the whole thing was when they made the promo video for it, and I wasn't invited, which I thought I would be after the contribution I'd made. In fact, the first time I even knew about it was when I saw the video on some Saturday morning kids' TV show, with my place on bass taken by my mate Johnny T, who wasn't even on the fucking record!

I felt hurt and let down by Doug. He was supposed to be my fucking pal and he went and did something like that behind my back. I didn't particularly care about being in the video, it was more to do with the way it all went down. Maybe my image just wasn't right?

So, what can I say about "Return Of The Ugly"?

Well, the first thing is I think a special mention must go to Steve Friel, who did all the artwork, which in my opinion is fucking mega. Steve told me that the only members of the band he actually drew for the front cover were me (flat top and headless bass) and Doug (fat and bald).

Fancy a quick Michael Caine moment?

On the album, Laurel Aitken played keyboards on "Sally Brown" and "Hey Little Girl". Not a lot of people know that!

179

A lot of people tell me that it's the last decent Bad Manners album. I don't know about that, but it certainly takes me back to a time when I was really happy making music. I felt that the band, and the whole ska scene in general, was moving forward in a very positive direction.

De La Soul	**"Eye Know"**
Rebel MC & Double Trouble	**"Street Tuff"**
Rufus & Chaka Chan	**"Ain't Nobody"**

We secured a deal for the album in America with the Californian label Triple X, which meant we were on our way back to the good ole US of A for another tour, but this time it was the whole band going along with Laurel as our special guest.

But before we go there, how about this for history repeating itself?

On the day before we were due to fly to America, Doug discovered his passport had expired (last year broken arm, this year passport). So, while the rest of the band flew out to Boston, I stayed behind with him to try and sort it out down at the passport office. Now, as everyone knows, these things take time. But Fatty, being Fatty, just signed a few autographs, did a few tongue-sticking-out photos with the staff, and hey presto, he had his new passport within a few hours.

We flew out the next day to meet up with the rest of the band and after some get together beers, Doug let it be known that it would make him a very happy man if everyone shaved their heads for the tour, which surprisingly no one seemed to mind doing, so the next morning we all indulged in some serious razor action.

"Don't knock the baldhead"

Unfortunately for us, this happened on the same day some racist skinheads decided to act like total wankers on the *Geraldo Rivera Show*, causing a storm all across the country and immediately making anyone who had no hair look like a total fascist in the eyes of the American public.

The abuse I got walking around the streets of New York that day was unbelievable. People were getting in my face, shouting at me, and I even got flobbed on! I was public enemy number one. I've never felt so glad to get back to my hotel room.

Besides Laurel, the other act on the tour was the Mighty Mighty Bosstones, who I fell in love with straight away. Every member of the band was a real character, but none more so than the lead singer Dickie, who almost immediately became my partner in crime when it came to getting drunk and acting stupid. Usually, when you have the same support band all the way through a tour, you'll maybe watch them a couple of times at most, but I stood at the side of the stage every night, totally engrossed in what I was seeing and hearing.

When the tour reached Detroit, Laurel pulled me to one side and asked if I would help him try and trace some of his relatives, who he thought lived in the area. So instead of going out on the piss with the rest of the band, I stayed in the hotel's reception area with a big pile of Yellow Pages, trying to help him hook-up with some long-lost family members. After three fruitless hours, I suggested maybe this was all a bit of a fool's errand, and we should go to our rooms and get ready for soundcheck, meeting back in reception in fifteen minutes.

When I arrived back downstairs with my guitar and stage gear, Laurel wasn't there. I asked the guy on the front desk if he'd seen him, and he told me that as soon as I'd gone upstairs Laurel had asked the guy to ring a taxi for him to take him to the airport, and off he went.

This wasn't good.

I jumped into a sherbet and made my way, not to the airport, but to the venue to give Doug the news, and when I told him what had occurred, he thought I was on the wind-up; but after a few minutes of me telling him the full strength, this quickly turned into: "What the fuck did you do to him?"

The truth was, fuck all. Laurel had simply fucked off, leaving us in the shit.

Why were we in the shit?

Well, if you have a contract with a promoter that has Bad Manners and Laurel Aitken to appear, that's what they want, and if one of the artists isn't there it gives them the perfect opportunity to knock you for your fee, and this was to happen on more than one occasion.

A few months later, I found out the reason for his sudden departure was he'd received a phone call from Mark Johnson, the owner of his current record label Unicorn, who'd just released Laurel's new single "Everybody Ska". Mark told him he had to come straight back to the UK, because he'd secured a TV slot to promote the single, and if he didn't it wouldn't be good for him or his career. Now, what you have to remember is that Laurel was in his late fifties, and I think he probably felt a bit vulnerable, and under pressure, so he jumped on a plane and fucked off home. I'm sure he didn't know how much trouble this was going to cause us, because Laurel was a decent man, but this wanker (and believe me he was a right wanker) put the frighteners on him, and so he did what he thought was the best thing to do.

As I've just said, it doesn't take a genius to work out that at every show we did after Laurel's departure the promoter would use it as an excuse to not pay a huge chunk of the fee, even though you could tell that some of them didn't even know who he was. During one conversation with a promoter, he actually let slip that he thought Laurel was a woman! The truth was, and I take no joy in saying this, the majority of people coming to the shows were there for Bad Manners, but a contract is a contract and so we didn't have a leg to stand on.

After Detroit, our next show was three days later in San Francisco, and some of the band made the decision to rent a car and do a 'see the real America' road trip. I did think about joining them, but instead took the easy option of flying, which allowed me to spend a few days sightseeing around the Bay Area, and what a glorious time I had, with most of my time spent in record shops, diners, and thrift stores.

When friends I'd made over there came to England, they were always getting me to take them out around London to search for rare reggae records. It was no different for me when I was over there, except it was for soul, funk and doo wop, and there were plenty of them to be found. I must have brought hundreds of the buggers home. I threw most of the clothes I took with me away so they would fit into my suitcase.

What's more important? A hard to find James Brown single, or a pair of trousers?

Our road warriors arrived in San Francisco full of stories about their trip, and I must admit that, listening to them, it might have been nice to have shared the experience, even though they all looked totally fucked and I felt as fresh as a daisy.

The Californian leg of the tour began.

The scene over there was great, and we were the only ska band from the UK they were getting to see. After a great show in San Francisco, we drove down to Santa Cruz, where I spent some time outside the club we were playing, with fans trying to get me to ride on their scooters. The idea didn't really appeal to me, but I didn't want to lose face. After receiving a few instructions, I jumped aboard and put my foot down. I must have gone all of ten yards before skidding straight into a brand a new Porche that belonged to the club owner. The bad news was, he had witnessed my pathetic attempt at being Barry Sheene and came running out of the venue screaming at me: "What the fuck have you done to my car?"

Luckily for me he turned out to be English, so when he started giving it large, asking for some big wedge compensation, I just looked at him and said: "Don't give me all that bollocks, you cunt. Your insurance will fucking pay for it, so I ain't giving you a fucking penny and if you keep on acting like a mug, we ain't fucking playing tonight."

Fuck is a great word to hammer home a point isn't it?

The geezer knew he had to back down, because there were about two thousand kids standing outside his gaff waiting to get in. I knew my 'no show' line was a winner. He did get to see a very good show though, and in a complete turnaround at the end of it, he invited me into his office and stuck a load of trumpet up my hooter.

Another reason I liked playing over there was we got to play a different set from the one we did in Europe. Tracks like "That'll Do Nicely", "Suicide" and "Bang On The Drum", really freshened things up a bit. It was also fun playing with all the US bands, because they all had a great attitude. Although their music was a little fast for my liking, I still enjoyed hearing something different. I've already mentioned The Mighty Mighty Bosstones, but I loved Let's Go Bowling and Skankin' Pickle, they were always great fun to be around. Our new label, Triple X, were really enthusiastic about the record, and wanted us to come back over again in 1990 for a much longer tour.

I'd had a great time out there, but I was happy to get back home mainly because my "Revolution '70" album was due out, and I wanted to promote the fuck out of it. Not just because I thought it was a great album, but because it was also my job.

I was now the Bluebeat Records Press Officer, and fuck me did I work my bollocks off to promote it.

I circulated all the old fanny I'd made up about the King's humble beginnings, and the press swallowed it up like a good 'un. And I'm not just talking about the ska and reggae mags, but the trendy ones at the time like *ID* and *Soul Underground,* which helped it to become Bluebeat's second biggest selling record, just behind "Return Of The Ugly", which was not bad going for a first release.

If you thought the "Sally Brown" fuck up was good, wait until you hear this one...

We'd been out and about on a huge tour of the UK, which had started in the last week of October, running all the way through until the third week of December. So why the fuck did Bluebeat decide that the best time to release "Christmas Time (Again)" was on December 21st when the tour was all over?

"Madness, madness, they call it madness"

How do you honestly expect to make any kind of impression on the charts with a Christmas single, if you don't release the fucker until a few days before the bearded one comes down the chimney for his glass of milk and plate of biscuits?

The B-side of our festive offering was a new version of "Skinhead Love Affair", which was basically the same backing track with me adding four new vocal harmonies to it. The 12" version featured "You Fat Bastard", a song that started off as something the audience would sing at our gigs and so by simply adding a little piece of music to the start of it, I was now the proud composer and 50% owner of this terrace chant that I've heard sung a million times at football grounds all over the country.

I don't know who it was that came up with the idea us touring Scandinavia in January 1990, but whoever it was needed a slap. For fuck's sake, it's cold enough in England at that time of year, but in Norway and Finland it's freezing.

But, a tour's a tour, and so, on a cold and frosty winter's morning, I wrapped up warm and made my way to Heathrow in the company of Mr Alan Sayag. Now, just in case any of you reading this are not familiar with Mr Sayag, or his stage persona Winston Bazoomis, then allow me to give you a quick lesson...

Alan is an original member of Bad Manners (harmonica), and some say the true spirit of the band, and ever since the first time I met him at school he was, well, different.

I loved him.

He's one of the few people in this world that could make tears run down my face, just from listening to his endless stream of strangeness. His tracks on the early Manners albums were always the highlight for me. They were straight out of 'Junior Choice'.

Sadly, the years of constant touring and recording took their toll on him, and eventually he had to leave the band due to some serious mental health issues. Thankfully, because we lived in the same area, I would get to see him from time to time to spend a while in his wonderful world although I'm not so sure he thought it was such a wonderful place to be at the time. Sometimes, we would chat and he would come across as the Alan of old, but I can also remember times when I would be face-to-face with a man, staring blankly at me, without a fucking clue who I was. Then one day in 1989, I saw him sitting on a park bench opposite Doug's house, so I went over and chatted to him for a while and he seemed really well in himself, and so I said: "Come on, let's go and see Doug and give him a bit of a surprise."

We had a wonderful afternoon. Over the next few weeks his visits to Spring Hill became more and more frequent, which escalated to Doug asking him to come along with us to a few shows. He did, although he never took part, until one day Fatty took me aside and said: "He's playing with us tonight."

I wasn't sure whether this was the right or wrong thing for him to do, but what the fuck do I know, only that he'd been an essential part of the group, and if he thought he was up to it, well maybe it might make him better.

Although it wasn't exactly vintage Bazoomis on the night, it was certainly worth it just to see the joy on the fans' faces to see him back on stage, and on a personal level it also gave him the chance to make a few quid for himself.

Anyway, let's jump back on to the Piccadilly Line, and make our way to whatever terminal it was that we had to be at, for us to fly out to become ice-poles in Scandinavia.

I think it was about Barons Court when I noticed the only thing he seemed to be carrying, besides a plastic bag full of broken and semi broken harmonicas, was a smallish split in his slightly flared brown trousers that started at his crotch and measured about an inch and a half long. When I asked him where his clothes for the tour were, his reply was classic Alan: "I'm travelling light."

Indeed, he was.

Over the next three weeks, I had the pleasure of watching that small split blossom into a huge one, running from his crotch down to his ankle. Every day, I would gently suggest to him that maybe the time had now come for us to go into town and purchase a new pair of trousers for him, but this was always met with: "No, these ones will do me fine."

It was on this tour that I sat down with Doug to discuss what direction we wanted to go with our next album, and I got very excited about some of the ideas we came up with. We decided the next Manners record would be our 'White Album'. You know, twelve or so traditional band tracks, along with more off-the-wall stuff, maybe even invite some guests along to join us on our anything-goes trip into the unknown. This all sounded right up my street, but unfortunately, it was a street that would quickly turn into a dead end.

So, what the fuck happened?

Well I'll tell you, but because I'm trying to write a positive book here, let's have a high before a low...

In April 1990, we were invited to play a Greenpeace benefit at The Greek Theatre in Berkeley, a show I still consider to be the best concert I've ever done. We were led to believe that we were joint headlining with The International Beat, featuring Dave Wakeling and Ranking Roger, but when we got there it was quite obvious we were definitely going to be playing second fiddle.

We didn't give a fuck. It was a result for The International Beat though, because it had only been about three months since I'd seen them play at The Dublin Castle, in front of about thirty punters, as The Elevators. Now here they were, playing in front of fifteen thousand in the glorious Californian sunshine.

The night before the show I went with Louie and Alan to watch blues legend Nappy Brown perform at Slims. Nappy wrote the song "Don't You Be Angry" that Manners covered in 1981, and which was still very much a highlight of the band's live show.

Do you want the good news, or the bad news?

Ok... The bad news was, there was hardly anyone there to see this great artist.

The good news was, he was fucking great, and afterwards we got to say hello to him backstage and told him all about the band and how his song always went down well at our gigs, and we even invited him along to our show the next day, but he told us he was working, which was a shame because it would have been so great if we could have got him onstage with us.

186

Even though the show was over twenty five years ago, I'm proud to say that I can still play the whole day back in my head like it was yesterday...

I arrived at the beautiful amphitheatre around midday, which was a bit previous considering our stage time was 7.00pm but I just wanted to hang out and savour the whole of this very special day. I made my way out into the auditorium and walked around for a little bit before settling myself down on some large concrete steps, closing my eyes and letting the sun shine down on my face. Ziggy Marley's "Tomorrow's People" came over the sound system, and for those few minutes I felt like I was the luckiest man alive, but that moment of perfection had to be brief, because I was due to hook up with a guy I'd met in Rasputin's on Telegraph the day before, who'd offered to trade me an eight-ball for three tickets.

I didn't give a fuck about all the joint headline bollocks that had gone on before the show, because we'd been given what I've always considered to be the best position on a festival bill, and that's just as the sun goes down. We didn't even wait to get an introduction from the MC, we just ran out on to the stage and went straight into our first song. The audience went fucking mental, and continued to do so with every song we played. When they sang along to "Don't You Be Angry", I can remember thinking: "I wish Nappy was here to see this."

For me, the stand out moment of that night was (and I will go on record now to say it's one that I would put above all the many others I have been lucky enough to experience over the years) just before introducing one of our songs, Doug lifted a giant inflatable globe above his head announcing to the audience: "This is our world. We've only got one of them, so let's take care of it."

Cue fifteen thousand people going ape-shit. At which point, he turns to me behind this huge thing that he has in front of his boat, and gives me the tongue.

It was classic Doug.

I was supposed to go to some big after-show thing at the end of the night, for a load of backslapping, but instead I ended up in a gay club, dancing with a couple of birds I'd pulled at the gig.

"We spent the night in Frisco, at every kind of disco"

The next day, I went out for a drive in the Height District with one of the girls. I switched on the car radio to find out that all the stations in the Bay Area had gone Manners mad!

"Hey man, Bad Manners rocked that show yesterday, so here's another one of their tracks..." To say we had created a good impression would be a bit of an understatement, so it came as no surprise when our agents got in contact with us to book a huge tour in the fall.

Dream Warriors	**"Wash Your Face In My Sink"**
The La's	**"There She Goes"**
Black Box	**"Ride On Time"**

So, that was something to look forward to, but before then we were booked to record our new album, remember the one? The 'anything-goes-open-your-mind-and-your-ass-will-follow-free-spirit' record we were gonna do?

Well, all those good ideas we came up with somehow turned into a shameful piss poor collection of dodgy cover versions. Bluebeat decided it wasn't the right time for a "His Fatanic Majesty's Request" type album, and decided it WAS right for a nice 'UB40 play the oldies style' one.

Joy oh joy.

When I asked Doug what tracks he wanted to do, he chose some great songs, but I didn't think any of them, besides "Wet Dream", really suited his voice. Also, the stupid idea of giving Manners 'modern production values' was a big mistake. I just didn't see us as a drum machine/sample kind of band, but that's what "F** S*****", original title "Labour of Lust", is. Everyone, including co-producer Longsy D, did their best on it, I just don't think it sounds right. But that's just my opinion, I'm sure there will be people reading this who like it.

Should I mention the sessions for the album would usually start at 10.00am and (wait for it) after eight hours, we'd swap engineers and carry on until about 2.00am?

Can you believe that? That's sixteen fucking hours!

My ears would usually be shot by early evening, and if you add all day drinking and drugging into the mix, well you really don't have the best ingredients to make a decent record.

The recording of "F** S*****" went on for ever and ever and ever, and when it was all over, the only good thing about it was, it didn't actually come out until after I left the band. But it still has my name on it, and I'd rather it didn't. I've never hidden the fact that I don't like doing cover versions, I think it's a waste of precious studio time. If you are going to go down that road, at least try and make the songs your own.

When our US agents said they were going to get us a huge tour, they weren't fucking joking.

"The road is long, with many a winding turn"

We were booked for NINE solid weeks performing SIX days a week all over the States and Canada, and I'm not teasing you when I say I could write a whole book just about that tour, but for the sake of my sanity and chapter length, I will just stick to a few reminisces that make me smile.

But before I do, let me tell you about a very important personnel change in the band.

After a few years of having drummers who I never thought were really up to the gig, we finally struck gold when Doug asked me to go down to a rehearsal studio and audition someone who was interested in joining.

From the moment I walked in the room to meet Perry Melius, I loved him. He was charming and funny; but the question was, could he cut the gig? Before we began to play our conversation went something like this:

Me: "Have you ever played ska music?"

Perry: "Nah, what's that?"

Me: "Well, have you ever heard this?"

I played him "My Girl Lollipop"; it was the only thing I could think of.

Perry: "Oh yeah, that's the music my Dad used to listen to."

He picked up his sticks, got behind the kit, and began playing the song better than any drummer we'd ever had.

But was it a fluke? I had the entire set with me on cassette, so we listened to every track once, maybe twice, and when we began to play it, each time the result was the same.

Absolute perfection.

As a bass player, the drummer is your partner. You're Regan, he's Carter.

I really wanted Perry to come and play with us, but I played it cool. For some reason, I'd got it into my nut that this young black guy out of the East End wouldn't be interested in working with people who were quite a bit older than him, playing a kind of music that was even older than that. So, I told him that I'd be in touch. I went back to tell Doug what had happened, and I think it was because he'd never seen me enthuse so much over a musician that he rang Perry straight away and offered him the gig. The band immediately sounded ten million times better.

We headed out across the Atlantic to spend nine weeks together on a bus, a very smelly bus, in the company of some very smelly people, in some very smelly bunks.

Get the picture?

It was smelly.

The bus was christened 'The Happy Bus' by Louis, and for a few weeks I suppose it was. The Tour started and ended in New York, and in between I saw places that I'd either never heard of, or places I never thought I would get the chance to play in. Boise, Little Rock, Rockport… And I loved every fucking minute of it.

As soon as we arrived in town I would be off to explore the place, always making sure that my sightseeing involved having a couple of beers in the freakiest bar I could find. The winner of the Freakiest Bar Award has to go to the Déjà Vu, which was (is) a titty bar in Nashville, that had the words "100 Beautiful Girls and 3 Ugly Ones" on their marquee. It made me laugh that the first girl I saw gyrating on stage in the home of country music was not to the sound of Loretta Lynn, but to The Rolling Stones' "Faraway Eyes".

One thing's for sure, it didn't matter to me if the venue we were playing was packed, half full or empty, I always made sure that I gave a great show.

Well, I think I did! It's hard to tell sometimes, because from the first gig of the tour to the last there was always someone there who wanted to buy me a beer or powder my nose, but I'm pretty sure if I wasn't up to scratch Doug would've said something to me about it.

After every gig the road crew would award a member of the band the accolade of either 'man of the match' (which I won a lot) or 'cunt of the gig' (which I won once, but more of that in a minute.)

The drive time between shows would sometimes be as much as fourteen hours. These hours were usually spent either sleeping, watching videos, or playing cards, with 'Cheat' being the favourite.

NICK'S TOP THREE FILMS ON THE 1990 US TOUR

1. **"Clockwork Orange"**
2. **"Blue Velvet"**
3. **"Spinal Tap"**

There were times though when I had to indulge in the disgusting activity of 'wimping out'. Which was basically me trying to get some sleep after a night on the trumpet. This proved pretty fucking hard until I discovered the delights of Nyquil, a 'cure for the common cold'. If you drank half a bottle of it along with a couple of beers, you might get you a couple of hours' shut eye.

Vancouver was a laugh. Well it was for me anyway.

We were playing a venue called The Town Pump, which was a nice little gaff, and before soundcheck I got friendly with a barman who sorted me out with a bit of gear. Anyway, while we were chatting away, he mentioned to me that there was a good club in town owned by the singer Long John Baldry.

"Are you joking mate? My dad used to make records with him!"

And five minutes later, I was making my way out of The Pump, into a cab, and on to the club. On arrival, I told the lump on the door: "Oi mate, tell the big man that Nicky Welsh is here."

And the next thing I know, this giant of a man is standing in front of me, of whom my old man once said: "If you drop a sixpence in front of him, don't pick it up son."

I didn't feel the need to tell him I was Nicky Welsh Junior, not Senior, but did anyway, and immediately it was hugs all round and drinks on the house… A lot of drinks on the house.

He talked fondly about my old man and laughed when I told him the sixpence anecdote. It was a lovely evening. So lovely in fact, the thought of playing a gig later on had completely gone out of my head and it wasn't until he said: "What time are you on tonight?" that I went into my best roadrunner impression.

BEEP BEEP!

So, I was an hour late, and The Pump was rammed. I could see that Fatty wasn't a happy man. He wasn't remotely interested in my childhood memories of the sixties, or my thoughts on how beautiful the Pye label's artwork was. He just gave me: "Get on stage Welsh."

What do you think was the first thing I did when I took centre stage for "Echo 4-2"?

Well, you win a coconut if you guessed that I fell straight into my large Ampeg stack, knocking it and myself to the floor.

When you think about it though, it's not a bad entrance, and although it was fucking painful I still seemed to find my act of ska-slapstick quite funny (well you would do if you were legless wouldn't you?), and I wasn't alone in thinking this, because the entire audience did too. But you know me readers, I'm an old pro, and so I dusted myself down and with the help of our roadies got myself and my amp vertical, plugged in the Steinberger, and I was away. But when Doug arrived on stage, the first words out of his gob were: "You fucking wanker."

I don't think I'd be wrong in saying it was aimed at me. In fact, if my memory serves me right, I got to hear those three little words quite a lot over the next hour or so.

Talk about one rule for one, and another for the others. The amount of times I'd covered his arse when he was fucked up has to go into double figures, but over the years I've learnt that if you're the singer in a band you can get away with that kind of stuff because you get classed as a 'character'; but if you're just a humble musician you're a drunken cunt.

And that's why, on that night, I was bestowed the honour of 'cunt of the gig'.

The two nights I spent at The Golden Bear in Huntington Beach are another time that will always bring a smile to my face. The Bear was the first of ten dates in California, but, hold on, it gets better, because the shows were all double-headers with the originators of ska: The Skatalites!

Me? Excited? Just a little!

Although I said I spent two nights there, we only played one at The Bear. But don't worry, I haven't made a mistake in all my excitement. As usual, everyone in the band wanted to get to California as soon as they could, so we drove overnight from the previous night's show in Phoenix (via The Joshua Tree) and parked The Happy Bus on the beach opposite the venue, giving me a whole day to get up to whatever I fancied.

And I didn't have to look far to see something I fancied.

Even though it was mid-October, it was really hot, and the beach was rammed with girls all sporting that classic Cali look, you know, blonde, pretty and very fuckable, and it only took about five minutes before I got invited over to join some right tasty ones. They were about six handed, and get this, all sitting around a little fire they'd made.

A fire for fuck's sake, it was fucking boiling!

As soon as I opened my mouth I got all the usual: "Oh my God I just luurrrvvve your voice." That was something I always seemed to get that over there. I usually went for my tender, sensitive and meaningful 'David-Essex-deflowering-a-virgin' type voice, and it never let me down, but the problem with these kind of girls was, they always seemed to want to talk all that star sign bollocks and I wasn't really in the mood to play that game; and so I dropped my 'I'm a lonely English musician in a band' lyric early doors.

Now, this will alienate some birds, who don't want to appear like a cheap groupie in front of their friends, but there will always be at least one on the firm who will be impressed enough to make the going 'a little easier'.

I don't want to come across as some kind of third rate Oliver Tobias, but come on, let's have it right: if you're young and fancy a bit of casual leg-over, what's wrong with that?

Well actually quite a lot really, because at this time Aids was very much front-page news.

Long story short, I pulled one of them, and arranged to take her out later that evening.

Question: Where does a skint musician take a bird out on the cheap?

Answer: Easy! The venue you're playing the next night!

And so, that's exactly what I did. Don't get me wrong, I wasn't being a total skint boat, I did take her to Denny's for a quick Denver Omelette before making our way on to The Bear for a few complimentary drinks in the company of Mr Don "American Pie" McLean.

Now, you tell me, what more could a girl want?

Well, for one she probably doesn't want her date for the night to turn into 'Mr Lairy' the unfunny, cockney heckler, who the moment he gets a little bit of bugle up his beak and ten Brandy Alexanders down his throat becomes a completely obnoxious cunt. I think the straw that finally broke this little Californian camel's back (enough to make her shout right in my face that I was no longer a 'really sweet guy' just 'a fucking asshole' and leave) was my attempt to harmonize, very loudly from the bar, with Mr McLean on his beautiful song "Vincent".

I wouldn't mind, but she didn't even hang around to hear my version of "Crying".

And neither did Don. Well, that's what his roadie told me when I drunkenly tried to make my way into his dressing room after the show, for what I thought would be the beginning of a beautiful relationship.

But don't be too sad people, my night doesn't end there.

I left the club and staggered the few yards back to the beach, where there were even more beautiful women sitting around fires (I suppose it was now 2.00am and a little bit colder). Once again, it didn't take long for me to get invited to another intimate gathering of tasty females, which poses these two questions…

1. Where the fuck were all the geezers in this town?

2. Why would anyone want this lagboat sitting with them?

You know what it's like when you're fucked up, but you're trying to look like you're not. Well, that was me that night on the beach. My charade didn't last too long though, because as I tried to sit down after accepting their kind offer of company, I tripped up and fell straight into the fire, but because I was so fucked it actually took me a couple of seconds to realise it.

I'm being serious, my arse was on fire!

So, like any stoned person on a beach with a burning bum hole, I ran to the cooling comfort of the sea. As I sat there looking up at the Californian sky, wet and very sore, I knew it was time for me and my good friend Nyquil to go to bed. As you can probably gather, I didn't really sleep much that night.

In a perfect world, I would have liked to have been in slightly better shape to meet up with The Skatalites the next day, but as the old Rolling Stones song says:

"You can't always get what you want"

I'd met a lot of artists in the ska and reggae world by then, who deserved the name 'legendary', but the problem here was, I was now with a whole room full of them! I kind of sussed maybe Tommy was the leader, but I adored them all.

The cool thing was though, I got on with all of them. As a gesture of friendship, I invited Roland to come onstage and play his song "El

Pussycat" with us and was over the moon when he accepted. When the big moment arrived, Roland came onstage and played beautifully; unfortunately, what I'd forgotten to mention was that we segued the song into "Ne Ne Na Na Nu Nu", and when we did, all poor Roland could do was just stand there looking at us in amazement, as we went into this super-fast slice of ska 'n' b.

And then it got worse… I'd also forgotten that every night when we played the song, Martin would come out from behind his keyboards to strangle someone in the band, and you've guessed it, that night's victim was Mr Alphonso; and we're not talking Louis Alphonso here, this was to be Roland's turn!

The poor guy didn't know what the fuck was going on.

I managed to signal to someone at the side of the stage to help him off, but the damage had already been done and he never joined us onstage again.

Besides Martin's impersonation of The Boston Strangler, all the other dates went off without a hitch. I couldn't really pick a gig out of those dates I could say was the best, but the two nights we had at Slims in San Francisco, where we performed two sets a night, would be hard to beat.

As I said a little earlier The Happy Bus was indeed a happy place to be for the first month of the tour, but as it dragged on into the second, little cliques began to form and pretty soon the bus became home to many heated arguments. Some escalated into full on fist fights, with one of them involving me and my close friend Louis.

It happened in a dressing room in Detroit, in a venue I'm reliably informed was the last place the great escapologist Houdini performed at. I can't remember what kicked it off, but at some point during the argument Louis called me "musical scum", a thinly veiled reference to my recent participation in a session I did for Jive Bunny, in the plush surroundings of Central Studios in Birmingham, where along with some other musicians I went about recreating some of 2-Tone's biggest hits for one of Jive Bunny's 'Megamixes'.

What can I say?

For me it was nothing more than a paid gig that turned into a very well paid gig. My fee was topped up by producer Roger Lomas when he asked me to sing like (impersonate) Suggs on a couple of Madness tracks, "Baggy Trousers" and "Night Boat To Cairo".

"It's just gone noon, half past monsoon."

195

I'd been told by everyone that Suggs was on the firm, but apparently in the period between him agreeing to do it and the actual recording, he began managing a group called The Farm who started having some considerable chart success and so he passed on the project. But thinking about it now, I think it's more likely that he just knew it was a load of old bollocks.

At that moment in Detroit, I didn't really like being called musical scum by one of my closest friends, and so I answered him in the only way a boy from Woodberry Down knows how to:

Throw a bottle at his fucking head.

It was an action I immediately felt ashamed of, because I loved the geezer, and in my defence, it probably happened because nine weeks is a fucking long time for ten men to live together in such close proximity and it's pretty obvious there will be the odd 'straightener' between pals, and to be honest I'm surprised there wasn't a lot more of it.

It was after that incident that Louis came up with the great idea of turning the back room of the bus into a 'Culture Corner'. A little sanctuary, where members of the band who didn't want to stay up all night destroying their liver and nostrils could go for a bit of peace and quiet with a book rather than a bird or a wrap of gear, and as the tour neared its end, I became a much more frequent visitor to it.

I could be here a lot longer if I was to go into more detail about all the ins and outs of those two months spent travelling around North America, but I think some things are best left where they are: buried somewhere deep in the wilderness of my mind. But before I bury those memories though, let me tell you about how I got home…

After spending the day before returning to Blighty relaxing in New York, we arrived at JFK around 11.00 am and waited in the bar for our call to go down to the departure lounge.

Flight delayed for an hour. A few drinks.

Flight delayed for another hour. A few more drinks.

It was 9.00pm before the flight was ready to go, by which time I was well cunted. I said, to no one in particular: "I'm just going for a piss, see you down there."

Apparently, I was found twenty minutes later, in the toilet, lying in a pool of sick with my trousers around my ankles and my bum bag, which I was carrying my wages in, on the floor with dollars from it spread all around the urinal.

Why? I will never know.

Martin told me a few days later he'd found me in there and cleaned me up the best he could, pulling up my trousers and putting my money back in my bum bag, before carrying me down to departures.

This doesn't exactly match what the other two band members told me. Their story went a little more like this...

Yes, Martin was there while I lay unconscious on the toilet floor, but it was them who undertook the not-very-nice task of tidying me up. All that Martin did was try and pull my trousers down in an attempt to take some cheeky snaps of me. I don't suppose I will ever get to the bottom of what went on (see what I did there) but for me the unbelievable part of the story is that the airline (Virgin) actually let me on to the flight in the state I was in, even upgrading me to first class, where I was woken up by a lovely trolley-dolly handing me a nice warm towel to wipe away puke I still had on my face, and telling me we were: "Just flying over Bristol, sir. You were in such a state we didn't think you'd be any trouble to anyone but yourself."

Which is one of the main reasons why, if I have to fly these days, I try to fly Virgin.

Don't take this as a complaint in any way, because at this point of my life I was a gigging musician, and that's all I ever wanted to do, but within a week of returning from that extremely long and tiring tour, I was back out on the road again.

This time for a month-long trek around the UK.

NICK'S TOP FIVE SONGS RECORDED WITH BAD MANNERS

1.   **"Skaville UK"**
2.   **"Skinhead Love Affair"**
3.   **"Since You've Gone Away"**
4.   **"Bonanza Ska"**
5.   **"Sally Brown"**

The first show on the itinerary wasn't a Bad Manners gig, it was a Buster's All Stars show at Wolverhampton Civic Hall, where Pauline Black and Neol Davies of The Selecter would join us to play a few of their old hits. This wasn't going to be a problem for us, because we'd been rehearsing their songs, and don't forget I was already familiar with their material due to all those musical-scum Jive Bunny sessions I'd taken part in a few months before.

Snide comments aside, the show was the dog's mate.

I don't think Pauline and Neol had played those songs in a decade, but they smashed it, and were really happy with the response they received from the crowd, and so it was arranged that we'd do it again, a month or so later at a festival in Belgium.

Although I enjoyed the rest of the shows on that UK tour, the Wolverhampton gig stuck in my mind. I always loved it when I got the chance to play with different artists, and here were two that had quite a few songs I really liked and so when the next gig came around I was really up for it, even though it was on Boxing Day and I don't like spending my Boxing Days in Belgium (and I have...twice). I've got nothing against the place personally, it's just that for those twenty four hours, I'm much more of a 'feet up watching *The Great Escape*, with a cold turkey sandwich in one hand and a drink in the other' kind of guy.

But let me take you away from the warmth of my cosy front room, and back to a two thousand capacity venue, where once again Joe Punter seemed to be overjoyed at getting a chance to see 'The Two Tone Two'. Even I was getting a few tingles down the old spine, especially when I struck up the bassline to "The Selecter" (I've always loved that song, for me, it's better than "Gangsters").

It was a long drive home after the gig, but I didn't mind that. I never do when I get that kind of musical pleasure.

The start of 1991 was taken up with me getting gassed on stage at the George Robey, and even more recording for the "F** S*****" album.

I'm sure by now you've worked out that a musician's life is one of ups and downs. I was just about to experience a definite up... A tour of Japan.

If there was one place in this big old world of ours I've always wanted to go to, it was Japan. Ever since I was a little kid I'd had an obsession with the place. I don't know why, it's not like I had a huge love of kabuki theatre or sumo wrestling, I didn't even desire the pleasures of a geisha girl. I just wanted to walk the streets of Tokyo, and that's exactly what I did the moment my feet touched the ground. I was out and about, living my dream.

I've never been the best at crossing roads, but I fucking excelled myself over there.

The first time I had to get from A to B, I must have stood at the lights for about five minutes before deciding it looked safe enough for me to cross. I got about halfway, when all of a sudden, another load of cars came hurtling towards me from a different direction and I had to run back to the safety of the kerb.

If you ask any musician who's ever toured in Japan, they will always tell you about the itineraries you get from the promoters. They usually go something like this:

18:00.   Leave hotel room.
18:02.   Get in lift.
18:03.   Arrive in hotel foyer.
18:05.   Leave for show.

I'm sure you get the picture.

The Japanese are sticklers for punctuality, and English bands always seem to like to play the game of making sure they're always a couple of minutes late.

Fuck knows why, because it's a fucking rude thing to do.

The gigs were weird. You'd be finished by 10.00pm, and some of the venues were situated in shopping malls! It was the first time I'd ever gone up to a show in a lift.

It was like: third floor - lingerie, fourth floor - gig!

Something that did throw us a little off-kilter at the first show, was when we finished playing our first song and the audience applauded loudly before stopping, just like that. It was like something out of a Benny Hill sketch, but you soon got used to it.

One thing that I didn't mind getting used to was the ultra-professional way that everything was run. For instance, how do you fancy...

Helpful and attentive stage hands.

Brand new, top-of-the-range back line.

Sound guys who don't read books during your performance.

Riders served by people who don't look like they live in a bush.

(I remember the first gig I did when I got back from Japan, at Dereham Memorial Hall. I was greeted by the sight of a PA man's fat arse, far too close to my face, and him informing me that his rig was fucked.)

Japan was everything I thought it would be. Everyone I met on that trip was as sweet as pie, except when I went to a few late-night karaoke competitions; boy do they take that shit seriously! Obviously, over the years, I've been to a few karaoke nights in the UK, full of over emotional birds 'singing' "I Will Survive" before jumping off stage to hit their ex-boyfriend over the head with a stiletto, or glazed-eyed geezers who think after ten pints they're Hackney's answer to Tom Jones, murdering "The Green, Green Grass Of Home" with all the charm and finesse of Charles Manson delivering an anti-natal class to a room of young expectant mothers.

I thought that, with my silky tones, I'd piss all over the other competitors, but when I found myself up against blokes giving it large in Elvis 'Vegas era' jump-suits, performing "Suspicious Minds", complete with all the King's karate moves; or some would-be-Sinatra, smooching his way through "Strangers In The Night" to a handful of swooning housewives... Well, what chance did an old cockney crooner have?

Goodbye Japan. I love you.

Hey, but get happy people, because there's good news coming my way. I managed to persuade Rico to come and play trombone with Manners.

He had just returned to England from Jamaica and was playing a few low-key gigs around town. I went down to see him play in The Weavers Arms, just down the road from my flat, and invited him to come along to play a few shows with us. I knew the audience would love him. And I was right.

He was the nicest guy you could ever know.

Even more good news came my way when I found out that there were a couple more BAS shows to do with Pauline and Neol. The first one, at Birmingham University, went pretty much the same as the previous shows we'd done, but it was at the second gig in Nottingham on Easter Bank Holiday Monday that my relationship with the two of them was cemented.

People still talk about that show.

The line-up was Bad Manners with Pauline and Neol guesting, supported by The International Beat, and even though it was a Monday night over three thousand people crammed into The Ritzy to see the show; and what a show it was.

The band moved up a gear when they joined us on stage. At all the previous shows, I'd played it straight because I didn't want to fuck up, but now I was Mr Confident, so I spent most of that afternoon tooting and drinking, but looking at the footage I have on DVD, you wouldn't have known it. After the gig, Martin asked Pauline and Neol if they fancied doing a few dates with him, me and Perry, which they must have done, because a couple of days later they rang Martin to ask: "What can you get for us then?"

His reply was: "A seven-date tour of the UK, followed by a three-week tour of America"

I'm gonna gloss over what happened next, because I thought it was all very nasty and unnecessary. What I will say is, it caused a big fall-out between Doug and Martin (who never played with Manners again) that was never resolved. Because of that, my love affair with Manners cooled quite a lot. I told Doug I really wanted to do The Selecter dates, which he didn't like the idea of, but reluctantly agreed to.

We carried on gigging together for another couple of months, but there always seemed to be a dark shadow hanging over our relationship.

"There's a shadow hanging over me"

For my last three shows before I went off, I got a bassist in to cover for me, who, I have to say, was technically much better than me. I moved to keyboards, to keep an eye on my 'dep'.

The last gig I ever did with Manners was at the Marquee in Charing Cross Road and from the moment I walked into the venue, the vibe between me and him was strained to say the least.

It came to a head when we were standing together for our 'warm up', and he changed his usual patter and started talking about how I was going off, and this was gonna be the last time anyone was gonna see me. I didn't get it, because in my mind all I was doing was going off for a couple of weeks to play a few shows with another band, and then I would be back with Manners.

But I suppose you never know what life is gonna throw at you.

Detroit 1990

Bad Manners 1990

THE DEVIL IN ME

I know that I hurt you, hurt you so bad, when I drank from the
well below,
Well no one would stop me, so I made my way, to places I shouldn't
go,
But now I'm older and I can see, the truth before us you know,
It's just the devil in me.

I felt the power to bang on the drum, and dance to a different beat,
The song that I sang to you back in the day, was I like to lie and
cheat,
But now I'm older and I can see, the truth before us you know,
It's just the devil in me.

I followed illusion, I need the high, when all I could get were lows,
I messed up the little things that I loved the best, I guess that's the
way it goes,
But now I'm older and I can see, the truth before us you know,
It's just the devil in me.

On the 1st July 1991, I travelled up to Coventry with Perry and Martin, to meet up with Pauline, Neol and Roger Lomas for a couple of days' rehearsals at The Tic Toc Club for our forthcoming tours of the UK and USA.

Looking back, I can't believe we only did two days' rehearsal, and one of those was taken up with filming a TV show!

It wasn't a problem though: the three of us had been playing together so much over the previous couple of years we were as tight as fuck and so it was more a case of the two of them slotting in with us, which of course they did with ease, and with Roger doing the live sound it was fucking easy.

A quick aside…

After the first day's rehearsal, I stayed at Pauline's house. The next morning, I woke up in her spare room a little blurry eyed and fucked up from the night before, but with an incredibly strong urge to knock one out. I was just about to finish my hand-shandy, when I suddenly remembered where I was and panicked. Luckily for me I managed to grab one of my socks off of the floor and gave it an unexpected gift, which was just as well really, because I don't think it would've been the best start to life in The Selecter if the singer had found a jizzy sheet in her spare room a couple of days later.

What I didn't realise at the time, was that this was not going to be just a three week love affair, but the beginning of a fifteen year marriage to The Selecter.

The UK part of the tour was seven dates in a row, starting at The Duchess of York in Leeds. The Duchess wasn't the biggest venue in the world, but the good news was it had sold out well in advance, which will always add a little swagger to a band's performance. However, when we were greeted by the promoter, John Keenan, he had a worried look on his face.

He took me and Martin to one side, and told us Doug had been on the phone to him all day telling him to cancel the show and send his band back home, which upset John, because he was friends with all of us and now he felt like piggy in the middle.

For the record, in promoter circles John is considered to be a bit of a leg end. He's the man who gave Nirvana and Oasis their first step towards stardom (well in Leeds anyway), and the brains behind the legendary Futurama festivals in the late 70s/early 80s.

We didn't bother telling the others what had been going on. I mean, for fuck's sake, it was our first show and we didn't want anything to fuck it up. As far as I was concerned we were here to play a show and that was exactly what we were going to do.

The crowd went mental from the first song, "Carry Go Bring Come", until the last, "Too Much Pressure". You couldn't have asked for a more perfect first gig but what was more important to me was the personal pleasure I'd got from the evening playing much more challenging material like "Celebrate The Bullet" and "Washed Up And Left For Dead".

After the show, I sat in the dressing room, totally knackered and covered in sweat, but as happy as the proverbial pig in shit. As we were making our way out of The Duchess, John handed us our night's wages and thanked us for a great show before adding: "I don't know if this will help, but I've given you an extra £100."

Although it was a really nice gesture from a really nice man, it wasn't going to help our situation with Fatty; but what it does show you is that there are some decent promoters out there!

And that's how all the gigs went for us on that first tour. No, not promoters giving us extra money, but playing packed shows to wildly enthusiastic audiences. None more so than the one we did in Coventry, which surprised me because all the gigs I'd previously done there hadn't been that great, but I suppose that's because Bad Manners weren't The Selecter, a genuine 2-Tone band from Coventry.

I think that night gave Pauline and Neol a real shot in the arm.

The last gig of the tour was at The Powerhaus in London. Once again, the show had sold out weeks in advance, and on the night there were untold touts outside the venue trying to make a few bob out of it.

So, we were kicking back in the dressing room post gig feeling on top of the world, talking about our forthcoming USA trip, when Martin opened his ever-present attaché case and handed everyone an envelope with their tour wedge in it.

Neol had a puzzled look on his face: "What's this?"

"It's your money from the gigs."

His reply really shocked me: "Do you mean we get paid for doing this as well?"

It gave me the distinct impression that maybe the first incarnation of the band had been taken for a bit of a ride by whoever was looking after them.

At the start of our American adventure I was greeted by the sight of Roger Lomas standing at the check-in desk at Heathrow dressed in a tight blue denim suit, no shirt (hairy chest) and white cowboy boots with brown heels.

I hugged him and greeted him with a genuine and heartfelt: "Looking cool Roger. Nice bit of denim you got there mate."

His reply was brilliant: "Well, I don't wanna be mistaken for one of you lot, do I?"

"I pull my blue jeans on, I pull my old blue jeans on"

The tour kicked off on the East Coast, and we went to all the usual places: Boston, Washington DC, Philadelphia, New York...

Let me tell you about New York.

On the day we played the Big Apple, it was so fucking hot I thought I was gonna die but even though it was fucking boiling, I decided to go for a walk around Greenwich Village, to have a few beers and check out all the great record shops in the area, both of which I managed to do with relative ease (you see, I can do things for myself when I put my mind to it) and after a couple of hours in the sunshine, I made my way back to the venue arriving at the stage door exactly at the same time as two fucking monsters, who looked like extras from The Sopranos, were trying to squeeze their huge frames into this one very small entrance.

I stood behind them, enjoying the cabaret, when for some reason I thought the right thing to do at that moment was to tap one of them on the shoulder and say in a camp voice: "Room for a small one?"

It wasn't!

They both turned around, took one look at me, and pushed me to the floor before departing with a more than slightly scary: "Fucking faggot."

As I picked myself up from the hot Manhattan pavement, I spotted a guy who worked at the venue and asked him: "Who the fuck were those guys?"

"They are people you don't want to know. They come, collect, and go."

I think I understood what he meant.

After the show, I took a taxi with the sound engineer to a transvestite cocktail bar he knew to pick up some totally mental gear, before going on to a great hip hop club in The Bronx. We both got seriously fucked up with the locals who I think (and I'm gonna let you into a little secret here) found my attempts at 'body popping' rather amusing.

I made my way back to my hotel at 5.00am, stopping in the middle of an unusually quiet and empty Times Square to take everything in. I felt like a fucking king.

The usually long and arduous distances between gigs seemed really easy to do, even though they were done in a Winnebago, a vehicle much better suited to short family holidays than taking a band on a coast to coast tour. I suppose that's why I can remember sitting in the desert just outside Salt Lake City at 2.00am, staring at the stars, while waiting for a replacement vehicle so we could continue our journey on to California. But that was just a small hiccup, quickly forgotten as soon as we reached the Golden State.

Those gigs were undoubtedly the best of the tour, with the highlight being San Francisco.

We were staying at The Phoenix, a gaff bands like to call 'the rock 'n' roll hotel', but let's have it right here, although I've always had a laugh there it's just another motel that charges a lot more than other places of the same standard, it has rooms furnished with dodgy 70s wallpaper, TVs with shit reception, and ice machines that never ever seem to have any fucking ice in them.

I could go on, but I won't.

As good as the gig was, this was to be one of those rare occasions where the show was overshadowed by the events after it.

When we got back to The Phoenix, we were serenaded by two dark figures leaning over a first-floor balcony singing "Three Minute Hero". At first, I thought they were fans who'd been to the show and gave them a wave, but as I got closer I realised that one of them was one of my all-time heroes…

Donovan.

I made my way up the stairs to say hello to the great man, who was standing outside his room with his stepson Julian. We shook hands and the first thing he said to me in that beautiful soft voice of his was: "Do you know Gil Scott Heron is staying here tonight?"

I couldn't believe my luck!

Here I am, in one of my favourite cities in the whole world, with two artists I've adored all my life staying in the same hotel as me and so obviously, the first thing that came out of my mouth was: "Well, let's have a party Don."

207

And the good news was, he was well up for it. Now all I had to do was get GSH on board and I would be in fucking heaven. I'd read many times that he was quite partial to the odd Russell or ten so I thought to myself: this will be a piece of piss. But when I rang down to reception to ask for his room number, all I got from the bird on the desk was: "I'm sorry sir, we can't give out guest's room numbers, it's against the hotel's policy."

The hotel's fucking policy!

See what I mean?

What kind of fucking rock 'n' roll establishment is that?

So, rather than banging on every door shouting "the revolution will not be televised" to grab his attention (which I didn't think would make me look too cool), I gave up on the idea of trying to make the acquaintance of Mr Heron and instead settled down for a mellow yellow evening in the company of Mr Leitch and son.

And what about this for a touch…

When he turned up at my door ten minutes later, he'd only gone and brought his guitar with him, which, after a few drinks, he took out of the case and suggested we play some music together, at which point someone in the room (I won't tell you who) asked him to play "Jennifer Juniper".

"Jennifer Juniper rides a dappled mare"

I felt myself squirming in my seat thinking: you can't ask the geezer to play one of his classics, well not straight away anyway, you have to pretend you wanna hear him do a couple of old Scottish folk songs or something, then hit him with a request from his greatest hits songbook. To his credit, he didn't bat an eyelid and went straight into performing a track I've loved ever since I first heard it coming out of my shitty little transistor radio way back in 1968, and I have to say, it was one of the most memorable musical moments of my life.

As Jennifer's final chord rang around the room, he handed me his guitar and said: "Now it's your turn to play something for me."

I knew he'd been good friends with Marc Bolan and I desperately wanted him to approve of my performance, so I decided to play safe and went for "Life's A Gas".

And twenty-five years later, I can still remember what he said to me at the end of it:

"I didn't think you'd have a voice like that, Nick."

Now, you can take that comment any way you like, but I'm looking at it in a totally positive light! So, the evening was going really well, with everyone drinking, chatting and chilling, when Roger decided to get up and go to the toilet. As he walked past Donovan he pointed his arse quite close to his face and made a loud farting noise (I never did get to the bottom of whether the noise came from his mouth or his arse) and guess what? Within a couple of seconds, the hurdy-gurdy man was thanking us all for a lovely evening, and was on his way out of the door quicker than a sunshine superman.

"For fuck's sake Roger, what did you do that for mate?"

"Don't worry about it Nick, he's alright, he loves a laugh."

"Really?"

And with that the party ended.

The next day I was relieved when I bumped into him and he gave me a big hug, thanking me again for a great night, and then he was off in a limo bigger than my flat.

So maybe Roger was right about Donovan being ok with his methane-based humour. I don't suppose I will ever get to the bottom of it (get it), because even though I've met him a few times since, I've never thought it was a good idea to ask him. What I do know though, is the memory of that night will stay with me for the rest of my life.

The day after the Frisco show, we made our way along the beautiful Pacific Coast Highway to Los Angeles, via shows in Palo Alto and Santa Cruz, to play two sold-out nights at Chuck Landis's Country Club.

After sound-checking on the first night, we all went across the street from the venue to a 50s style diner that looked pretty cool. As we sat there waiting for our burgers and fries to arrive, I looked out of the window to see a huge crowd of fans queuing to get into the show.

I pointed it out to Neol, who's reaction was: "We're not playing tonight unless they change that."

Which was greeted by a quartet of: "Change what?"

"That!" He said, pointing to the sign on the venue's marquee that read: TONIGHT... SOLD OUT...THE SELECTOR

But what was really funny was he was totally serious about it!

While I can understand that it was the name of the band he'd started that was being misspelt, for fuck's sake, we were being paid good money for the shows and it was only a couple of months before that he was sitting in Coventry not doing a hell of a lot.

That night we had the pleasure of being joined by the police onstage. No, not Sting and co, but some of LA's finest, to make sure the crowd didn't get too near the stage. When I turned around to look at Perry in the middle of "Street Feeling" (I always did), to see a shit load of old bill standing right behind me, it certainly straightened me up a little bit, if only because I'm not used to seeing geezers with shooters on stage with me.

At the end of the tour we all agreed The Selecter experiment had been a complete success and I hoped maybe there would be other times when we could do it all again, but for now it was back to England and Bad Manners.

Or so I thought…

I rang Doug as soon as I got home to arrange a catch up with him the following Thursday, at The Crown and Two Chairman in Dean Street, which was where we'd always go for a few drinks before going to Gossips. When we met, we hugged and started chatting in the same light hearted way we'd done for all our lives, but the laughter soon stopped when I said: "Listen Doug, if any more Selecter shows do come up, I really would like to do them."

His reply couldn't have been any clearer: "I don't want you doing any more shows with them, from now on it's me or nothing."

And that's where our lifelong friendship ended, because I had to say: "Well, it's got to be nothing then mate, because I can't let you or anyone else tell me how to live my life."

From that moment, in his eyes I was the on the same list as all those other people he thought had 'turned him over' and I was about to receive the prize of a lifetime membership to the 'Fatty cold shoulder club'; and although it really upset me, I felt that as a friend he should have given me a little bit more leeway.

It was time for me to move on.

As I've said before, at this point I didn't know if there were going to be any more Selecter shows but what I did know was that I would never ever stand on stage again with a large bald man throwing a bucket of water over the audience.

I think what really stuck the knife in that night was when we bumped into Chrissie Boy from Madness and he greeted me with a light hearted: "Oh hello Nick from Manners. Oh sorry, its Nick from Selecter now, isn't it?"

I could see from the look on Doug's face he was not a happy man; and then the last lunge of cold ska-steel that would tear the flesh out of our relationship was, while we were standing at the bar (in silence), all you could see were people wearing Selecter t-shirts. There were only about six or seven of them, which I know doesn't sound like a lot, but in a club the size of Gossips they really stuck out. I want to say here and now that none of this makes me smile: all I can think is, on that night I lost someone who I considered to be one of my best friends.

Crystal Waters	**"Gypsy Woman"**
PM Dawn	**"Set Adrift On Memory Bliss"**
Soho	**"Hippy Chick"**

After that US tour, I had no gigs in my diary, so I took the opportunity to go on holiday for a couple of weeks to think about what I was going to do next. Thankfully, the answer came on the day I got back when Martin rang to tell me that there were offers on the table for Selecter tours of Europe and the UK and was I up for it?

Well of course I was.

We all met up in London a couple of days later to record a live radio session for GLR, and afterwards we made our way to the nearest pub to 'talk about our future', and by the time the bell rang at closing time I staggered into the street a full time member of The Selecter.

Martin had sorted out a one-off single deal with Pagan Records, a label run by Andy Cowan-Martin (remember him?) and ex-Tubeway Army member Russell Bell.

He then in typical Stewart fashion also informed me that they were now our managers!

"The Other Side Of Love" and "Trouble In Paradise" were two new Neol Davies songs we'd been playing since our first gig and I immediately (but wrongly) assumed they would be the tracks making up the A and B sides of our record and even suggested as much to the company. And so it was a bit of a surprise when I arrived at the studio to put down what I thought was to be the first in a new era of Selecter music, to be told in no uncertain terms by the powers that be: "If the band are serious about making a comeback, you're going to record new versions of "On My Radio" and "The Selecter"." And because they were paying for everything, we had to swallow it.

I didn't say it at the time, but I will now…

Both tracks are a pile of shit and not worth the vinyl they're pressed on, and just as bad is the promo video we made for "On My Radio '91".

The director got me to do some kind of stupid hip hop type hand moves in it, which I did because I didn't wanna rock the boat, but I tell you, I wish I hadn't because it's so embarrassing I can't watch the fucking thing.

On the first day of the "Out On The Streets Again" tour, the Selecter vehicle curse struck again, when our van broke down after just fifty yards from where we picked it up. Now normally, with us being so close to the hire firm, that wouldn't be much of a problem and we'd just go back and get another, but it was a problem, because they told us they wouldn't have another vehicle available for at least another four hours.

So, it was 10.00am and we were stuck in South London in a broken-down van, and we had to be in Utrecht at 6.00pm for soundcheck. Now, I'm sure you'll forgive me if I miss out the next long and very boring twelve hours of that day; so long story short, we arrived at the venue at 11.00pm with just five minutes to spare before our first tour of Europe got under way.

I would be lying to you if I said that I could remember all the ins and outs of that first Euro tour, but the one thing that really sticks out in my mind was staying in a hotel in Lucerne that used to be a prison. Oh, and a night in Jena that has made its way into one of my lists...

NICK'S TOP FIVE SCARY RACIST GIG INCIDENTS

1.	**Le Mans, Bad Manners**
2.	**Valencia, Bad Manners**
3.	**Fresno, The Selecter**
4.	**Los Angeles, Buster's All Stars**
5.	**Jena, The Selecter**

Fuck, I forgot about being held at knifepoint in a Milan toilet!

Our second tour of the UK was just like the first.

Lots of sold out shows all over the country, finishing up with two sold out nights at The Powerhaus in Islington just before Christmas, which was great for me because the venue was only about five hundred yards down the road from my flat; but it was that short distance that turned out to be the catalyst for a huge amount of pain I was just about to endure.

At the end of the second show I was getting flavoured at the bar, boring everyone with the same line over and over again, which was: "I live so near to here, I could fucking hop home." And so when it came to throwing out time, in my pissed up, sniffed up state, that's exactly what I tried to do, but all I achieved was to give myself an unexpected Christmas present.

A twisted ankle!

Oh, and by the way, just in case you were wondering how "On My Radio '91" did...

Well I'm sorry to say that it sank lower than whale shit.

The new year began with me thinking: "Have I done the right thing here?"

There were a few reasons for this. The band were not going to be gigging for a few months because Pauline was back treading the boards in a play, and our next release was gonna be a live album "Out On The Streets", which was certainly no step forward for the band in my book. But the thing that wound me up most was thinking about a conversation I'd had with Neol a few weeks before in the dressing room at Scunthorpe Baths Hall.

He was fucking around on his guitar, and I thought it sounded really good. I asked what he was playing and he told me it was a new song he was working on. I took out my bass and played him a bass line I thought might work for it. He put down his guitar and looked at me like I'd just taken a shit in his coat pocket and said: "Thanks for the offer Nick, but I write the songs in this band."

"I write the songs that make the whole world sing"

I was a bit taken aback by what he said, but I suppose he did write all those hit songs that were basically the reason why we were all there and so out of respect for him as a songwriter/guitarist, I just left him to it, hoping he'd eventually come up with something decent, but he never did and that's as much as I'm prepared to say on the subject.

Knowing my creative input wasn't required, I began doing what I always do and that's writing and stockpiling songs, and once again within a month or so I had about ten of them, enough for me to start putting the wheels in motion to find myself a side project as a vehicle to play them, and when I found my vehicle it would be one I'd want to run side-by-side with The Selecter.

At the start of 1992, I bumped into Jennie Matthias, former lead singer of 80s girl group The Belle Stars who were a band mostly made up of ex-members of 2-Tone group The Bodysnatchers, with the addition of Jennie, a vibrant, energetic vocalist, possessing a beautiful voice perfectly suited to their timeless pop sound. If the Shangri-las had recorded "Sign Of The Times", it would probably be hailed as an all-time classic.

I'd seen Jennie around the clubs, but never had a proper conversation with her and the first one we had was hardly something we can look back and smile at, even though it did start us off on a lifetime's friendship.

I saw her sitting on her tod in the dressing room (kitchen) at The Dublin Castle, waiting to come on as a special guest with The Trojans. She'd just gone through the terrible experience of her boyfriend, Andrew (bassist in the band), committing suicide, and here she was just about to go out and do a show without her loved one standing next to her on stage.

Not very nice really.

I knocked on the door to say hello and she went straight into telling me all about Andrew, how much she loved and missed him, and this seemed to have a snowball effect on me, because I began going on about how much I missed my dad, which in the four years since he'd gone I'd never done. So there we were, two relative strangers pouring our hearts out to each other, but while it may have been therapeutic for me, I don't think it was the best way for her to get ready to do a show. I stood at the back of the room watching her work the crowd that night and all I could think was: "I really wanna work with this woman, she's like a little ball of dynamite."

We continued our conversation after the show and I just came straight out with it: "Listen Jen, I've got some great song ideas but they need lyrics, can you help? How do you fancy meeting up and finishing them off with me?"

She said yes, and that's how Big 5 started.

"This is the dawning of a new era"

We met up at her place a few days later, and after just a couple of hours we'd written our first song, "Shame", a track deeply rooted in that classic period of 60s UK girl pop music, just like The Belle Stars had been, but with a new cutting ska edge.

214

After getting blanked by Neol, meeting Jennie was a real shot in the arm for me. I'd found someone to write with, who was absolutely on the same pop wavelength as me. Over the next couple of months, we'd get together at least twice a week, to try and write some three-minute-symphonies of our own.

For me, the best of the bunch were: "Universe", "Outrageous" and "Sweet & Funky", which eventually all featured on our debut album "Popskatic". There were also quite a few like "Jesse James", "Pleased to Meet You" and "Get Smart", that were recorded but have never seen the light of day.

We discussed the idea of doing a London gig to showcase the songs, but that had to go on hold for a couple of months because The Selecter were back out on tour in the UK, this time under the banner "Pressure '92".

Pressure?

Thirty-six shows in forty days? Pressure?

I would say the only pressure was on the singer's voice.

To be honest, I don't know how Pauline got through it. Truth be told, there really was no need for us to play some of the shows we were doing. The gigs in the early part of the week were usually small venues with dodgy PAs, who weren't paying us a lot of money.

What was the fucking point of that? Maybe it was an ego thing, you know: "Hey, look everyone! See how wanted we are."

Ego tripping out.

Who gives a flying fuck about playing Swindon on a rainy Monday night, I know I didn't; especially when you've just been offered a tour of Japan with Prince Buster and The Skatalites!

Now, you know about my love for all things Japanese, and what a great time I'd had there with Manners the year before, but this was going to be better.

So much better.

After the first of two shows in Tokyo, Buster approached me to ask if he could come and perform with us, instead of The Skatalites. When I told the band what he wanted, they were all a little bit dubious about it, because although playing with Buster would be an honour, no one wanted to upset The Skatalites; but 'The Voice Of The People' can be very persuasive. And so, on our second night in the capital, The Selecter were joined onstage by Buster for a four-song set of "Madness", "Al Capone", "Orange Street" and "Rough Rider".

215

He loved it. We loved it. Everyone loved it.

And ten years later, Mint Royale must've loved it too, because they sampled some of Buster's performance for their dance track "The Sexiest Man in Jamaica", which made its way into the UK chart giving Buster the chance to perform it with them on *TOTP*.

One night, after a wonderful Chinese meal, we asked Buster if he fancied coming over to London to do a show with us and maybe, time permitting, some recording. Well, he must have liked the idea, because before I'd even finished my crispy duck he'd agreed, and just over a month later we were on stage together in the less than salubrious surroundings of The George Robey which was, strangely enough, at Buster's request. He'd got up on stage there a few years before and really liked it. The cost of the show (his fee, flights, hotel and support acts) really required a much bigger venue to make it work financially, but The Robey said they would make it happen. It wasn't until the night of the show that I discovered what their cunning plan was and I have to say it was absolute genius in its simplicity:

You simply let over a thousand people into what was at most a three hundred capacity venue!

I'm not joking, and anyone reading this who was there will back me up.

But remember Nick don't mention how great the gig was…

While he was over we struck up a deal, that if the band recorded some songs for him, he would come and do some tracks with us.

He definitely got the better deal…

We recorded about twelve songs in three days for him with Rico, Lester Sterling and Jennie all guesting on tracks. There were two cuts on those sessions that really stuck out for me, the cover of "What A Wonderful World" that Buster sang beautifully, and a psychedelic reggae jam (I can't remember the title) that dropped like a Funkadelic track, with Prince doing some weird shit over the top. It was a top groove.

And then it was our turn.

With only a couple of days' studio time available, due to Buster's other commitments, in my role as producer (me producing Prince Buster!) I decided it would be for the best if we recorded a song everyone knew, so we would at least get one track done; and that's why I chose "Madness".

It was Perry who came up with the idea of giving it a modern-day reggae rhythm on a drum machine, instead of doing it in the more

216

conventional ska style with a live kit, and I think it worked well. The funny thing is, we recorded "Madness" in the same studio Manners had used for the "F** S*****" album where I thought it took all the life and energy out of the band's sound. This time around it just felt like another facet of The Selecter's more complex musical personality. I've gotta tell you though, playing bass for Buster was a lot easier for me than having to sit behind the desk, giving him production pointers like: "Excuse me Cecil old chap, I think your diction could be a little better on that section."

But he trusted and put his faith in me, and it was an experience I will never forget.

Triple X released "Madness" as an EP, featuring three different mixes of the song, which was good for us because we were going back to the States for a five week tour.

I spent most of that summer either writing with Jennie or playing European festivals with The Selecter, in the company of real-deal legendary artists like Buddy Guy, Maceo Parker and Rufus Thomas, and it was at one of these shows that Martin was sacked from the band, with his charge sheet reading: Dismissed for trying to sell the singer's private parts to the promoter.

He was replaced for a couple of gigs by Bob Jackson, the former Badfinger keyboardist, but although he was a superb player he just didn't seem to slot in and so it was decided Martin's sentence would be quashed, and he was allowed back into the fold.

Two days before we were due to fly out to the USA, it was my turn for a band run in.

We were playing a big festival in Holland, and I was sitting bored in the backstage area so I decided to shave my head, before moving on to the next thing that would keep me amused until show time. Anyway, I was on my way to watch Golden Earring when I bumped into Pauline (literally) who took one look at a slightly flavoured bass player, with a freshly shaven head, drinking champagne straight out of the bottle, and went fucking mental.

"Look at the state of you Nick, you look awful!"

She tried grabbing the bottle out of my hand, but only succeeded in spilling the bubbly over both of us. I didn't give a fuck, but she got very angry about it. Angry enough not to speak to me for the rest of the day, or the three that followed. In fact, it wasn't until the morning after we'd played our second US show that we decided over breakfast maybe it would be for the best if we started talking to each other again, because we did have to spend the next five weeks together living in each other's pockets, but if you think that's musicians acting childishly, how about this for musicians behaving fucking stupidly...

The day after peace was declared, we were playing in Baltimore.

I'd gone clean for the first few gigs, but I was now getting that all too familiar urge to go and score. At soundcheck, I asked the promoter, who in turn asked the sound crew, who hooked me up with the lighting guy, who made the call that came up trumps. His man would be there in twenty minutes. We did the introductions and it turned out he was just the middleman, so all three of us jumped into a taxi downtown to a Days Inn, where I would get sorted out by his people. I was chatting away to them, about music and shit, and at no time did I ever think to myself: "Hold on old son, you're going to pick up drugs with two faces you don't know from Adam."

I didn't think.

And the reason I didn't is because when you're going to pick up, all you can think about is getting your gear. I tell you what though, I thought about it pretty fucking quick when the hotel door opened (chain still on), and all I could see was a pair of crazy-man eyes.

Was it too late for me to say: "Actually guys, I've changed my mind about all of this, can we take a rain check?"

You bet your fucking life it was too late, because the chain was off and I was in the room with Crazy-eyes. Sorry, let's change that to Crazy-eyes and three more of his crazy-eyed friends. But as I was brought up never to judge a book by its cover, I shook their hands in some kind of awkward hip hop street way, and accepted their kind offer to sit down with them on the sofa.

Unfortunately, I think I managed to raise all the eyebrows in the room (it has to be a guess, because everyone's face was hidden by an oversized baseball cap), by sitting on a huge pile of $1000 bills I hadn't seen all over the floor. Being the polite Englishman I am, I quickly dropped to my knees and tried picking up the worst financial mess since Wall Street, but I was quickly told not to. Somehow, in just a few minutes, I'd managed to turn this into some kind of comedy drug deal, with me playing Woody Allen as the first-time buyer.

My apologies were interrupted by Crazy-eyes pulling out what looked to be a very large bag of cocaine and asking me how much I wanted to buy. At that point my original eight-ball request just didn't seem enough

218

so I blurted out: "Oh, just a little half-ounce man, you know, enough to get me through the next couple of days."

Where the fuck did that come from?

I know I play ska, but I'm not fucking Scarface!

"Are you sure that's all you want? We've got a lot more than that."

I knew he wasn't just trying to big himself up or anything like that, because at the same time he was tempting me to up my drug-ante, he began opening suitcases containing many, many more large bags of Charlie. Sadly, I had to decline his kind offer on the grounds I was just a struggling musician, and that's when the mood in the camp changed.

You know, it's funny, I've met all kinds of people from different backgrounds, all over the world, and when they find out you're a musician you suddenly seem to become Mr Interesting to them, and luckily enough for me, it was going to be one of those days.

Crazy Eyes' mood changed from terrifying, to one of a helpful youth club leader.

He even offered me a free sample of his product, off the end of a knife that really should have still been behind the counter in a Harringay kebab house.

Fuck me that shit hit me straight away.

It was S-T-R-O-N-G!

While he weighed and packed up my purchase (see, it's not much different from John Lewis) I sat back and tried to relax (yeah right), and for the first time I noticed the way the room was decorated. I'm not talking about the wallpaper and curtains here, it was more the boxes of trainers that resembled a Nike Stonehenge, the endless piles of folding on the smoked glass table, oh and what's that leaning against the bedside cabinet? A fucking machine gun!

Handing me my bag, he said: "Hey man, after you done playing your show, come on back here and we can party."

And do you know what kids?

Sometimes it's ok to tell a little white lie, and so through the biggest and falsest smile I've ever given, I said: "Yeah man, that would be really cool."

Ziggy Marley   **"Look Who's Dancing"**
Prince   **"Sexy MF"**
Arrested Development   **"People Everyday"**

My 'don't look before you leap' behaviour continued all the way through the tour, right up until the final day when we played The Palace in LA. I'd arranged to go and grab something to eat with Pauline and Neol after the show near our hotel on Sunset, a block from the venue. We were halfway to hamburger heaven, when a group of fans who'd been at the gig stopped us to say how good the show was.

One of them kept saying to me: "Come back to The Palace and get high with us man."

The elder statespersons of the band made their excuses, but of course the chance to get fucked up with these kids was far too good an opportunity for me to turn down. I remember Pauline grabbing my arm and saying: "Nick, just leave it eh? Come on, let's go and eat."

But as usual, the seed had been sown.

The reason I think she became uncharacteristically protective of me, was that these 'kids' as I call them were obviously Mexican gang members, all tattooed muscles bursting out of tight fitting 'wife beaters' and so before you could say, well anything really, I was back in the upstairs 'celebrity' area at The Palace, doing tequila slammers and snorting toot off the bar.

Fuck me it was some night.

They were lovely though, even walking me back to my hotel before leaving me with a piece of well-intentioned good local advice: "Don't fuck the whores around here man. You'll end up with a big dick in your ass."

I think from here on my touring anecdotes will not be of a musical nature and the reason for this is simple...

The majority of shows I've done in the last forty years, whether it was with The Selecter, Bad Manners or any of the other artists I've been lucky enough to have worked with, have thankfully always been great, and usually played to a packed-out venue. Which is why I've chosen to tell stories that are not music related, but instead to try and show what my state of mind was at the time I was doing them and letting you know the kind of crazy things that can happen when you're out on the road.

I bought a book "The Last Days Of John Lennon" at LA airport at the end of the tour to read on my way home, and in one chapter, it told how John couldn't quite get the beat right on a song called "Kiss Kiss Kiss" and so he asked the book's author to go and fetch a cassette of an album he'd been listening to on a recent holiday in the Bahamas. That album was "Too Much Pressure"! He popped it into his blaster and tried to copy

220

the rhythm of the title track for his song. I think I must have read that paragraph about five times, before handing the book to Neol, sitting in the row in front of me. The geezer went into shock, but who can blame him; what an accolade for a songwriter to learn John Lennon had tried to rip him off!

It lifted our spirits on that long-haul trip, helped along by the endless refills of free brandy, and before we knew it, we'd touched down and my first thoughts were to ring Jennie and get our project up and running: "Let's just book a show somewhere, get some musicians in and do it."

The first part was easy, that somewhere was the George Robey.

Now, I just wanna say this about the place... I'd been getting pissed in there since I was sixteen and it was always good for 'afters' after closing time; the curtains would be drawn and I would proceed to get hammered in the company of characters as diverse as John Lydon, Screaming Lord Sutch or on one memorable night Gerry Conlon, but one thing was always the same, I'd never leave the gaff until the sun came up over Finsbury Park.

Alright, the bogs weren't the best and you did get the odd tear up in there, but you can get that anywhere. The most important thing for me was that they actually got off their arses and advertised the shows they put on. There wasn't an area of London you wouldn't see one of their posters on a wall, bus stop or a disused shop window. Plus, the owners were good people who I got on with. The fact I had a free bar tab in there after the Prince Buster show had nothing to do with it at all!

Right, so we needed some musicians and of course a name for the band.

We decided right from the off the nucleus of the band would be the two of us and Perry Melius, because the musical road we were going to take was a ska/reggae meets soul/funk one and Mr Melius was the perfect man for that. I played safe and went for Martin on keys and Louis Alphonso on guitar. Jennie got Leslie Shone from The Belle Stars to do backing vocals alongside brother Richard, who'd carved out a decent career for himself in that role, working with Marc Almond, The Brand New Heavies and Boyzone.

The name Big 5 was a last-minute deal because the adverts for the show were just about to go to press and we needed a fucking name.

Why Big 5?

It's my favourite Prince Buster album. Simple as that.

And with no small thanks to the Robey's advertising, the place was rammed.

My only worry was maybe punters would turn up expecting a set made up of familiar numbers due to all the 'ex this and ex that' nature of the gig's promotion, because we weren't doing any of that. It was all new gear, with just a couple of Jennie's favourite songs, "Stupid Cupid" and "Mr Big Stuff", thrown in for good measure, but it went down a storm; in fact I'd say the vibe in the room was one of light relief that we weren't just trotting out dodgy pub-versions of "Iko Iko" and "Lip Up Fatty".

We were even joined onstage by one of the pub owners, Bryan Aldwinkle, a fantastic traditional Irish musician, playing flute on the final song of the evening, "Free", a sort of 'acid jazz meets Jethro Tull' track which went on for about twelve minutes and was fucking phenomenal.

Tragically, I've only just heard in the last week that Bryan passed away in 2014.

We managed to slot in another couple of Big 5 shows before I had to go back on the road with The Selecter for another month long schlepp around the UK. If I'm being honest, at that time I would rather it had been with Jen and co, but I knew I had a few months' break away from all things Selecter at the start of the following year, when we could gig away to our hearts' content.

My last Selecter show of 1992 was on Boxing Day as special guests to Steve Harley and Cockney Rebel at some festival in Belgium. That's not the reason I'm gonna grant the gig a few lines here, it's because we had to hire two private planes to get us there!

Now, before you start having visions of me lording it up thirty thousand feet in the air, in something resembling Elvis's *Lisa Marie*, let me say you'd be well wrong. In truth, when I turned up at the remote airfield somewhere in the middle of Essex for the flight, my first reaction was to turn into a cockney Mr T: "I ain't fucking getting on no plane like that!"

But after a calming conversation with the pilot over a couple of large brandies, I ended up sitting next to him in the cockpit for the whole flight, while he explained everything that was going on, and I have to say that the time just flew by. (Sorry.)

I don't remember much about the show, except I got well pissed in the backstage area and kept shouting in an ultra-camp Mick Jagger type voice: "Oi, has anyone seen my fucking pilot?"

222

Maybe you had to be there to appreciate its full comedic value.

I wasn't so flash on the return trip though, because I let Perry take a turn in the front while I sat in the back, where I heard and felt every noise and bump the aircraft made.

In the words of the great Sir Alex Ferguson it was 'squeaky bum time' or more accurately:

"Fresh trousers for Mr Welsh please!"

Japan 1992

THE FREAK SHOW IN YOUR HEAD

You don't believe in love, you don't believe in hate,
You really rack me off, you little two and eight,
Because you never change, you just simply rearrange,
The freak show in your head you have grown,
You have grown.

You got a good idea, but it's out of date,
When everything goes reels, you say it's down to fate,
But you never change, you just simply rearrange,
The freak show in your head you have grown,
You have grown.

You say your glass is full and your life is sweet,
But I can see your hand on the word delete,
Oh, you never change, you just simply rearrange,
The freak show in your head you have grown,
You have grown,
On your own.

The next project mooted for The Selecter was to record an album of covers.

For me that was just about as low as I thought we could go, even lower than re-recording your own back catalogue, or releasing a desperate stop-gap live album, but thank God it never actually happened, because the band were about to undergo some quite radical changes.

I'd begun writing new material with Pauline, and this was because Neol was no longer in the band, and let me go on record now in saying we never did adequately replace him in the line up. When I heard the news I was shocked, but to my detriment, I was far too busy getting fucked up to even care, so shame on me.

To be honest, I was more upset when Perry left us a few months before, but at least that blow had been softened with the knowledge I'd still be playing with him in Big 5. Luckily for us we replaced Perry with Winston Marche, a superb drummer who was, and still is (on occasion), a joy to play with and a great geezer into the bargain.

After Neol's departure the band's original co-vocalist, Gaps Hendrickson, made a welcome return into the fold, bringing with him untold energy and a wonderful stage presence to our live show. As far as I was concerned this was now year zero in The Selecter.

Chaka Demus & Pliers	**"Tease Me"**
Shabba Ranks	**"Mr Loverman"**
House of Pain	**"Jump Around"**

I always knew people mainly came to our shows to hear the old songs, but I now felt I could give the band a little more than just bass and backing vocals and although our first few songwriting sessions didn't really produce anything of note, we started to get to know each other a little better, finding out our strengths and weakness, and before long the songs started to flow.

And so "The Happy Album" was born.

I won't bore you (or me) with all my recording reminisces, but I will tell you my co-producer on the album was Grammy award winning producer Jimmy 'Senya' Haynes, and what an eye-opener and learning curve that was for me. He taught me so much about making records in such a short time. And I can't possibly talk about him without saying what a guitarist he is. I can still picture him doing the solo on "California

225

Screaming" on a twin neck Gibson guitar, decked out in a string vest, bowler hat, ultra-tight jean shorts and funky cowboy boots!

I've never worked with anyone that good before or since.

Jimmy was all about the spaces and I took that all on board.

I'm sorry, I lied to you, I'm going to reminisce.

There was one day when I had to leave Jimmy on his own and that was because I'd decided to take a couple of 'love doves' (along with some really strong sniff and a bottle of Moet) that brought on an uncontrollable case of the shakes, and so I had to pussy out of the session and fuck off home until I was back on planet normal.

I was extremely proud of the first batch of Black/Welsh songs, particularly "Whip Them Down", "Neurotica!" and "Mother Knows Best" that formed the backbone of "The Happy Album", which I still think is the finest work I ever did as a member of The Selecter.

I'd no sooner finished mastering the album, when I was back in the States for the 'Skavoovie' tour, sharing a bill with The Toasters, Special Beat and The Skatalites, with whom we also shared a tour bus, them down the front and us up the back.

I really enjoyed that tour.

The bloody-minded Selecter would open up their forty-five minute set with four or five new songs instead of relying on our more 'heritage' material. We'd play "The Happy Album" to anyone who came within two feet of us, because we were so proud of what we'd produced.

I felt the future was bright, the future was Selecter.

"The future's so bright I gotta wear shades"

Check this out: two weeks into the tour our bus broke down (see, even when other people were in charge of the transport it went tits up) and so everyone had to grab their suitcases and make their way to a hotel that had been hastily booked. I think that was the moment I became Roland Alphonso's unpaid butler! Watching him struggling across the car park with his huge fucking bag, while none of The Skatalites seemed remotely interested in helping him, sort of upset me, and so I took it upon myself to give the geezer a hand. I guess I saw it as some kind of duty of honour, and that duty carried on for the rest of the tour.

While we were sitting waiting for a replacement bus, our tour manager came up and told me our driver had been sacked for racist behaviour. I wasn't gonna stand around arguing his case, but I did say I'd never seen

226

or heard him do anything like that, but he assured me he'd been out of order on more than one occasion, so I took his word for it.

A couple of minutes later the driver came walking towards me. I asked him what had happened and in a slow Southern drawl, this is what came out of his mouth...

"Work for a fucking nigger, treated like a fucking nigger, son."

You live and learn, don't you?

When the new bus turned up, we all piled back on and I jumped into the first available bunk, unpacked my stuff and put my head on the pillow to get some kip. Within seconds I could see a pair of eyes staring at me through the curtains of the bunk and a voice saying: "Nick, this is my place."

It was Tommy McCook.

Apparently, I'd got into the same bunk in the same position that he'd occupied on the previous bus and so out of respect to Tommy, I picked up my bags and found myself a new home. Well you've got to, haven't you?

It was a great tour although I could never understand how Special Beat headlined over The Skatalites and neither could Tommy, because on more than one occasion he bent my ear while they were onstage, suggesting that it was 'sabotage' and 'espionage' on their behalf to stop the originators of ska from headlining a tour called Skavoovie. It wasn't, but I would still nod my head in agreement (fucking crawler).

I knew how that shit worked. A band featuring ex-members of The Specials and The Beat was a much easier sell for the promoters, and you have to take into account that The Skatalites were touring all over America regularly; but come on, let's give respect where it's due.

We signed a deal with Demon records for "The Happy Album", a label I really respected, and when my suggestion of doing the photo-shoot for the album cover in my old childhood haunt of Abney Park Cemetery in Stoke Newington was accepted, I was well pleased. I thought it was a place that would complement the album's darker mood.

Unfortunately, it turned out that Demon were to be the first in a succession of labels that didn't really know how to market the band (or maybe it was the band not knowing how to market themselves) and "The Happy Album" sunk without a trace.

I was fucking gutted, because I felt we had a little gem there, but if the great unwashed don't want it, you can't really force it down their throats.

"And the public gets what the public wants"

Good news and bad news…

Bad: Perry decided to jack in Big 5.

Good: I persuaded my good friend John Bradbury to get on board with us.

On the Skavoovie tour, me and Brad used to hang out and get merry, and he would tell me he was thinking about quitting Special Beat because: "I don't like watching "Ghost Town" being turned into a bird pulling exercise."

Fact.

Brad was the most exciting drummer I'd ever had the privilege of sharing a stage with. He'd hit his kit like he hated the fucker. His only downside was (if this is a downside), he made everything sound like The Specials!

We shared a dry sense of humour.

When the audience saw it was Prince Rimshot behind the kit, they'd call out his name and he'd treat them to a few seconds of "Concrete Jungle" which would always raise a huge cheer. Big 5 shows would often turn into chaos. Sometimes Jen wouldn't arrive until halfway through the gig (she wasn't a great time keeper) but that didn't matter because there was never a set list; we just made it all up on the spot. It was a fucking great band to be in, and with Brad giving it all of his 2-Tone attitude it changed the band's sound from a ska/soul/reggae groove, to a full-on ska/punk vibe.

I always felt that, if there was one place in the world that would accept The Selecter for what it was now, rather than what it was in 1980, it was gonna be America.

We kicked off our next coast to coast of the States in Hawaii.

This was, along with Japan, another place I'd always wanted to visit, basically because as a kid I used to watch the TV show *Hawaii Five 0* religiously every week without fail, but for some reason as I got older, I got it into my head the only music they liked over there was Elvis, so when I found out that our two shows were both sold out, it came as a bit of a shock.

Once again, I have a DVD of those shows and I watched it recently.

The first thing that struck me was that I seemed to think it was ok for me to go on stage with shoulder length hair, shamelessly tied back in a pony tail. The second was seeing how young (and mostly female) the audience were. I remember thinking this was a good thing, because a younger crowd has a more open mind when it comes to listening to new music and I was right, because they didn't give a fuck if we played "California Screaming" or "Missing Words"; if it was good, they went for it.

I have quite a few DVDs from that tour and one of them I found particularly interesting was from The Belly Up in Solana Beach.

A couple of years later Gwen Stefani told me she was at the show, and described it to me as: "One of the best gigs I've ever been to."

I went to the club the night before our show, to see Paul Rodgers, who I consider to be one of the greatest singers in rock history, and I arrived just as he was singing the classic Bad Company song "Seagull", but because I'd been on it all day my attempts at a duet with him from the bar (just like Don McLean) didn't go down too well with anyone in the venue, or on the stage; and I think it's just as well I was no stranger to being turned away from Californian dressing rooms by an artist's assistant, usually accompanied by "Hey, so and so (fill in any artist's name you want) is a little tired right now. I'm sure you know how it is."

Yeah, of course I do. They don't want some flavoured-up cunt trying to steam into their rider, and generally being a fucking bore to everyone in a confined space.

When the tour reached Vancouver (what is it with that place), my lifestyle caused a problem. Not for me, but another member of the band. I'd just come offstage and was standing outside the venue by our van, chatting and posing for photographs with some of the fans. A few minutes later Pauline came out and said "Put my bag on the bus" to me and fucked off back inside the venue, which I should mention was bang in the middle of a busy red-light area.

But before I could remember to do it, I got distracted by a couple of brasses waving at me and shouting "Why don't you come over here baby, we'll give you something you won't forget."

And even though I thought it sounded like I was being offered the chance to join up to some rare-sexual-diseases-club, I still walked over to have a butchers at what they looked like. After turning their offer of a good time down at least three times, I said goodbye and got into the bus to prepare myself for my other far less glamorous job in The Selecter...

Keeping the driver awake on long overnight drives to our next show.

My job consisted of chopping out huge lines and pouring out large brandies to the driver.

We arrived at our hotel the next morning, where we parked up and took all the luggage out of the van with the only thing on our minds being grabbing a few hours' sleep before the next show. Well, I think you know what I'm gonna say next.

Pauline's bag was missing!

Fuck me did I take some verbals off her that day which of course I had to accept because I suppose it was down to me; but I've got to say I wouldn't hand all my possessions over to someone who'd just stuck an eight-ball up his hooter. But who knows, maybe some good came out of it.

How?

Well, maybe the working girls might have been able to charge a little bit more for their services with a nice bit of Prada on their backs.

I never thought my intake of all things party was a problem. I just saw it as part and parcel of being in a band. I used to get my dealer in London to jump on a train and bring me gear to gigs all over the UK. There was one time when I ran out of bugle halfway through a tour, and couldn't get in touch with him. I was ringing the geezer every half hour, leaving my usual cryptic message but he wasn't picking up. When he finally got back to me, two days later, I was mid pony at Watford gap services. Fuck knows what the people in the other cubicles thought when I shouted: "GET YOUR FUCKING ARSE UP HERE!"

Another part of my life that was getting a little bit naughty was the number of women I was seeing. When I say seeing, I mean birds I was picking up at gigs and after a quick two drink courtship, would slip off with to the toilets for a quick nosh.

I just considered this to be the sort of behaviour that was par for the course in a musician's life but truth be told, I never felt that great about it afterwards, and I never treated any of them like a cunt but if I ever went back with a girl to her place, I always found it difficult when she started cosying up to me in the morning, talking about possible future dates as if this was the beginning of a brand-new relationship, because I didn't wanna mislead anyone.

Now that's not me being big headed or anything, I know women like casual fucks just like men do, it's just the only thing I was looking forward to having a relationship with when I woke up was a full English in the nearest café.

Everything was getting a little bit fucking mad, probably best demonstrated by a night that started off with me taking a girlfriend up the West End for a nice meal and a few drinks, but ended up with, well, let me tell you...

After a nice evening out, we were in a taxi on our way back to her place; well, that was the plan, but when we pulled up at the traffic lights in The Angel, I opened the door and jumped out telling her I had to go and see someone (true) and that I would be round to her place soon (not true). I went straight round to score some gear at a dealer's flat I knew and after a couple of toots, I decided to go to The Powerhaus in Liverpool Road for a few drinks, and the next thing I knew I was getting my cock sucked in the ladies' toilet.

I basically came back to earth with some bird's mouth around my knob.

No, think about it... To get to that stage of the game, I would've had to have gone from the geezer's flat, to the venue, had a few drinks at the bar, and chatted up this girl for long enough to persuade her that having a quick lavatory liaison with me was in her best interest, and I couldn't remember doing any of it.

And get this: when I was back in the land of the living, I asked her to stop!

I can see the headline now in the Sunday Sport: "Man asks woman to stop sucking his cock."

As I'm reading through what I've just written, my reaction is to hit the delete button, because I think it makes me sound like a right lowlife, but let's be honest, all men can be pretty low when they want to be, and will basically stick their dicks into anything that moves; and if you put being in a band into the mix, well, you will definitely get the opportunity to slip into more birds than you would do than say, if you were on the other side of the barrier at a gig.

I guess if I added up all the time I was spending in toilet cubicles back then (tooting, blowing and of course shitting and pissing) I'm surprised I had time to make any music, but I did, and I have to say I wasn't happy with some of the results.

"If you don't wanna fuck me baby, fuck off"

We followed up "The Happy Album" with "Pucker!", but instead of it taking us one step forward, it was definitely more of a two-steps-back scenario. Although the songs on "Pucker!" were a lot better than on its predecessor, there were two main reasons why the album didn't cut the mustard:

1. The brief I was given was to let the musicians in the band play the parts, no matter what, because it would make it easier to reproduce the songs on stage, which wasn't a problem in the keyboard department, because Martin could always come up with something, but the guitarist we had in the band at the time, well let me say he was no Jimmy Haynes; no, fuck it, he was piss fucking poor, with no imagination for creating riffs or solos, in short, he was a hired hand who came into the band with the MO of trying to recreate Neol's sound on stage, which he never managed to achieve.

2. The overall sound of the album is fucking pants, and that's because the producer was taking far too much sniff at the sessions and that stuff really affects your hearing and judgment and that's why "Pucker!" sounds like it was mixed by Daniella Westbrook on a two-week bender.

I wasn't deliberately trying to fuck our shit up, far from it. I always tried my absolute best in anything I did for the band, but at that time my state of mind was at absolutely rock bottom; but there was no one else to take the helm and so for two months I'd get to the studio every day at 11.00am and work right through until 11.00pm. Band members would drop in, do their parts and fuck off home, but I was there for the long haul. I was always ok until about 6pm, but then I would start getting the taste and that's when I should've just downed tools and fucked off home, but I wouldn't, and that's when the problems began because when you're high in the studio, you think you're making the best music the world is ever gonna hear, and you start adding more and more instruments to songs that don't need it. The best example of this is "Vicky's Magic Garden", which is a fine little tune, but by the time Islington's answer to Phil Spector got his increasingly sweaty hands on it, it sounded like a low-fi ELO.

There was one time though when I didn't need any chemicals to get me high and that was when the legendary pedal steel player, B.J. Cole, came down to do his thing on our version of the Nancy Sinatra song "Sugar Town".

Getting the chance to work with him was all the buzz I needed that day.

I'd seen his name crop up on so many of my favourite records: Elton John's "Tiny Dancer", "No Regrets" by The Walker Brothers and the one that really sealed the deal for me on the T.Rex album "Zinc Alloy & The Hidden Riders Of Tomorrow".

When he arrived for the session he turned out to be an absolute delight to record with, an absolute sweetheart. He only had to listen to the track once, before laying down four takes of spine-tingling pedal steel for me to 'comp' together, and although the whole thing was over within an hour, it was definitely the highlight of an otherwise sad experience from which I learnt this lesson:

Don't take drugs when you're recording in the studio in the hope they will magically turn you into David Bowie's more talented brother. It's much more likely they will make you just another druggie making substandard music.

I do look quite hot on the cover though.

But don't despair, it's not all doom and gloom because the next two albums I made were very happy experiences for me and what's more, they were both done and dusted within a month. Let me tell you about them in chronological order of recording…

1. BIG 5 "IN YER FACE"

This is one of the finest albums I've ever made.

Do you remember when I told you that after Brad joined Big 5 we inherited a much harder sound? Well, that's what you get on "In Yer Face". From the moment Jen and I wrote "Pussy Whipped" at a soundcheck in Northern Ireland, we knew it was the direction we had to go in. There are a lot of good songs on "In Yer Face". I love "Amphetamine Rush", "No, No, No" and "Outrageous", but my favourite has to be "Wired To The Moon", a three minute declaration of what my life was all about at the time.

We went into the recording with everyone on the same wavelength and so there wasn't really that much for me to produce; I just had to give a few musical pointers here and there, like making sure the guitars were as loud and nasty as possible, except on the beautiful "Bad Karma", which I thought needed a more gentle touch.

We shot the cover for the album in the bogs at The Mean Fiddler, with me dressed in a black Ralph shirt and bleached Skinhead jeans, and Jen in all her leopard-skin glory. But when I saw the finished product I was well disappointed, because it looks like I'm covered in fucking makeup, which I wasn't (honest guv), and for some reason best known to himself,

233

the artist erased the tattoo on Jennie's arm, which I felt was totally unnecessary, but even worse, it upset my mate.

If you haven't got "In Yer Face" in your collection, have a look for it online and if you see a copy grab it, because I give you my word that you won't be disappointed.

I think if I'd had the bollocks to take time off from The Selecter to promote the album properly, we could've taken Big 5 on to a different level but I didn't, because I am a stupid fucking bastard. And with that, let's move on...

2. JUDGE DREAD "DREAD, WHITE & BLUE".

This has to be one of the most enjoyable albums I've ever made.

I'd known Alex (Judge Dread) Hughes for quite a long time, and so when he asked me at a record company piss up in Soho: "Nick, how do you fancy producing my next album mate?" I jumped at the chance.

What I didn't know was it would be the first album he'd made since the passing of his long-time friend, co-writer and producer Ted Lemon; all I had in my mind was I wanted to make a great album for him.

On the first day of recording "Dread, White & Blue", I placed lots of saucy seaside postcards around the studio to try and create a vibe for the album and it must have done the trick because by the end of our first session we'd finished "The Ballad Of Judge Dread", which Alex called his reggae/folk song.

As I pulled down the faders on the final mix, he put his hands on my shoulders and said: "Do you know, that's the first song I've written that isn't credited to Lemon/Hughes" at which point a shiver ran down my spine, and my mind was sent racing back to my childhood, sitting in front of my Dansette in my bedroom, studying the labels of all the records going round and round on the turntable and Lemon/Hughes were two of the names that I used to see a hell of a lot.

I got Rico to come in and blow on the song, alongside my friend Dave Hillyard from The Slackers. I would like to take this opportunity to apologise to him, because his name was left off the album credits and as producer I have to take the blame for that.

Sorry Dave x.

The sessions were a fucking blast from start to finish.

234

Sometimes, while I was sitting at the desk, I'd look around to see Alex behind me writing down lyrics and laughing hysterically to himself. One time I said to him: "Another classic there mate?"

His reply was brilliant: "You try writing the same fucking song two hundred fucking times."

Anyone who knew him personally would know he was very keen on telling the odd story and in those two weeks I must have heard them all. There were some mornings when he came in and didn't even bother to say hello to me, he just went straight into some surreal anecdote like "Did I ever tell you about the time I was in Bali with Andy Gibb?"

If you can find a job where you can't wait to get to work, you should be happy, and that's how I felt with this gig.

"Dread, White & Blue" was finished in just under two weeks, but I wouldn't have cared if it had gone on for another six months. It was an absolute joy to do and when the album came out Alex told me it was the only one of his records his missus liked.

I think that was only because it was slightly cleaner than the rest!

And I have to give top marks for the cover, it was tackiness personified.

A few months after the album was released, Alex asked me to put a band together to play a few shows to promote it. I did, and do you know what, it didn't matter if there were a thousand people at the gig, or only fifty, he was never anything less than a total pro, a real old school entertainer, and the time spent travelling to shows seemed to fly by, courtesy of all his stories. I didn't really care if they were true or not, but I tell you one thing, I will never think of The New Seekers in the same way again.

Edwyn Collins   **"A Girl Like You"**
Pulp   **"Common People"**
Supergrass   **"Alright"**

The next Selecter album to feature any new material didn't show its face until 1998, and so for the next three years I spent my life gigging and promoting compilation albums that really shouldn't have seen the light of day, like our barrel scraping second live album "Back Out On The Streets". It was just product, put out to enable us to keep functioning as a live entity.

I still had the belief that all the hard work Pauline and I had put into The Selecter would eventually pay off at some point and although it had nothing to do with our new music it was certainly the case when we were invited to be special guests on No Doubt's 1997 "Tragic Kingdom" tour. At the time they were probably the hottest ticket in town, which meant we would be heading out for a taste of life on the arena/stadium circuit. Apparently, we got the slot because Pauline was one of Gwen's idols when she was growing up in Orange County.

It was on the flight out to America for the tour that I became a ridiculously fearful flyer.

Up until then, I'd have to say I'd never really had any bad flying experiences and I'm talking about a man with a lot of air miles under his belt. I used to just strap myself in and get pissed, without giving a flying fuck about being 35,000 feet in the air, but for some reason on that day (where once again nothing scary happened), I began crying like a baby. I don't know why and what's even more stupid is that when we touched down and got into our bus to take the ten-hour road trip to our first show, I saw at least two fatal car accidents along the way, but they didn't bother me because I was on the ground and felt safe.

On this tour, we had a new drummer, Al Fletcher.

A beautiful man with a great sense of humour, but more importantly, he could play.

At our first rehearsal, we only played for about an hour before it became obvious to everyone in the room he'd done all his homework and knew the set inside out, and so we all fucked off down the boozer for a nice afternoon's socialising.

Before we joined up with No Doubt, we had a gig of our own in Cincinnati, at Sudsy Malone's, a venue that used to be a laundry and still had all the washing machines and dryers in there to prove it. We really cleaned up that night (that's pathetic Nick) in front of an audience of about five hundred, but the next time we stepped out on stage to play our opening number "My Perfect World", it was to a crowd nearer to the TWENTY FIVE THOUSAND mark, which is a little bit of a leap!

Besides the huge jump in crowd size, let me give you a couple of examples of what it's like when you're in that league. I was sitting in our dressing room just before show time, when there was a knock at the door and in walks a geezer, dressed up like a waiter in an upmarket burger restaurant.

"Is everything ok for you Sir?" he politely enquired.

236

"Yeah fine mate," I shrugged nervously. (I fucking hate it when people call me Sir.)

Hold on, let's take a break, I feel another list coming on:

NICK'S TOP FIVE THINGS HE HATES BEING CALLED.

1. **Geez.**
2. **Matie.**
3. **Boss.**
4. **Bruv.**
5. **Sir.**

He walks over to this huge ice bucket, full of beers and sodas, and sticks his hand in it for a few seconds. I thought the bloke must be a fucking head-case or something, so I asked him what he was doing.

"Oh, I'm sorry Sir, it's my job to check your ice is always just right for you."

Fuck me, I've got my own personal ice checker!

On the first night, they arranged a party for us.

Their roadies set up a room with all this special lighting. I presume it was so they would look great, not for us, but for some of the fans who'd entered various competitions to meet them, and after they'd had twenty minutes they were shown the door, leaving us to it.

I spent about an hour with Gwen, chatting about the late 80s ska scene in California, and the show we'd done together almost a decade before when No Doubt supported Buster's All Stars at The Variety Arts Center in LA. They had certainly moved on since those days.

The next day Gwen pulled me to one side and whispered: "Is Martin ok? Has he got problems?"

"Yeah loads mate, but nothing serious, why?"

"It's just that last night I saw him walking around with a brandy in one hand and a beer in the other."

I'm glad she hadn't seen him on a normal night!

It was an incredible series of dates, consisting of us playing in shitholes, arenas, stadiums and of course, revamped launderettes. We ended the tour at Tramps in New York, a wonderful club that I'd played a few times, but never with a band that define the word reggae as much as The Skatalites define ska…

The Wailers.

237

Now, here were a group of musicians at the very top of my 'to break bread with' list and they didn't disappoint. I got to spend time with Aston 'Family Man' Barrett and Junior Marvin, and I'm not ashamed to say I was totally in awe of them. They told me stories about their early days that were absolutely fascinating, and just like the show they performed that night, it was a little piece of reggae heaven for me. It really was a fantastic way to end a very memorable tour.

Even though I wasn't making any new music with The Selecter, there were still some highs to be had gigging with Desmond Dekker, Laurel Aitken, The Ethiopians, Toots & The Maytals and Prince Buster, at ska and reggae festivals all over Europe. It wasn't all reggae and ska though: we smashed the Roskilda festival in Denmark, just before Jimmy Page and Robert Plant went on stage.

And how about this for a line up at a show we played in San Diego.

Ladies and Gentlemen, I give you...

The Selecter

The Monkees

The Village People

What a bill eh?!

I couldn't believe my luck, because like most people my age I grew up buying Monkees records and annuals, and their TV show was essential viewing to my generation. They were probably one of the first boy bands: four guys put together by answering an advert in the trades for basically a Beatles rip-off, but they were so much more than that.

The only downer was, the line up didn't include my favourite member Mike 'Wool Hat' Nesmith, but as I made my way into the backstage area that was soon forgotten, when I saw the small but beautifully formed Davy Jones. Now, I knew he was small because I'd read that he'd trained as a jockey when he was young, and of course from the "just 'cos I'm short I know" intro of "Daydream Believer"...

But fuck me! He was REALLY small!

Even more shocking to me, was the loud, canary coloured suit he was wearing, but that didn't stop me from making my way over to say hello; but as I got near to him I was stopped by some big fucking gorilla shouting at me: "Move away from Davy. No one goes near Davy."

"Alright, keep your fucking hair on. I only wanted to say hello to the geezer."

Now, I'm not sure if it was my English accent that did the trick, but Mr Jones stepped forward and said: "It's ok man, we're just gonna have a little chat."

Which was really nice of him, but that big fucking ape had already ruined the moment for me, and so (and this still annoys me till this very day), I turned around, leaving them with a very loud, cockney: "Fuck the lot of ya!"

Oh, and just for the record, apparently a couple of us upset Micky Dolenz by trying to hit on his daughter, although I don't remember that, and as for Peter Tork, well he just didn't want to talk to anyone.

What is it they say about never meeting your heroes? Well maybe there is something in that, because it had only taken about twenty minutes to turn a lifetime love affair into a messy divorce.

Nah, I'm being over the top there.

Their show was ok, if a little cabaret. Bad stage gear and awful cheesy intros: "Here's one we used to play when we were on tour with a little-known guitarist called Jimi Hendrix. I wonder what happened to him?"

When you have that amount of brilliant songs in your set, it would take a lot of hard work to make it shit, although they gave it a good go.

I'll tell you who was nice though, The Village People.

We chatted for quite a while, and they laughed when I asked if they used to get a lot of disco cock back in the Studio 54 days. I got them to pose for a few snaps with me on my newly acquired piece-of-shit-throwaway-Kodak-camera, but because I got right off my tits after the show I fucking lost it and so the only memories I have from that day are in my head.

Of course, if it was today, those pictures would have been uploaded in seconds to my Facebook page, but you have to remember this was 1996, when people had to take their snaps to the chemist and get them developed.

In 1997, I got a call from a German agent asking if I would like to put a band together to back Laurel Aitken and Dave Barker on a tour of Europe, with the icing on the cake being I would open the show with a King Hammond set. As you know, I'd played with Laurel loads of times, but Dave Barker, fuck me this was a dream come true.

The band was basically the current line up of The Selecter (why make hard work for yourself?). I knew with Al and Martin there the legends would be in good hands.

239

I was told by the agent Dave was a very religious, so could I make sure the band didn't drink or swear in front of him, but this was blown out of the water when we came face-to-face on the first day of the tour, and he invited me back to his hotel room to share a bottle of brandy.

The shows were long, very long, three fucking hours long.

I would go on first and do a thirty minute King Hammond set, which included a version of Paul Nicholas's "Reggae Like It Used To Be", that I claimed as my own to the unsuspecting European audiences. Then it would be Dave's turn to do his stuff, and what a voice that man has. I was back in 1971, with the real deal; and then it would be time for Laurel to close the show, always ending with "Skinhead" to send the people home happy.

It was a buzz playing with these guys, and even though I only got to do a short King Hammond set, it got me thinking maybe there was a market for my kind of music; but it was only a thought, because I was far too busy with The Selecter to bring the King back to life again.

Another thing to suffer because of my Selecter activity was Big 5, and that still niggles me to this day. Whenever I could slip in a few local shows, or the occasional European date, I would. But the offers became fewer and fewer and I put that down to our set not being exactly what the promoters or indeed the audience were expecting. Because we were always being booked as 'ex this, ex that', I'm sure everyone had the idea it was going to be a trip down memory lane, and not the full-on, razor-edge, guitar-blazing set of new material they actually got. Thinking about it, one thing Big 5 were rich in was drummers.

Here's a few of them…

Perry Melius
John Bradbury
Winston Marche
Fuzz Townsend
Al Fletcher

On the flip side of the coin the last person I can remember behind the kit was a guy called Martin Ward, who I only gave the gig to because his dad was the songwriter Clifford T Ward, who I loved dearly. Unfortunately, his son didn't have his gentle touch when it came to holding a beat down, and after completing a not very enjoyable Italian tour with him, we decided to call it a day.

240

NICK'S TOP FIVE BIG 5 SONGS

1.   "Universe"
2.   "Shame"
3.   "Pussy Whipped"
4.   "Beautiful World"
5.   "It Sucks!"

I hope one day "In Yer Face" gets the dusting down and re-release it deserves, because I think what we achieved on that album was a little ahead of its time and maybe now it might get the attention I thought it should've got back then.

Always great fun with Alex

SO LONG AGO

I was so dumb,
Too fast, too young,
But that was so long ago.

Bad days, mad nights,
But now it's all right,
That was so long ago.

So long ago,
That was so long ago.

I can't explain,
The lies and shame,
That was so long ago.

You won't go back,
To make it all right Jack,
That was so long ago.

So long ago,
That was so long ago.

The UK was riding on a wave of New Labour bullshit, when Pauline rang to tell me about a lyric she'd written, "Cruel Britannia", describing the way she felt about all the 'cool Britannia' bollocks the papers were giving it at the time. I thought was a great title and a good starting point for us to begin work on a new Selecter album.

We arranged a meeting in Coventry, to see what we could come up with, and I think the break we'd had from writing together had done us both a bit of good, because within a couple of weeks we had an album's worth of songs in the bag. We decided that this time we'd rehearse and demo the new songs with the band before actually going into the studio, which was something we'd never done before, and it turned out to be a good move, because Snapper Music heard some of the demos and offered us a one-album deal.

But just before the sessions were due to start, Gaps decided to leave the band, which was a bit of a shock; although unlike Neol, we never tried to replace him, and so it was left to me to try and fill his big boots on stage, doing all the 'de killa' stuff on "James Bond" and the odd bit of toasting here and there. It wasn't so bad doing it live, but I certainly wouldn't do it on record.

I came up with the idea of asking Dave Barker to come down and give us some of his trademark vocals on a few of the songs, and I'm glad to say he did. I thought the blend of Pauline and Dave's vocals worked well together, but a few years later Pauline told me she thought it wasn't one of my better moves.

Listening to "Cruel Britannia" in 2017, the thing that strikes me most is that it has a much harder sound than either of our previous two releases and I would put this down to Al Fletcher and the use of live drums. If you check out "Bad Dog", "Musical Servant" or "Respect Yourself", they have, dare I say it, more of a 2-Tone vibe to them and for a band like The Selecter that's not a bad thing; but it was the final track on the album, "Blind Leading The Blind", that really moved me, and was unwittingly a taste of where my musical life would be heading in the near future.

Of course, having a new album meant going back out on the road, which was cool because I loved gigging, but I began to notice we were going to the same places, and venues, at the same time every year.

Snapper were playing the game though, giving us a lot more support than our previous labels had. They got us a fair bit of TV/radio and magazine coverage, which is what you get if you employ a decent publicist, and in this case it was the more than decent Judy Totten.

One of the TV shows she got us was an interview on VH1 that I did it with Pauline the day after I'd been on a serious two-day bender, which explains why at one point I nearly fell asleep on the sofa! But once again it was to be the same old story. Even with a decent record company giving us far better promotion than we'd ever had before, "Cruel Britannia" still did fuck all. And that pissed me off big time, because I thought we'd made a good album sounding the way I thought people wanted The Selecter to sound, and yet we still couldn't have it off.

Was it all worth it?

Madonna	**"Ray Of Light"**
Cornershop	**"Brimful Of Asha"**
Radiohead	**"Karma Police"**

Sunday mornings had become very predictable in my house. The phone would ring about 9.00am and I'd get up, knackered from a gig the night before, to pick it up and hear the familiar sound of Alex 'JD' Hughes on the end of the line.

Me: "For fuck's sake mate, I didn't get in until four."

Alex: "Never mind about that boy, have you heard about so and so?"

And for the next fifteen minutes I'd listen to him telling me all about what an ex-member of The Rubettes had been up to. Fuck me, Alex did love a gossip, and so, when the phone rang on 15th March 1998, I thought it was going to be more of the same.

I was wrong.

It wasn't Alex's voice on the end of the line, it was Martin telling me Alex had suffered a heart attack the night before on stage in Canterbury and was dead.

Fuck me, that ruined my Sunday roast.

He was a friend I was proud to have.

I guess the public knew him as 'the geezer who does all that nursery rhyme stuff', but there was so much more to him than that. For a start, he put on the first Ethiopian famine concert at the Edmonton Sundown in 1973; that's twelve years before Live Aid. He also recorded a single, "Molly", with all the royalties going towards helping those poor people who were suffering and even though "Molly" didn't have any rudeness

244

in it, the BBC still banned it, which is something I could never understand.

I mean, it's not like his songs were filled with loads of fucks and cunts or anything like that, they were just harmless bits of nudge, nudge, wink, wink fun, from an era when people flocked to the cinema to see the latest *Carry On* film; and let's not forget the musicianship on those records was superb, and that's because it was executed by some of the greatest players on the reggae scene.

Don't judge a book by the cover. I love and miss you mate x.

My next production job was Dave Barker's "Kingston Affair".

First of all, I wanna get something off my chest. "Kingston Affair" was originally supposed to be a "Dave Barker & King Hammond" album, but was changed by the record company, Moon Ska, to "Dave Barker & Friends" which fucking wound me up, but I agreed to it because all I wanted to do was get in the studio and make music with Dave. And then, on the morning I was due to start recording, I got a call: "Nick, we want the album to be credited to "Dave Barker & The Selecter."

I told them I thought it was a shit idea and I wanted what we'd originally agreed on, because musically it made much more sense but all I got was...

"Yeah, but we think The Selecter carries a lot more weight than King Hammond."

"Well of course it does. But we're going to record a skinhead reggae album, and that has nothing to do with what The Selecter is about."

I went off to the studio, hoping they would eventually see my side of the argument when they heard some of the roughs.

They never did.

I suppose it's like the Skatalites/Special Beat thing on the Skavoovie tour: people will always follow the route they feel is gonna work best for them financially and so, it was fuck art, let's call it "Dave Barker & The Selecter".

I had to go and ask Pauline if this was ok with her and I think it was more out of friendship to me than liking the idea she said yes. Thinking about it now, I shouldn't have even asked her and I should've just told Moon Ska to fuck off, but I always try to do things honestly, even when it's not what I want.

I'm starting to get a bit angry about it now and my outraged sensibilities are in need of a large one. I'll be back soon.

"To eyes that are bright as stars when they're shining on me"

Ah, that's better.

The first time Dave got behind the mic to vocal a song, I had what this London boy would call a 'spiritual fucking moment'. Playing live with the guy was one thing, but getting the chance to work the controls for a man whose voice caressed my youth, was another. "Kingston Affair" is a great album and I will always be grateful for getting the chance to make music with an absolute giant in the history of reggae, and who knows? One day it might even get a release under the proper moniker.

Talking of music that caressed my youth…

Trojan Records came calling to offer The Selecter a three-album, cash-in-your-pocket, no-royalties-ever, take-it-or-fucking-leave-it deal, to record some of their back catalogue.

I remember not being that keen on the idea, because no matter how hard you try, you ain't ever gonna get anywhere near the perfection of those original records; so I can only assume I must have needed some quick drug money because I said yes to it.

The only good things about those sessions were that they didn't take up too much of my time and they gave me another chance to work with Roger, who as luck would have it was also working with Roy Wood at the time, and knowing I was a big fan he invited him down to the studio, without telling me, to hang out.

When he walked into the control room, the first words out of my mouth were: "Fuck me, it's the wizard!"

I think the session only went on for about another fifteen minutes before we all decided the best plan of action was to go down the pub and get pissed.

For someone who I consider to be one of the best songwriters ever to come out of the UK, Roy is one of the most down to earth guys you could ever hope to meet. He told me stories about working with Hendrix, Winwood and Bolan, but never in an 'I'm a fucking star' kind of way. Maybe it's a Brummie thing, because I've seen his ex-band mate Jeff Lynne on TV many times talking about his life in the same 'I can't believe this has all happened to me' way.

It was all absolutely fascinating stuff.

I think it was after my sixth large brandy, that I plucked up the courage to ask if he fancied doing a Wood/Selecter single, with Roger producing. I'd like to think it wasn't just the drink that made him say yes, but when he did, as far as I was concerned, it was a done deal. Unfortunately, like most plans hatched between pissed people after several hours in the boozer, it never came to fruition. However, I did go home that night and write a melody I thought would be suitable for both artists to record giving it the title "Symphony Of Love".

I have the trilogy of CDs in front of me and I can honestly say I can't remember recording about 90% of the songs on them, and there's about forty-odd of the fuckers! The funny thing is though, over the years, I've had lots of people telling me how much they like those albums, so what the fuck do I know?

I'll tell you what I do know…

I don't like wasting studio time, recording piss poor cover versions that are never going to be anywhere near as good as the originals. One of the things I love about the original records (and I know there are a lot of purists out there who wouldn't agree) are the strings that were added on to tracks like "Young, Gifted and Black", to apparently make them palatable to a white audience, just like I think Chris Blackwell's idea of adding an element of rock to the Wailers' sound on "Catch A Fire" and "Burning" was a stroke of genius.

But there was to be no such inspiration on "The Trojan Songbook". In my book, there are only a couple of tracks worthy of a mention, "Blood & Fire" and "Sun Is Shining", both from volume three, because at least they sound like we're trying to make the tracks our own.

At the start of 2001, we took a six-month skabatical from The Selecter to recharge our batteries and I thought this was the perfect time to meet Martin for a drink because I wanted to tell him that I was thinking about taking a much longer break from the group, to try and step out on my own musically.

This didn't go down very well with him.

He quizzed me about my plans, and when I told him I had an idea of going out on my own, armed with just an acoustic guitar, and playing a kind of stripped-down ska and reggae, that, dare I say it, would almost border on the blues, his response was…

"Who the fuck would wanna listen to you, doing that?"

That really hurt me.

"Everyone I know goes away in the end"

I don't know what I expected him to say, but it certainly wasn't that.

Although we were never that close outside of the band, when we were on the road together we were fucking soldiers. I think I was just looking for his approval, you know, something like: "Yeah, go on mate, that sounds great."

I'm also forgetting to mention that all the time I was trying to pour my musical heart out to him, I was being interrupted every five minutes by a voice sounding not unlike Rob Brydon's 'small man in a box,' saying things like "can you do a pick up from Kingsland Road?" because while I'd been musing over the next stage of my life, Martin had already made the decision to spend the next six months of his as a motorbike courier. I didn't have a problem with that, but like a lot of people I've worked with over the years, it seems to be one rule for them and a completely different one for me. He always knew there was going to come a time when I would eventually drop out and start writing and performing in my own right. I wanted to improve as a songwriter, producer and performer. After our meeting, I went straight home, picked up my guitar and began to write.

Of course, Martin could've been right, maybe no one would be interested in listening to what I had to say, but I thought if I could just write for myself like I've always done, what did it matter: as long as I was happy, why should I give a fuck about what he thought?

After a week of going at it like a man possessed, I had what I thought were a few really good songs: "One Step Forward", "Goodbye Piccadilly", "Parallel Road" and "Jet Black Tourniquet", which have all made their way onto albums of mine over the last ten years.

With everything coming together, I thought it would be a good time to ring Pauline to let her know what my intentions were, which I did; but get this, by the end of our conversation, my solo project had turned into a duo!

She said what I wanted to do would be something of interest to her, and what did I think about us maybe doing it together? I suppose I should have said: "No, I wanna do this thing on my own."

But I didn't.

I don't know why; maybe in the back of my mind I thought Martin was right and I could take some kind of shelter with Pauline. When we did team up though, it started a new and much more fruitful writing and performing relationship for us, which I really needed, because this was a time when things in my life were very much on the down side.

Why?

Mum had been diagnosed with breast cancer, and she didn't seem to understand the severity of the situation. I used to plead with her to do something about it all the time but she just didn't seem to acknowledge what was happening to her, and what did I do to get through this heartache?

Well, it's obvious, isn't it?

Self-medicated myself with copious amounts of brandy and cocaine.

This was the time of the World Trade Centre horror, and when Anthrax scares were the norm in America, and there was me in the relatively safe surrounds of Islington, getting all kinds of white powder delivered to me in envelopes through my letterbox!

I would tear them open and stick it all up my hooter, but it didn't matter how much shit I was taking, if I wasn't on tour I would still go and see Mum every day, mainly because my constitution for all things naughty was pretty large, and so I could still make my way round there, even after a heavy night on the trumpet. Even if it was just for a few hours I would go and sit with her to chat, watch TV, and make her lunch, you know, generally be a loving son (which of course I was) and then it would be "Goodbye Mum, see you tomorrow", and off I'd go to give my liver and nostrils a fucking good hiding.

Also, at the same time, my best mate Brian had developed a brain tumour, which was a fucking double whammy to say the least. Thankfully the doctors got to it in time, and I'm happy to say he's still my best friend today and will be until the day I die.

Besides giving it the obvious by telling you caning the powder every day isn't the best thing you can do for yourself health-wise, I was also knocking about with a few mates who seemed to have an even bigger death-wish than me. One night, I was out with a pal having a drink in a pub just off Brewer Street, when his dealer came in and started digging him out. Apparently, he'd had about two grand's worth of sniff on the books, and was getting a bit pissed off because he thought my mate was mugging him off. I knew this guy and he was a right nasty cunt although I didn't think he'd iron him out for a two grand debt, but he certainly would have done him a bit of damage.

I took the geezer to the nearest hole-in-the-wall and gave him a monkey to 'clear the air' and my mate promised he would sort the rest of it out in a couple of weeks. Long story short, my so-called pal never came through with the cash, and surprise, surprise, soon went on the missing list and I never saw the mug again; but you see, that's what drugs can do to you... turn people turn into untrustworthy little cunts whose only aim in life is to get their next wrap, no matter who they have to stripe up to get it.

Gorillaz	**"Clint Eastwood"**
Outkast	**"Ms Jackson"**
Afroman	**"Because I Got High"**

Before we even got to perform as a duo, Pauline and I somehow become a quartet by inviting my old mate Dave Farren to come along and play double-bass, and ex Big 5 guitarist Simon Cookson, to help pad out what The Guardian once called my 'pub strumming'!

I hired the Hope & Anchor in Upper Street, Islington for our first show, and I can feel my face going red when I think about the name we came up with for ourselves for the gig: 'Me & You'.

This appalling name came from one of the many, "So, when are me and you gonna get this thing going then?" conversations we had on the phone.

What the fuck were we thinking of?

It sounds like a wine bar act, covering Captain and Tennille songs.

Even though The Hope is a very small venue, I worked my bollocks off promoting it because I wasn't sure what people would make of our acoustic venture, and so I did about three times as many posters and flyers as I'd normally do for a gig that size and the result was long queues around the block, way before the doors were due to open.

When the people who normally promoted at the venue saw the size of the crowd, one of them came over to me and said: "Right so it's the usual deal, fifty/fifty, yeah?"

"No mate, I've hired the gaff, this show is fuck all to do with you."

"Well I know nothing about that, I better check with my boss."

And off he went coming back a few minutes later: "Look, I can't get in touch with him now, so let's just do the normal deal and if I'm wrong I will sort it out with you later."

"Look cunt, I'm trying to be Cat Stevens here, but if you don't fuck off you're gonna get a spanking."

He fucked off.

The set felt fresh and exciting.

Our new songs, "Unbeaten And Unbowed", "Symphony Of Love" and "Roll the Dice" didn't sound out of place against crowd pleasing covers like Marley's "Lively Up Yourself" and Desmond's "Israelites" and I needn't have worried about people not taking to this more laid-back version of ska and reggae, because they loved it, and more importantly so did Me & You, sorry, me and Pauline.

It was a very welcome distraction from all the heartache on the home front.

Thankfully by the time we played our next show, Me & You had become Selecter Acoustic and were now a duo. What's more we booked ourselves into a little studio in Hackney with me back in the producer's seat, although to be honest there wasn't a lot of producing for me to do because most of it was recorded live with very few overdubs. We started recording the songs that would make up the "Unplugged for The Rudeboy Generation" album. The sessions had a happy, laid-back atmosphere with tracks like "Heavy Rain" and "Symphony Of Love", having, (sorry Pauline), a Wings-Ram-era-type-vibe to them. At the end of the final track "Roll The Dice" you can hear the postman knocking on the door, but instead of doing another take we just let it ride.

It was a very pleasurable album to make.

Even the cover has a real warmth to it.

As I sit here writing this I'm remembering the enjoyment I got from the shows we did together. It was a very tight ship. We'd pack our equipment into the back of Pauline's car and she would drive us to the gigs, which were mostly nice little art centres that are a real joy to play: great sound, nice facilities and audiences who actually listen to what you are doing.

Oh, and it was usually all over by ten-thirty!

We had some good 'banter' going on between us on stage and it helped that I was totally clean. I felt I had to be because I didn't want to let the side down.

These shows led to an agent, Myke Stevens, approaching us to see if we were interested in forming an 'acoustic supergroup' (his words not mine) called '3 Men & Black' (his name not mine).

And when he told me the other artists taking part were J.J. Burnel from The Stranglers, Stiff Little Fingers frontman Jake Burns, and Buzzcocks guitarist Steve Diggle, well, I nearly shat my safety-pinned trousers! And so just a few months after being laughed out of my local for wanting to go down this route, it was now looking like a very interesting journey indeed.

251

Myke didn't fuck about. Within a couple of weeks, a ten-date tour of the UK had been arranged, with a couple of days' rehearsal booked at The Stranglers' studio in the West Country.

I don't know why, but as we drove down to meet up with our new bandmates, I felt a little bit nervous, which is not like me because I don't do nerves. Maybe it was because this was a different arena I was about to enter. Playing with the ska and reggae legends that I'd idolised as a kid was different to this: these were artists from the era that had made it possible for me to play in a band.

The first person we met was J.J. Burnel, and although he didn't look as threatening as I remembered, he still cut a very daunting figure. Jake was already there, but sadly Steve Diggle wasn't. He'd fractured his wrist a few days before and had to pull out, which was a shame because I'd met him a few times around the clubs and always got on well with him.

We put his non-appearance down to a wanking accident, or as Jake put it: "A problem with his masturbatory mitt."

Rehearsals went well.

It helped that I knew most of the songs anyway, and I got the same 'how the fuck did I get here?' feeling from playing "Go Buddy Go" as I did from "Al Capone".

After a few hours, we did what all musicians do at rehearsals, and that's go to the pub, and that's when I realised Mr Burnel was the most alpha-male I've ever met. Fuck me, as soon as we were in the boozer the geezer had all the barmaids running after him: "A little more ice in your drink J.J.?"

"Is your ploughman's ok J.J.?"

"Would you like me to suck your cock J.J.?"

The last one was never actually said, but it wouldn't have surprised me if it had been.

So, let's get my obvious jealousy out of the way and talk a little about the tour. We were always going to be, as Pauline put it, 'third banana', but at the end of every show we'd always come away having made a lot of new fans.

I think J.J. thought our music was a bit childish and so he never really bothered to learn our songs. At one of the early shows, after we'd finished playing "Too Much Pressure", he leaned over towards me and said: "It's great what you can do with two chords isn't it?"

"Yeah it is mate. One of my favourite records is "96 Tears.""

We bonded immediately.

He loved to play little mind games with me, like following me down hotel corridors whispering in my ear: "I'm coming to your room later to fuck you up the arse."

And although I think there might be quite a few people out there who would have liked to have some of that I was more a 'snuggle up with a good book' kind of guy.

"Too many teardrops for one heart to be crying"

Over the years, I'd heard so many stories from people in the industry about his rock 'n' roll behaviour, I would have been very disappointed if he'd turned out to be a pussy, and it was all an act. You have to remember, I'm a bass player, and he's the geezer who came up with those brilliant bass-lines for "Straighten Out", "I Feel Like A Wog" and the best of the lot, "Peaches". For fuck's sake, of course I'm gonna love him and wanna be his mate!

Jake was different.

He was the easiest person in the world to get on with.

To be honest I didn't really know that much about SLF before then. Shame on you Welsh!

Yeah, of course I'd heard "Alternative Ulster" and "Suspect Device" on the Peel show, but it shames me to say the majority of their music had somehow passed me by. That was all to change when he sent me a CD of the songs he wanted 3 Men to play. It was like discovering a huge bag of emotional amphetamine rock at the end of the punk rainbow.

How could I not have heard "Nobody's Fool" or "Listen" before?

It was fucking obvious that Green Day and a load of other bands had!

Jake was always keen to add his own parts to our songs, and encouraged me to do the same with his, and like a lot of his fellow countrymen, he had a real gift for storytelling that would have the audience literally hanging onto every word he said.

Mind you, I was the same and I was hearing them every night!

We would come onstage and J.J. would introduce us as: "The Wog, The Frog, The Mick and Nick." Not very politically correct I know, but fucking funny.

The Roses Theatre in Shrewsbury is a beautiful venue, and is also the place where Eric Morecambe tragically died in 1984. Even though it's a place with sadness attached to it, I was still thrilled to get the chance to

253

perform there, because it plays a huge (if unpleasant) part in Eric's history and I'm a massive fan. It had been a really hot day and I couldn't be fucked getting changed into my stage gear, so I went on wearing my t-shirt, shorts and sandals. A few songs into the set, J.J. started slating my footwear to the audience, telling them: "I didn't fight the punk wars to end up playing next to someone wearing sandals."

It got the laugh he was looking for and I knew he was just taking the piss, but it gave me a little food for thought and so when we came out for the second half of the show, I waited until everyone was back onstage before I made my entrance… in bare feet.

What a response it got.

The punters stood up and gave me a short ovation, it was fucking mint.

I don't know why the idea came into my head; maybe it was Eric's spirit entering me so I could have a personal moment of comedy gold.

No, bollocks, it was just me not wanting someone to get a bigger laugh than me.

I enjoy playing with artists further up the food chain than me, because I know I have to up my game and show that, given the chance, I won't let anyone down. Unbelievably, I've known musicians (no names please, we're British!) who actually like working the other way around, not because they're kind hearted souls wanting to help out shall we say 'lesser musicians' by showing them a few licks and handing out a little advice that may help them out later on in their journey, but because they're stupid, self-obsessed wankers, with a fully paid up membership to the big-fish-in-a-small-pond theory.

A dick will always be a dick.

Hold on, let's take a quick break from all things music, because I've just realised that I haven't made a list of my favourite TV shows.

NICK'S TOP TEN TV SHOWS (In no order)

1. 'The Sweeney'
2. 'Minder'
3. 'Bilko'
4. 'The Thick of It'
5. 'Fawlty Towers'
6. 'Yes, Minister
7. 'Scotland Yard'
8. 'Dad's Army'
9. 'Morecambe & Wise'
10. 'Top Of The Pops'

Those first ten days with 3 Men really worked wonders for me, and I returned to The Selecter with a much more positive outlook about myself, and what the future might have in store for me. I still hung on to the hope that somewhere along the line the band's fortunes would take a turn for the better, although I think deep down I knew the whole thing was just being run into the ground.

Another shot in the arm for me was when I got a call from Dolphin Taylor, the boss of Extreme, a company that specialised in library music, asking if I was interested in writing some new original ska and reggae music for possible use on TV or radio, in fact anywhere where they could place it. I'd been recommended to them by Lol Pryor, the former owner of Link Records, who said: "If you want someone who can write melody that sticks in your head, go to Nick Welsh."

Thanks for the recommendation Lol.

I really enjoyed the experience of having to write to order. The library world is basically all about making music that is as close as damn-it to some well-known song that everyone knows. The bottom line is that companies don't have to pay X amount of pounds to a label for using something like say "Ghost Town" in an advert, they can just get someone like me to give them something similar for half the price. The ground rules of the genre were a little hard to get my head round at first, such as the track should last no longer than two and a half minutes, and fade-outs were a definite no-no. On one of the songs I got a really good saxophonist to blow all over it and I was told:

"We're paying you for the melodies in your head, not to musically wank all over them."

I have to say that any time I heard one of my library tracks on TV I felt really proud of myself because it was all my own work. I was especially proud when one of them, "Hey You", made its way into the Keira Knightly film, *Domino*. I reckon that's the closest I'll ever get to her! Besides making lots of appearances in TV shows and adverts, that song has also been used in computer games, most bizarrely as the entrance music for WWE's Brian 'Spanky' Kendricks.

The band were back in the studio after saying yes to Captain Oi's offer of putting out a new Selecter album. I now expected fuck all in terms of sales from anything we put out, whoever the company was, and it sort of freed me up mentally to just go in the studio and make music, without the hindrance of all my usual high hopes and grand expectations. Just as well really, because although the whole experience of recording "Real to

255

Reel" was a good one, and our new guitarist Toby Hoskin played some nice stuff on it, the album is a little bit pants.

There are a couple of tracks on it I like: "Peace Crisis" and "Algebra"; but most of it is mediocre at best. All it really achieved was to give the band an excuse to go out on the road again, the prospect of which didn't exactly fill me with excitement.

Mum's condition wasn't getting any better, but like the good band member I was, I once again went off to play all the same old venues and, it has to be said, ever decreasing crowds. Even going to America didn't have the same buzz for me. Maybe it was something to do with the conversation I'd had with Martin just before we went: "We've been offered a tour of the States as special guests to some band. It's not great money, but the agent says it will be good promo for us."

"Who's the band?"

"I can't remember, I think their name has something to do with water."

"Well, are they a ska band?"

"I'm not sure, but on our days off we've been asked to open for someone who used to play with Bill Clinton or something. There's not much money involved, but it would mean no down time. It will help pay for a hotel and some diesel to get us around."

"That doesn't sound like a great deal mate. Why don't we just do the other dates? Find out who the band are to check out if we're compatible."

I found out a week or so later that the water-based headliners were some old friends of mine, Reel Big Fish, which was great, but imagine how pissed off I was when I discovered that the other dates, which I'd told Martin to cancel, were not in fact with an old musical friend of the president, but with none other than one of my all-time heroes, Bootsy Collins, the space-age funk brother of George Clinton!

I didn't let that one go for months…

Now, if I was the best fucking writer in the whole world, I could still never do justice to describing the weather conditions when we flew into Denver to start the tour. Before we could touchdown, the plane had to circle for what seemed to be about thirteen weeks (but was probably only about forty minutes), because it was snowing like I'd never seen before. The airport staff had been doing their best to try and clear the runway for us to land, but there was still a lot of fucking snow on the ground.

When we eventually did land, let me tell you, that was the easy bit. We then had to travel about a hundred miles from the airport to our hotel.

On a normal day that would be what? A two hour trip? But this was no normal day my friends: on that cold, cold, Denver day we were stuck in our freezing van for a marathon twelve hours! As we crawled along the freeway, I looked out of the window to see what I thought looked like giant plates of bangers and mash, but were in fact twenty-foot snow drifts (mash), with random vehicles sticking out (bangers). It was fucking mental.

I have never been so happy to reach a hotel and a warm bed in my life.

So anyway, the tour gets underway and you know what? For the first time in my life I feel old. Like a fish out of water. After only a couple of shows, all I wanted to do was go home.

How fucking sad is that?

I was in my favourite place in the world, getting to play venues like The Fillmore and The Palace, places that are on most musicians' bucket-lists, and bollock chops here wanted to bale. But I've never run off to leave everyone in the shit, that's not me. The truth was, though, I no longer had any heart for what I was doing.

Over the years there'd been plenty of times when I wanted to just jack it in, but I always pushed those thoughts to one side and carried on. Not this time, and I can tell you exactly where and when it was, that my final decision was made.

Las Vegas.

"All you need's a strong heart and a nerve of steel"

I'd just come offstage after playing at some ska festival, and was sitting at the side of the stage watching all the young kids in the mosh pit, jumping around to their generation's version of ska and reggae. All I could think was: "Why doesn't anyone play the kind of music that I grew up with?" Those skinhead reggae rhythms that would get me to try and rub my unwanted, sticky, teenage erection against any girl who would dance close enough to me when the lights went out, in the back room of my local youth club. That's the music I really love. That's what made me take this musical trip in the first place.

So there I was, in the gambling capital of the world, finally deciding it was time for me to roll the dice and leave The Selecter behind. I wanted to be my own man, playing my own music. I couldn't go on playing sidekick Hank to frontman Larry, and although it wouldn't come to fruition for a little while, the seed had been sown.

Mum succumbed to breast cancer on 22nd January 2005.

I was heartbroken, but in some way the pain was eased a little by the fact I knew it was coming. As I watched her take her final breath to leave this precious earth, the feeling I got was one of 'at least she's not going through all that pain anymore.'

I don't think you'll be that surprised when I tell you I spent that night drinking and sniffing.

Exactly what my mum wouldn't have wanted me to do.

But fuck it, that's the only way I knew how to block things out in my life, even if it was just for a few hours.

Mum, you were the most loving, caring person I've ever known. x

Just like it had been with Dad, the day after Mum's funeral I was back out on tour again with 3 Men. It was probably the best thing for me to be honest, because it kept me focused, and straight, and now more than ever I needed some sanity in my life, which probably explains why Skaville UK came into my mind and on to fruition.

My vision for SUK was for me to be surrounded by old friends, playing original skinhead reggae with a hint of glam and punk, or, as guitarist Louis Alphonso described it: "A middle-aged rampage."

Louis was the first person to sign up for SUK. For me there was no one better at playing that "Wreck A Pum Pum" style of guitar. I knew he wasn't the best when it came to solos, but I had plans of getting a second guitarist in to do that.

Now hold on, that ain't right.

Al Fletcher was the first to come aboard. We came up with the idea of starting a band together on a very pissed up night out.

Yeah, that's what happened, and then Louis came along a little bit later.

Old friends.

My phonebook wasn't giving me too much joy in the lead guitarist department, so I widened the net a little by asking other musicians if they knew of anyone who, besides having the ability, also had the kind of personality they thought would fit in with the three of us. We did manage to put a few faces in the frame, but on meeting them for a drink or two, I didn't really think they were that suitable.

Martin had been bending my ear about me leaving The Selecter, because he thought if I fucked off the whole thing would stop. Which I thought was basically bollocks. He also made it obvious to me that he wanted in on SUK, but that didn't really appeal to me because then SUK would have two members of The Selecter in it (three if you include Al). I didn't really want that, but let's cut right through it here: the man was going through the worst fucking time of his life. His wife, Penny, had recently passed away, and he must have been in great pain. Against my better judgment I asked him to join, hoping that it would be of some kind of help to him. I'm not bigging myself up here, I just thought that it was the right thing to do.

I was absolutely wrong.

As soon as the four of us got together to chat about the direction we were going to go in, he started saying how we could get more, and better paid shows, if we just played a few Bad Manners songs, or threw in a couple of Prince Buster and Lee Perry covers.

I knew it. I bloody knew it.

Of course, it makes sense to do that if your only aim is to gig a lot and make a few quid. But I didn't want to leave a band I loved to go and play "Wooly Bully" at some 80s night in Rotherham.

Don't ask me how, but that's exactly what happened.

No, I'll tell you why it happened, it was because I struck up a deal with Martin, that if we did what he suggested for a few months, we could earn enough money to go and record all the new songs I wanted. Like some weak-willed pussy, I agreed.

I'm looking at a set list from one of our early shows and it's so top heavy with Manners material, it reads like a fucking tribute band: "Inner London Violence", "My Girl Lollipop", "Suicide" and "Can Can". The only new songs of mine I can see in there are "Hey You" and "(I Wish It Was) 1973", but I kept schtum and got on with the job in hand.

Oh, and if that wasn't bad enough, Martin started bringing his new bird out on tour with us. As I said before, the geezer was going through a really bad time, and his head must have been all over the shop, but one of the things we'd all agreed, right from the off, was that SUK was gonna be a bit of a boys' jolly. I had nothing against the woman in any way at all, her presence just sort of put a bit of a dampener on everything.

There was some light at the end of the tunnel though, because we did manage to raise enough dosh from those gigs to record our first album, "1973". We chose to do it at Pat Collier's Perry Vale Studios in Forest Hill. Pat was the original bassist in The Vibrators, before going on to form his own band The Boyfriends. In the mid 80s he decided he wanted to work behind the desk, not in front of it, and that's what he's been doing (very successfully) ever since. I knew he was really good at getting a drum sound that would jump out at you. That was exactly what I was looking for, and that was exactly what I got.

Fuck me Nick, people don't wanna read about drum sounds you boring cunt.

Ok, I'm sorry, you're right. I'll just mention a few of my personal highlights from the album: I loved the title track, I loved getting the chance to work with Jennie again, I loved our take on "Memory Train", I loved the little adverts, but I didn't love the cover.

While all this was going on, I was still doing shows with The Selecter and it was at one of these gigs in Holland that I told Pauline I'd be calling it a day at the end of the year, which would give her six months to find a decent replacement for me. I have to say, it didn't go down well with her and our relationship cooled a little from that day on, which really saddened me because I considered her a close friend. She is someone I have great respect for as a writer and performer.

Now, I could be completely wrong here, but maybe (like Doug) she respected what I had to offer the band, and thought I might be a tough one to replace? Or is that just me being a bit big headed? I dunno, but what I do know is that it made for a very strained six months.

Madonna	**"Hung Up"**
Kanye West	**"Gold Digger"**
Gnarls Barkley	**"Crazy"**

My last Selecter performance was at Rock City in Nottingham on 17th December 2006. We were on with Stiff Little Fingers, The Damned and King Kurt, which was a great bill to be on to say goodbye to a band that had basically been my life for fifteen years.

NICK'S TOP FIVE SONGS RECORDED WITH THE SELECTER

1. **"Whip Them Down"**
2. **"Blind Leading The Blind"**
3. **"Neurotica!"**
4. **"California Screaming"**
5. **"Musical Servant"**

After the show, we drove back to London, dropping Pauline off first at Watford Gap Services, to be picked up by her husband, Terry. We got out of the van and Pauline said her goodbyes to everyone. I knew this was gonna be a huge turning point in my life, but I didn't want it to be a sad one, so just before she turned round to say goodbye to me, I tried adding a little levity to the occasion by dropping my trousers round my ankles and doing a cockney dance, which I think got a laugh.

But even if it didn't, as far as goodbyes go, it might not have been *Casablanca*, but it was fucking memorable one!

The Upsetter

DANCING IN THE GARDEN OF EVIL

Dancing in the garden of evil,
Swimming in a sea of sin,
Dancing in the garden of evil,
I don't know where I'm going or where I've been.

I was just a young boy, when I left my home,
And bought myself a ticket, to the last days of Rome,
It's not a new religion, it's a place to go,
And so I hitched a ride, and went to hedonism row.

I could be a rich man, but that's not who you are,
It's been a lifetime party, with the Marquis De Ska.

Dancing in the garden of evil,
Swimming in a sea of sin,
Dancing in the garden of evil,
I don't know where I'm going or where I've been.

One of the biggest disappointments of my musical life was what happened to SUK over the next two years. What was supposed to be the start of a new and exciting adventure for me, ended in what would best be described as a damp squib, which is why I'm not going to spend too much time talking about it here.

Focus on the positive.

We made two more albums after "1973", one of them "Decadent!" with Martin, and "Devil Beat", without.

I got a phone call from him one morning telling me he was sorry, but he no longer wanted to be in the band because his health wasn't too good. I totally understood, and told him to look after himself, and his last words to me were: "I'll come and see you at a show in a few months."

That was eight years ago. I haven't seen or heard from him since.

It totally fucked up the gig side of things because he booked all the shows, and when we did finally hit the road again, I made sure it was with a second guitarist instead of a keyboard player, because I didn't think I could replace him adequately; because for all my little niggles about the geezer (and I'm sure he had plenty about me), Martin is definitely a one off in terms of personality and musicianship.

I could now have the line up I'd wanted right from the start for SUK, making our offbeat sound the loudest in town. For evidence of this check out our version of Vince Taylor's "Brand New Cadillac" on YouTube, from a show we did in Paris.

It fucking rocks!

With Martin off the firm we began recording what I consider to be our best album, "Devil Beat", but before I'd even had the chance to master the fucker, it was Louis's turn to tell me he was pissing off. His reason was he felt musically limited playing just ska and reggae, which I found a bit odd because on "Devil Beat" our musical door was well and truly thrown wide open to any new ideas that came along.

I was beginning to get so pissed off with everything I didn't even bother to try and change his mind, we just hugged and said goodbye.

Where are all my friends today?

NICK'S TOP FIVE SKAVILLE UK SONGS

1. "(I Wish It Was) 1973"
2. "Devil Beat"
3. "She's Mad About The 80's
4. "Thank God I'm Not Like You"
5. "I Threw It All Away"

263

That's the way life is sometimes, but do you know what? It turns out that SUK was just a tasty starter to a much more interesting main course.

It was a gift to a friend at the start of 2010 that set the whole thing rolling again.

I was booked to perform at a mate of mine's fortieth birthday party, and I wanted to give him something memorable as a present, seeing as it's considered to be one of the big ones, as birthdays go. I knew Mike Cornwell was a big fan of The Specials, so I popped into a studio a few days before his party and recorded a version of "A Message To You Rudy", changing the song's title and chorus to "A Message To You Mike C".

Well, the gift certainly had the desired effect, because I watched him get a little tearful listening to it, but it was something he said that really got me thinking: "That's got a proper King Hammond feel to it."

I can only assume that's why, two days later, I found myself in the same studio, doing the classic reggae trick of recording a new song over an old backing track and in one three-hour session "A Message To You Mike C", became "Cool Down Your Temper", a song about the rise of knife and gun crime amongst Britain's youth.

I personally think it was a lot more naughty on the streets of London when I was growing up in the 70s, but the difference now is the consequences are a lot more serious. Youngsters aren't just coming home with a black eye or a broken nose anymore (although I'm sure they still do), what we are talking about here is a fucking terminal turn out. Families are being torn apart because their kids are getting involved with gangs and all their postcode related bullshit, and that can sometimes end with parents having to go through the ultimate pain of seeing their baby lying on a cold mortuary slab. There didn't seem to be a week go by without me seeing bunches of flowers attached to a fence or lamp post somewhere in my area; usually surrounded by bereavement cards and pictures of some kid whose time on earth had been drastically cut down by some stupid, senseless act.

What a tragic waste of life.

Although the track was tinged with sadness, I could also take some real positives from it.

The main reason I'd avoided doing any new King Hammond recordings was because I didn't feel comfortable singing songs about pum pum, vampires and exorcism as I fast approached my fifties. Now, call me thick, but it never entered my head that maybe I could keep the skinhead reggae vibe, but change my lyrics to slightly more grown up subjects.

Exactly like "Cool Down Your Temper".

I don't wanna sound like a ponce here, but something almost spiritual happened to me when I listened to the first playback of the finished track. It was like there was a huge fucking finger pointing at me from the sky, and a voice saying: "This is the real you Nick, why has it taken you so long to realise it?"

I knew there and then that for the rest of my life I was going to be King Hammond. The stupid thing was, I always had been, I just didn't know it.

The next song I recorded was a slice of big-beat ska, originally called "Session Man", as a tribute to my dad and all those guys like him, who made a living in the 60s and 70s, going from session to session, playing whatever was asked of them, but somehow it ended up as "Mr Easy Talk", with me venting my anger on the politicians' expenses scandal that was big news at the time. I'm glad to say my old man wasn't totally dropped from the track, because the drum loop I used for it was taken from one of his records.

Over the next couple of months, I went into the studio two, maybe three times a week, always recording for just three hours (just like the 'good old days') and very rarely did I ever leave without a finished track. I found it easy and a lot of fun to do.

A big help in all this was Steve Crittall because all the recording was done at Racknaphobia, which is his studio bang in the centre of the big, bad, ever-changing place they call Soho.

Steve is one of the good guys.

I first hooked up with him when someone stuck him up as a possible guitarist for The Selecter, and I went to his gaff to check him out. We hit it off straight away. He had a 'Joe Brown' haircut, which I thought was a plus, so when the position became available a few months later he was the first name I thought of, and he never ever let me or the band down. Steve was a great support to me when I was getting back in the studio saddle, coming up with some great guitar lines, and lots of unique off-the-wall mixes. I swear, at times I thought the geezer could read my mind.

I'm still recording with him nearly ten years later, which is proof of the trust I have in him.

Ten years of letting him share my chips. Ten years of listening to him go on and on about his dodgy knee.

The fruits of our labour resulted in "The King & I", which sometimes gets referred to as my comeback album.

'Comeback'? Who am I? Fucking Frank Sinatra?

I wish.

Because I was funding everything, I played safe and just got a thousand pressed up. This was mainly due to lack of ackers, but also because I wasn't sure what kind of response the album was going to get. I'd received a lot of positive comments from all the 'teasers' I'd got my computer savvy friend Paul Willo to post on YouTube but kind words are one thing, getting someone to actually dig deep and buy a 'physical copy' of an album in these dirty 'I want my music for free' download days is another.

But I was about to be overwhelmed, because "The King & I" flew out of the door and sold out within a couple of weeks of release with all the proceeds going towards recording the next album, and seven years down the line that's still how I operate.

The Punk in me is proud to say that, in 2017, King Hammond's world is still very much a DIY hand to mouth one, which, hand on heart, is just the way I like it.

With the album out, my attention turned towards putting a band together to play some shows to promote it, and I have to say I must be quite a good band leader, because the first person I got to join The Rude Boy Mafia (even though she's female) is still with me today.

The first time I met trumpeter Wendy Jane Bridger was when her band The Skanx supported Skaville UK. I fell in love with her at first sight, because quite simply, she is the sweetest thing you could ever want to meet, and it's not only me who thinks that, because I've never seen an audience that doesn't immediately fall in love with her.

My first show was at a scooter rally in Great Yarmouth, which was great because it meant I would be playing to the people who'd supported me and my music through thin and thin.

The gig was ok.

Just ok.

Why?

Some of the guys I'd got in to play let me down big time. There's no point in me digging people out here, because what's done is done, but what I will say is this… It was supposed to be the beginning of a new era for me, but the standard of performance and commitment I got from them that night pissed me off big time. However, unlike a few years before, when I would've buried my head in a big bag of Percy, I just chalked it up to experience and moved on.

Thankfully, the next show was a lot better.

When I stepped onstage at The Gaff in Holloway Road on 30th July 2010, to hand out crowns to the packed-out audience, I didn't realise it was the first King Hammond show in London for twenty-one years. Thankfully, this time the band rose to the occasion.

It was lovely to get such a warm and loving reaction from the crowd, especially when you think my set (other than "Skaville UK" and "King Hammond Shuffle") was made up of songs from the new album, and even a couple of tracks I hadn't even recorded yet like "Chicken And Chips" and "Riot In London Town".

Oh, and while it's on my mind, I just wanna clear up something about "Riot In London Town". A lot of people have asked me in the last few years which riot I was writing about. 1981 or 2011?

It's neither.

The 'riot' I'm referring to is an architectural one, which I think is destroying the city I love.

NICK'S TOP THREE LONDON EYESORES

1. City Hall. Looks like a cheap portable CD player from the 90s.
2. The Gherkin. Looks like a juicer you've got from Argos.
3. The Shard. Looks like a very expensive cheese grater.

Come on, you have to admit that if you were to put any of these up against say, The Tower Of London, or the beauty that is St Paul's Cathedral, they'd come a pretty poor second.

It's like Morecambe and Wise sharing a stage with fucking Hale and Pace.

I might not be Hubert Gregg, but I've written quite a few songs over the years about London. Some good, some maybe not so good, but the one thing they all have in common is they all come straight from the heart.

"I get a funny feeling inside of me when I'm walking up and down"

With the help of a lot of good online reviews for "The King & I", and the success of London show, it was pretty much known on the ska 'scene' that King Hammond was back and apparently in good health. The good thing about my newfound freedom was, everything was down to me. If I wanted to bung out five albums a year, and only do shows dressed as an onion, well that's the way it was gonna be.

The next King Hammond album was the slightly darker "Jacuzzi!".

I started having a lot more fun lyrically. For instance, all the characters in the title track were people I'd seen every day in my local gym. The Mirror Man... Was a well-built, handsome guy, with a massive cock, who used to stand naked in front of a full-length mirror for ages, stroking his hairless body. The Fruitcake... This lady used to sing opera, while soaping and rubbing her tits vigorously in the communal showers next to the jacuzzi. The Kung Fu Kid... An Asian kid who used to jump into the swimming pool Bruce Lee style.

Another favourite of mine from the album is "Tattoo Girls", which was me trying to write a 'Stones play reggae' type track, with its lazy slide-guitar and affected vocal.

And in case you couldn't hear it in the music I put two Stones album titles in the title.

On release, "Jacuzzi!" was very well received, and after putting my money where my mouth was, I was more than happy when it sold out as quickly as its predecessor.

I did a few more UK shows in 2010 (including another London sell out), but most of the interest I was getting was from promoters in Germany, Spain, USA, and Canada. Which of course was great, because after all these years I still enjoy travelling, but limited finances meant heading out on my own, to play with local bands; which was fine, but obviously my first choice would always be to be onstage with The Rude Boy Mafia.

When I wasn't undertaking my royal duties abroad, I would slip in the odd "Life & Times" solo acoustic show wherever I could.

"The Life & Times Of A Ska Man" was another outlet for me to express myself musically. That's a lot easier to do when the venue you're performing at is an arts centre or a club specialising in acoustic music, where audiences are used to keeping schtum while you're showing them your darker, more introspective side. It's a lot fucking harder when you're onstage in some noisy pub, trying to fight for ear space against the sound of pissed-up office birds screeching loudly to each other,

268

sounding like chalk on a blackboard, or geezers on their mobiles, trying to find out what time their dealer's gonna be there to sort them out: "That's a definite, yeah? Twenty minutes? Ok mate, I'll meet you in the car park."

The stupid thing is, I know that's exactly how it's gonna be before I even turn up to those type of gigs because I usually only say yes to doing them because the landlord/promoter is an old pal/fan of mine.

The "The Life & Times Of A Ska Man" album has been released three times in the last few years, all with different track listings and sleeves, and every one has sold out and received great reviews.

Right, time for a break, I'm off to the West End to get pissed with my brother Jake (Burns).

P. J Harvey	**"Let England Shake"**
Josh T Pearson	**"Last Of The Country Gentlemen"**
Kate Bush	**"50 Words For Snow"**

Fuck me that was a good night out.

I'm not sure writing with a hangover is a good idea, but here we go. Now, where were we?

Oh yeah, so it's 2011, and with a couple of good albums under my belt, I get invited to the Ink 'n' Iron festival in Long Beach, California.

As I said before, when I go abroad I usually have to play on my own with the promoter getting a local band to back me, but on this occasion, I was able to take my keyboard player, Richie Downes, along for the ride. I didn't really want to play a big gig like that without having at least one person on the firm I could trust. The two of us flew in to LAX and drove down to Chula Vista, to plot up at the house of Jorge Jimenez, our guitarist for the tour. I'd first met Jorge nearly twenty years earlier, when his band, Tijuana No!, supported The Selecter on some Californian dates.

Jorge is one of the good guys. Not only did he make his home our home for the tour, he found all the musicians for the band and booked two more shows for me to do, one in San Diego and another across the border in Tijuana.

After spending a day kicking back, the three of us drove down to Tijuana to meet up with the rest of the band and rehearse. Everything went well for the first couple of hours: the songs were sounding good, and everyone was getting on well.

Then we took a break.

269

As I was making my way out of the studio to grab something to eat, I was stopped in my tracks by a guy with a pen in one hand and a copy of "Blow Your Mind" in the other. "Would you please sign this for me Mr Hammond?"

"Yeah of course mate, no problem." I signed it and handed it back to him.

"Mr Hammond, I have a present for you."

"Oh, that's nice of you mate. What is it?"

"Can I give it to you inside?"

And that's when the rehearsal came to an abrupt end, because his present was a gram of some of the strongest gear I've ever fucking had and after a couple of lines, I was well and truly out the game; so we all pissed off to a bar and got totally hammered.

The Ink 'n' Iron festival was a gas.

We played on a stage that was in front of a huge ship, to an audience made up of beautiful tattooed Rockabillies (boys and girls). We were on the same bill as Fishbone, who rocked like it was 1987, and after their show I had a good catch up with singer Angelo Moore who's someone I've admired ever since I first clapped my eyes on the mad fucker.

I didn't hang around the festival for too long though because I'd arranged to go and see another artist I've admired for more years than I can remember, and he's someone I'm proud to call a friend, Dave Wakeling, who was playing at The Belly Up in Solana Beach, which has always been one of my favourite venues in California, with his band, The English Beat. After doing all the showbiz hugs and kisses in the dressing room, he got one of his people to show me to my seat in the VIP area, right next to the stage. Halfway through his show, the old schmoozer sprung a little surprise, by asking me to stand up while he introduced me to the audience, who gave me such a wonderful round of applause I got a bit tearful.

I've always considered Dave to be right at the top of the 2-Tone talent tree, which is why it annoys me a little that we haven't carried through the threat we've been making for many years now, to write some songs together.

Dear Dave,

If you ever do take a break from your never-ending tour, let's do it.

Love Nick x

The day after the Ink 'n' Iron festival was our Tijuana show.

I love the place and have had a fascination with it ever since I played there back in the 80s with Buster's All Stars. I don't know if I've just watched too many films like *A Touch of Evil*, but whenever I've walked along the streets of Tijuana, I get that film noir feeling and so it was quite fitting that the gig was in an old, burnt out, rundown 50s cinema, although I have to say I can't remember a film of the genre where one of the scenes features hundreds of young Mexican rudies doing the conga to skinhead reggae.

It truly was a moment I will never forget.

These kind of shows make everything worthwhile.

"Time can't erase the memory of these magic moments filled with love"

We had all the usual trouble getting back across the border, with some people fucked up, and some going missing, but I suppose it wouldn't be a Tijuana show if we didn't have all that malarkey. In the end, we managed to get across to play our final show in San Diego.

The stand out moment of the gig was when I decided that I'd make my stage debut playing the ukulele, and led the audience in a sing-song of "Pressure Drop".

So, without any managerial financial backing or record company help, I'd managed to take King Hammond to the USA and Mexico, and it happened because I had good people around me, who believed in what I was trying to do. They put everything they had into helping me to make my dream come true, for which I say:

Thank you, I love you all x.

I have never taken touring for granted, and I'm not going to start doing it now, because I always knew I had no divine right to be on any stage. I'm grateful for every show that comes my way, and let me tell you something else: when I got those chances to play all over the world, I always performed like it was gonna be the last show I'd ever do; and I still live by that code today.

I would love to work more in the UK, but my chances are few and far between. Promoters seem to want to go for either the more established 2-Tone artists, or one of the many ska and reggae cover/tribute acts up and down the country and unfortunately for me, I seem to fall somewhere in the middle of that. Gig promotion at the level I'm at has changed a lot in the last twenty years. In the old days, promoters would flyer

271

everywhere in their area, and nine times out of ten would come up with interviews for the artist on local radio or press.

Nowadays it seems to be more like: let's bung it on Facebook and see what happens.

Sometimes I get the chance to be special guest to one of the 2-Tone bands and I always go down well. That's not me being big-headed, it's just I've been doing this for a hell of a long time and I'm bloody good at what I do.

I do have to admit a few years ago I did have a bit of a downer on the whole cover/tribute thing, but that was mainly because whenever I had that type of band supporting me, it made my job a lot fucking harder.

Why?

Well, if the group playing before you have just banged out a set that is basically the soundtrack to the audience's youth, and then you go on and play a load of new material, well it doesn't matter how good your songs are, it's always going to be an uphill struggle.

I've cooled on that now though, because you know what, if people want to go and see them, and they have a great time, well what's wrong with that? However, I will say this: if you're gonna be in a band like that, make sure you try and do it right, because fuck me have I seen some real shockers in my time!

One thing no one could stop me from doing though, was writing, recording, and releasing new material. I was going for it, with all the passion and commitment I used to show chasing my next wrap, or a new bit of skirt.

I only released one album "Showbiz!" in 2011 (you lazy bastard!), which was basically me just treading water with some more skinhead reggae scorchers, like the autobiographical "Rocking On Ridley Road" and "Easy Lovin'" both of which I'm immensely proud of. All good stuff, but in my opinion, it wasn't until the following year I finally made a King Hammond album I felt ticked all my boxes.

I returned to America at the end of that year to play two shows on the East Coast with The Hard Times as my backing band.

The first gig was in a wonderful club in Harlem called The Shrine, which was the kind of room you'd expect to see John Shaft come strutting into with a couple of hookers in tow. Sadly, for me though, he didn't show, but it was the perfect warm up for the following night's gig in Brooklyn at a warehouse party.

272

Once again, it was to be one of those times when I close my eyes and think: "How lucky am I to be here and doing this?"

You know what I'm saying?

It was nearly twenty-five years since I first gave birth to the King, and here I was, playing in a packed-out venue in NYC, and the crowd were going fucking mad for it.

I may not be a big noise, but I am blessed.

Nick Cave	**"Push The Sky Away"**
Scott Walker	**"Bish Bosh"**
PIL	**"This Is Pil"**

If you just take a few seconds to look back at my foreword, you can see what I said about the book's title and the reason behind it and so with that in mind, let me try to explain to you my thinking when I began the writing and recording of "Dancing In The Garden Of Evil".

I've always banged on about how you should write about what you know, and for some reason as I entered 2012 (after a decent period of behaving myself), I started to slide back to some of the dark places I thought I'd left behind, and so I decided to address the situation on the album. The title track was written after I'd been on a three-day bender, where I'd woken up and couldn't remember where the fuck I'd been for the last seventy-two hours. All I knew was I'd gone into my local Monday lunchtime for a couple of drinks, and woken up on the Thursday morning feeling like dog shit; but I would always justify my behaviour if a good song came out of it. The same thing applies to "Downbeat On Upper Street".

I'm not saying that's the right way to think, it's just what I do.

The problem was my good intentions of just having 'a couple' would always get hijacked by some well-meaning local whispering "Have a little bit of this Nick, it's pucker" in my ear and a new journey would begin.

I'm particularly proud of "Jet Black Tourniquet".

It wasn't that hard for me to write about depression and self-harm, because I'd been at it for fucking years! Other stand-out tracks for me are "Chutzpah!" and "Parallel Road", which was the first song I wrote after deciding to try my hand at acoustic based mùsic, but on this album the road took on an almost world music type path.

I've always wanted to take ska and reggae music in new and different directions.

The way I see it, when ska took Jamaica by storm in the early 60s it was a hybrid of rhythm and blues, calypso and mento, with an added exciting youthful offbeat that complemented their songs of repression and struggle perfectly, just like the 2-Tone movement did at the end of the next decade, when it mixed ska and reggae with punk and soul.

Something that really winds me up is the way people label anything that has an offbeat as ska. I was being interviewed by a reporter from a regional newspaper when "Dancing In The Garden Of Evil" came out and he asked me what my favourite ska track was. Before I could answer, he told me his was the Harry J classic "Liquidator".

This is the conversation that followed:

Me: "That's not ska, it's reggae."

Him: "No, it's ska and I'm surprised someone like you doesn't know that."

Me: "Listen mate, it's reggae, or if I'm being really pedantic it's fucking skinhead reggae."

Him: "I don't think I've ever interviewed anyone as rude as you."

Me: "Well then, it won't come as a surprise when I tell you to fuck off."

And I put the phone down.

Luckily for me, having that rare unprofessional moment while nursing a hangover with a reporter from the Norwich Nonce, or whatever the local rag was, didn't stop the album from selling out again, and so once more I had the necessary folding to go towards the next release.

That's one addiction I'm not trying to fight off.

I get even more pleasure from the writing and recording process than I do from a gig, because no matter how good or big a show is, when it's over you're on a high but it only lasts until the next show, whereas when you have a new track of yours that you consider to be 'the dogs' in your sweaty hands it's a high that will stay with you forever, and hopefully give others a high long after you've gone.

To promote my next release, "Hot Skin Music", I performed in Germany, Switzerland, Spain and another one of those places I never thought I'd get the chance to go to…

Argentina.

A few years earlier I'd guested on a single "Bring Down the Birds", with the Argentinian band The Crabs Corporation and as a thank you the group's main man, Gustavo, promised me that one day he'd get me over to his country. Well, it might have taken a few years to happen, but when it did, fuck me was it worth the wait! Buenos Aires has to be one of the most beautiful cities I've ever been to, and the people are so warm and friendly. Oh, and the steaks are out of this world!

I'll tell you what else was out of this world too, the venue I was playing at. La Confiteria Ideal is a beautiful building, which has played a major role in the history of the wonderful dance they call... The Tango. All the masters of the art have performed there, and its marble columned ballroom has been used in films like *Tango* and *Evita*.

And now they've had me!

I don't know what it is with King Hammond and South America, but the people just seem to love my music out there and they certainly have no problem in showing it. I suppose it has to be down to the power of the internet, which allows me to go halfway across the world, to play a show in a country I've never been to before, and yet still be greeted by a room full of people who know and sing along to "Rocking On Ridley Road" and "Riot In London Town", because I'm pretty sure none of them are familiar with that market in Dalston, or spend time wondering why there are no Wimpy bars or record shops in London anymore, but here they are in front of me, dancing like nutters, and singing every chorus with the same passion as a drunk sings about his favourite football team at closing time.

It was a fantastic night; sorry I should say morning, because I didn't actually go onstage until 3.00am, but with the help of a bump or two I gave Buenos Aries a show to remember, even though having coke before a show was supposed to be a thing of the past for me.

I'd knocked it on the head altogether in England, which was a lot easier to do than I thought it would be. It was helped by the fact that the standard of it was now so piss poor, I was getting more of a buzz when I washed my bum-hole with that mint and tea tree shower gel. In Argentina though, I got the impression that having a line together was a bond of friendship thing, just like it used to be back in the 80s. I didn't get to bed until 8.00am, but it didn't really matter because I couldn't sleep anyway!

I wonder why that was Nick?

And so I went for a nice early morning stroll around the city for a couple of hours, although I had to make sure I was back at the hotel by noon because that's when I was being picked up to be taken to watch Boca Juniors play Gimnasia La Plata at La Bombonera, and because I didn't want to miss out on that experience I thought it would be for the best if I had a little early morning medication just to keep me going.

And what an experience it was.

I've been to grounds that have what commentators like to call a 'cauldron-like atmosphere', but none that compare to this gaff, and by all accounts, it wasn't even an important game!

It was an afternoon of never-ending chanting, tribal drumming, smoke bombs, fire crackers, you name it they had it, and it was just as well because the game was fucking pants.

Dodgy burger on the way to the game?

Nah, try half a fucking cow in a bun and you're getting warmer!

Argentina, I hope to see you soon x.

Another country I'll never tire of going to, who also love a late gig, is Spain.

I remember playing there once at 5.00am with Bad Manners in a swimming pool! That was back in the 80s though, when I was in my early twenties; it's a lot fucking harder to do when you're in your fifties. It wasn't quite as late as that when I got to perform at the Rototom Sunsplash festival, but it was as near as damn it; but as any musician will tell you, time goes out the window when you're performing. I can remember many, many times, sitting in a dressing room before a gig, feeling like death warmed up, but the moment I went on stage I was absolutely fine.

It's musical magic!

Well not really, because you can bet your last tenner that when it's all over and you're back in the dressing room, you feel like fucking shit again.

Anyway, it doesn't matter if you're cream-crackered or if you're suffering from a bad case of the shits, how can you not be up for it when there are thousands of people out there wanting to P-A-R-T-Y and you're the person they expect to show them how?

Bollocks, we've just gone 2-0 down to Everton.

In 2014, I released a vinyl only single "Skaville Ole" / "Gimmie Some Soul" on the Spanish label Liquidator, and went on a six-date tour of the country to promote it. I even managed to get the acoustic out and do a "Life & Times" show in a small club in Madrid, and a live session on the radio, both of which were a great success, despite the language barrier. But although I had a great time there, and the gigs were very enjoyable to do, my health was starting to become a major worry to me.

I seemed to be getting very tired, very quickly, and constantly finding myself short of breath, which for a singer (or indeed anyone) is no great thing; and so for the first time in my life, I welcomed having a few days off in between shows, to try to get my head together and relax.

Plotting up in the middle of the capital gave me a good chance to get to know a city I'd visited many, many times before, but never with enough time to see what it had to offer. The Prado Museum is a wonderful place.

No hold on, that's not good enough...

The Prado Museum is a fucking brilliant place.

It's home to not only a shit load of Goya, who I love with a passion, but also to what has to be my favourite painting... EVER! Step forward Hieronymus Bosch and take a bow, because 'The Garden of Earthly Delights' is, and will always be, top of my pops mate.

Full time Everton 3 WBA 0.

Bloody hell. That result would be a lot easier for me to take if I was sitting in the calm, relaxing surroundings of Madrid's Botanical Gardens, instead of my little flat in N1, watching that wanker Matt Le Tissier telling me how shit we've just played.

I can't think now. I'm too upset.

Oh yeah, Madrid is a great place. Try and go there before you die.

Fuck it, let's talk about London. I usually try and do two London shows a year, and my preferred choice of venue is small, hot and smelly, which is why I use to love playing the 12 Bar Club in Denmark Street so much, because it ticked all those boxes.

Here's a classic quip from a punter to me, after one very hot and packed show there:"Great show Nick, where are you playing next... a broom cupboard?"

The 12 Bar closed down in 2015 as part of the architectural annihilation of Denmark Street, because no one seems to give a fuck about history anymore.

Especially musical history.

For fuck's sake, we're talking about Tin Pan Alley here mate. You know, that little street off the Charing Cross Road, where songwriters used to go to try and flog their songs to some unscrupulous cigar chomping publisher for a few bob. The home of Regent Sound, where the Stones recorded their first album, and bands like The Kinks, Jimi Hendrix, Elton John and Genesis rubbed shoulders with hundreds of other artists who didn't quite make the grade.

277

I went there a few times with the old man but he never liked it there much, he preferred the far grander surroundings of somewhere like Abbey Road (in his defence you couldn't really fit a thirty-piece orchestra in Regent Sound!); and whatever happened to the TPA Club, where he'd take me after a session, for a coke and a quick stare at Jimmy Page or Pete Townsend?

"There's a place where the publishers go"

This street should be cherished, preserved and its story told.

I know I might sound like a naive dreamer, but I'd like to think that in fifty years' time, you will still be able to see some fifteen year old kid, with his face pressed against a music shop window, trying to work out how he's gonna get the wedge together to pay for that great looking guitar he's just fallen in love with.

And who knows, maybe that kid is blessed with a unique talent and could go on to take the world by storm, making millions of people laugh and cry to his musical vision of the world. But that ain't gonna happen if you turn everything you see into luxury lego flats for the rich, or open yet another coffee shop for people to sit around in, talking shit and poncing around on their laptops; but that's what going down baby so it's time to wake up and smell the shit.

I saw more and more London venues closing down and so I decided to start a ska and reggae night of my own called 'Reggae Riot' in some of the capital's iconic venues like The Hope and Anchor or The Dublin Castle, where you can see four artists for a tenner. I'm proud to say that in just two years I managed to put on five 'Reggae Riots', featuring a mixture of legends, like my favourite female reggae singer of all time Susan Cadogan, ex-Specials guitarist/songwriter Roddy 'Radiation' Byers, and my old mate Jennie Bellestar alongside new and exciting talents, Millie Manders and Enne.

I've had the pleasure of performing on stage with Susan Cadogan, and her voice still sends a shiver up my spine, just like it did when I first heard "Hurt So Good" at the Tottenham Royal back in 1974. We also had a lot of fun when we recorded a 'live and loose' version of The Clash's "Bankrobber", for the Specialized charity album "Combat Cancer".

Susan, it was an honour.

And as for Roddy…

Roddy is a Rocker. Roddy has an edge. Roddy is my friend. But you never know what you're gonna get when you're onstage with him.

Some nights, he'll be totally on the money, looking cool, playing great guitar and throwing shapes like Johnny Thunders' long lost brother, but there are times when he looks like a lost soul, desperate for someone to give him a hug.

We recorded a track together at Roger Lomas's studio in Coventry for Specialized called "Get Specialised!" under the name '3 Men' with Jake Burns making up the trio.

I wrote the song after meeting Michelle Mcguffog at the second Specialized weekender. This very special lady had recently lost her beautiful teenage daughter, Leila, to cancer, and I could only stand back and admire her dignity and bravery, and when I told Roddy and Jake about her tragic story they were more than happy to join me in recording a little something for her, and for everyone who's ever lost a loved one to that horrible illness.

Anyway, back to the man with quiff.

Personally, I don't think Roddy gets the respect he deserves. For a start, he wrote "Rat Race", "Concrete Jungle" and "Hey Little Rich Girl", which in my mind are three of The Specials' best songs. He also has a guitar style that is uniquely his own.

Roddy, you are one of life's true originals, don't ever change mate x.

Hey, do you remember I told you I was having some health worries?

Well, say hello to my two new friends: type two diabetes and ridiculously high blood pressure.

When my doctor told me, I can't really say I was that surprised. I mean we are talking about nearly forty years of bad (good?) living here, and even I know there's gonna be some kind of payback from that kind of excess. Call me stupid though, I just didn't realise how serious diabetes can be.

I just thought it would mean a few more pills to add to my daily dose of Citalopram.

Keith Richards   **"Crosseyed Heart"**
Father John Misty   **"I Love You, Honeybear"**
Paul Weller   **"Saturns Pattern"**

I've just noticed something...

My random lists of music from the times of my life I'm writing about, have shifted from singles to albums. Is this an age thing?

More and more bands had started doing my kind of music, even using tricks like putting scratches at the start of their tracks. Although I can't take the credit for invention, it just all felt a bit too close to home. So, for my next album "The Outsider", I fancied a move away from shall I say my 'vintage reggae' sound, to a more contemporary one, and to make sure this happened I found a new studio to record in. As luck would have it, not only did I find a really good one, it was only a three-street walk from my flat!

What a result.

Sublime Studios is owned and run by one Mr Charles 'Chicky' Reeves, an American producer, engineer and master mixer, whose CV includes collaborations with…

Radiohead
Tito Puente
UB40
Grace Jones
Prince

Impressed?

Well I am, the geezer's worked for Prince for fuck's sake!

I worked at a much slower pace with Charles on "The Outsider", slower than I'd ever done on any previous King Hammond album, and this definitely complemented the music I was now trying to make. More time was spent on mixing, whereas before I felt my skinhead reggae tracks benefited from a 'get it down as quick as you can' work ethic.

No room for a picture, let's have a list instead.

NICK'S TOP FIVE KING HAMMOND SONGS

1. **"Dancing In The Garden Of Evil"**
2. **"Out Of Control"**
3. **"Cool Down Your Temper"**
4. **"Jet Black Tourniquet"**
5. **"Rocking On Ridley Road"**

2016

It was a cunt of a year, it was a cunt of a year,
The bombs kept dropping, the economy was rocking,
And the world lived in fear,
It was a cunt of a year, it was a cunt a cunt of a year,
I hope the next one's better but I just don't see it from here.

The politicians kept lying, while innocent people were dying,
Everyone seems to be heading for world war three,
We made our Euro exit, when Britain voted Brexit,
It's the great unknown, but what will be will be.

We hid our heads in the sand, when England lost to Iceland,
I think what we need is another Bobby Moore,
The voice of the people departed, to leave us broken hearted,
It's the great unknown but what will be will be.

It was a cunt of a year, it was a cunt of a year,
The bombs kept dropping, the economy was rocking,
And the world lived in fear,
It was a cunt of a year, it was a cunt a cunt of a year,
I hope the next one's better but I just don't see it from here.

2016 was certainly a cunt of a year with a lot more lows than highs for me. It started with sadness and got a lot fucking sadder as it went along.

I was absolutely in bits when I was told John Bradbury had suffered a heart attack at home, and passed away on the 28th December 2015. It was only a few months after Rico had left us, which meant my first day out of the year was gonna be spent at Golders Green Crematorium, saying goodbye to a much-treasured friend.

On the way to the funeral I bumped into Suggs from Madness and as we walked along, we both had the same story to tell, and that was how fit and healthy Brad looked the last time we'd seen him. It was standing room only as Brad made his entrance, to the theme music from 'The Long Good Friday'.

I wanted to laugh out loud, but contained myself in case it was taken the wrong way!

My mind raced back to many a drunken night, when we would talk about forming a punk band 'Diabolical Liberty', who only played songs with titles taken from the dialogue of this classic British film.

Brad's personal favourite was, "A Grand And A Bubble Bath".

The ceremony was short, sweet and, in the case of Terry Hall's eulogy to his friend, beautiful.

Goodbye JB it was a gas knowing you. We had some times, didn't we mate x.

Just to make things a little worse, Brad's funeral was held on the 11th January 2016, the day the world woke up to the news that David Bowie had died.

Hold on a minute, Bowie doesn't die. Bowie is forever.

I'd been playing his latest album, "Black Star", constantly in the days leading up to his death and loved every moment of it, but unlike a lot of people, who after the sad event began giving it: "Oh, we knew he was dying, the clues are all in there if you look" I didn't get that vibe at all. The only thing I could hear was an artist nearing his seventieth birthday, still making great cutting-edge music.

I hated all his bearded blokey bollocks 'I'm-just-the-singer-in-the-band' cobblers of filofax rockers Tin Machine. I want my Bowie to be a distant star, light years away, alienated from us mere mortals who occupy the 'real world' and that's exactly what I got from "Black Star". And when it was time for him to go, he made the greatest showbiz exit since the late great and extremely funny Tommy Cooper.

NICK'S TOP FIVE DAVID BOWIE TRACKS

1. "Lady Grinning Soul"
2. "John, I'm Only Dancing"
3. "Black Star"
4. "Aladdin Sane"
5. "Where Are We Now?"

Love on ya starman x.

Now, I don't wanna go on and on about all the musicians who passed that year, because I'd be here all fucking day, but I do think Prince deserves a special mention. I fell in love with him in 1979 when I heard "I Wanna Be Your Lover" in a Ruislip disco.

I saw Prince as Marc Bolan's new-age, funk, soul, brother. If you check out "Cream", it sounds just like "Get It On", dressed up in the emperor's new clothes.

My friend, Charles Reeves, had just come back from a month-long tour with Prince, doing his front of house sound. He told me a few stories of the Purple One's behaviour that didn't surprise me at all. The man was a master craftsman, and I think a little (or large) bit of eccentricity goes with the territory.

NICK'S TOP FIVE PRINCE TRACKS

1. "Sign Of The Times"
2. "I Wanna Be Your Lover"
3. "Paisley Park"
4. "When You Were Mine"
5. "1999"

For me, it was business as usual, which meant weekly recording sessions for an album of bluebeat music I was planning to release, and doing the odd show here and there. Then the gods dealt a blow that I don't think I will ever get over.

The last time I saw Al Fletcher was at a gig we played together in Ipswich. The day went something like this...

Al arrives to take me to the show.

Al comes up to my flat and fixes my bathroom plug.

Al drives me to the gig.

Al rams his car into my legs at a service station.
Al (as always) gives a fantastic performance.
Al drives a very pissed Nick home.
Al gives Nick a big hug and says goodbye.
And that was the last time I saw him.

A couple of weeks later, his wife Rebecca rang me and her first words were: "There's no easy way to say this, but…"

She went on to tell me that Al was on a life-support system after developing a fever. We later found out it was due to the extremely aggressive, and life-threatening condition, sepsis.

When I arrived at the hospital I was asked to chat to him about things personal to us.

Which of course I did, but as I looked at him lying there all I wanted to do was hug him and I'm not ashamed to say when I left the room I cried like a little kid.

"You stay a little while and then you're gone"

Over the next week I visited him most days, hoping at some point he'd open his eyes and give me one of his beautiful smiles, but he never did, and it wasn't long before I got the call I was dreading, telling me they were gonna pull the plug on him, and when they did it only took a couple of minutes before it was all over.

How the fuck did it happen?

Al was a fit man. I mean, you have to be to play the drums!

He was also ten years younger than me; yeah he liked a session or two, but there was no way he should've left us that early.

And so, I did what I always do when I want to release my pain… I wrote a song for him, and went straight into the studio to record it.

The result was "My Beautiful Friend". I sent the song to his wife Bex, who played it to Al's mum, and this resulted in them wanting me to sing it at his funeral which I considered the ultimate honour; although at that moment I think I'd rather have been in the back row blubbing away like a good 'un.

But a man's gotta do what a man etc, etc. And so, while my mate was lying in a wicker-coffin within touching distance of me I sang for him like I'd never sung before and since this was also gonna be our last ever performance together, I thought we'd do what we always did on stage…

Get the people to singalong with us.

It was the hardest gig I've ever had to do.

Al had a beautiful humanist service, where lots of people, including myself, said a lot of nice things about him. I even managed a smile when "Jet" from "Wings Over America" (edited a few days before by Steve Crittall) filled the crematorium, and when it was all over after the hugs and kisses, I went home feeling empty knowing that I'd never see my mate again..

I understand it's all part of the game, but sometimes it's so hard to accept. Everyone I love is going to die.

I think about you every day mate x.

Cards on the table, I never felt like gigging much after Al passed.

It's not so bad when I go abroad, because Al was never gonna be there, but back home, although I've been lucky enough to have good drummers on the firm who are also great guys, like Rob Coates, they would be the first to admit they're not my beautiful friend.

I miss the whole Al package, not just his incredible drumming ability; I'm talking about driving to shows together talking absolute cobblers, inventing sketches for comedy shows that would only ever see the light of day in his car. The last one we came up with was about a Bowie obsessive, who worked as an undertaker. It was fucking funny and kept us amused for hours on the road.

Al, I hope we'll meet again one day, but not too soon eh mate! x

So, that's two friends of mine, both drummers I loved dearly, that I had to say goodbye to in 2016. It really was a cunt of a year. What else have you got lined up for us then?

Well, in September, it was Prince Buster's turn to get heaven dancing.

The Prince departed hadn't been in good health since 2009, when he had suffered a stroke leaving him unable to walk, and in a selfish way, I'm glad I hadn't seen him since then, because the memory I want is of a strong powerful man, who I looked up to and was proud to have as a friend. I still treasure the time I got to spend with him, especially the laughs we had at his house in Miami.

Buster, thanks for allowing me into your life x.

NICK'S TOP FIVE PRINCE BUSTER TRACKS

1. **"The Virgin"**
2. **"The 10 Commandments Of Man"**
3. **"One Step Beyond"**
4. **"Hard Man Fe Dead"**
5. **"Bald Head Pum Pum"**

But it wasn't all doom and gloom (thank fuck I can hear you say), because in October I was invited by Jose Olan to come and guest with his band Out Of Control Army on four shows in Mexico, with the highlight being The Non-Stop Ska Festival in Mexico City.

We warmed up for the big one by playing two shows in Monterrey, which turned out to be a very warm, beautiful and friendly place. Although the people looking after me told me not to walk the streets on my own I didn't pay any attention to them because one of the little pleasures I enjoy when I'm out touring, whether it's Monterrey or Macclesfield, has always been to get out on the streets, even if it's just for an hour, and see a few things I'm not going to see back home.

The first gig was at Café Iguana, a club that had recently been decorated with bullet holes from a gangland drug related incident. The second was at a slightly smaller festival than Non-Stop, but it was no less fun to do. I find Mexican audiences warm and responsive, and on 15th October 2016 there were thirteen thousand of them making me feel me like a King that night.

For the first time ever, I let someone else (Jose) choose my set, which is why I performed "Skinhead Love Affair" and "My Girl Lollipop" and boy did Jose get it right, because the crowd went fucking mental for those songs and I went mental for the crowd, giving them every ounce of whatever it is I've got; and they loved it.

I tell you what was a strange though, sharing a stage with The Selecter.

Don't get me wrong, those days were now a distant memory for me.

Today, the band are a completely different proposition to the one I was a part of and to be honest, I think they're a lot better than we ever were… they just don't have me!

I went out front to see their set, but didn't get a chance to watch them because for the hour they were on stage, I was too busy shaking hands, signing autographs, and posing for pictures with Mr and Mrs Punter. It's a wonderful thing to be able to get that kind of reaction from an audience even if I did wanna watch the band, but from what I saw it kicked bottom!

After the show, I got hammered with my old pal Jorge from Tijuana No! and a couple of guys from Richie Ramone's band, in the fuck-off five-star hotel we were all staying in. It was the perfect end to a perfect day. However, I'd forgotten that I had a little club show to do the following night, which ended up being a bit of a struggle for me throat wise; but the crowd didn't seem to notice, so who gives a fuck!

I will treasure the memory of that tour for the rest of my days.

Why?

Because it was me they wanted, not an ex-member of Bad Manners or The Selecter. Little old me. And that's what I've been working towards for all these years.

"Follow every rainbow till you find your dream"

At the tail end of the year I released two albums in two months, and they couldn't have been more different.

"The Beat is Blue" was a kind of concept album featuring a soundtrack of bluebeat, blues and psychedelia. It was aimed at trying to paint a musical picture of what I thought a typical night out at a Mayfair discotheque would be like in 1968. Originally, I had the idea of having dialogue in between each track of a guy trying to pull a girl; but in the end, I fucked it off because I thought it might end up sounding like a poor relation of Sham 69's "That's Life" album.

"This Babylon" was a much more eclectic piece of work, taking in elements of dancehall, hip hop, reggae and funk. Listen to what I consider to be the album's highlight: "Move Me, Groove Me, Touch Me, Hold Me, Soothe Me", and you will hear one of the most danceable tracks I've ever made.

Oh, and I mustn't forget to mention my end of year single "2016".

I didn't use the word cunt just for a little shock value to try and sell the single, or to show the world a new low in my songwriting abilities. It just really was the best way to accurately describe my (and a lot of other people's) feelings on that horrible year. I tried a lot of other words, but none fitted as well as the C word.

I know "2016" is a short chapter but I just felt that like "(I Wish It Was) 1973" and "Girl At The Roxy", it was a year that deserved to have a chapter all of its own, and although I hope there won't be too many more years like it in the future, I somehow think the world's got a different agenda in store for us.

MAY YOUR GOD GO WITH YOU

Those endless nights,
On sleepless flights,
To be near you,
May your god go with you.

Through heavy rain,
And heart again,
Just to see you,
May your god go with you.

There'll come a time,
There'll come a day,
When we will fly,
We'll fly away,
Until we do,
We'll be with you,
And when you're dreaming,
May your god go with you.

Well, that's about it, but before I go there is something I haven't talked about in this book and that's the most important thing in my life (yes, even more important than music) and that's my family.

No not Mum, Dad and Richard, but my own family.

I have an extremely caring and loving wife, to whom I would like to point out, that all the stuff concerning female company from my Manners and Selecter days, happened while we were, as they say on the Jeremy Kyle show, 'on a break'.

She fucked off and left me in the late 80s and I don't blame her one little bit, because I had started to act like a complete and utter cunt. Thankfully, we got back together in the mid 90s and ever since then, I have been one act of sexual goodness.

And then there are my two wonderful children, who have given me four beautiful grandchildren.

There's not a day goes by that I don't speak to my daughter, who I'm sure wouldn't mind me telling you, has always been a little bit of a Daddy's Girl.

It's a bit harder with my boy, because he emigrated to Canada a few years ago, but we 'Skype' each other every week, and me and the missus go over there to visit him and his family on a regular basis.

Before he deserted his heartbroken parents, he bought us a present and his name is Dandy. Anyone who's a Facebook friend of mine will know all about Dandy, due to the ridiculous amount of pictures I post of this beautiful King Charles Cavalier.

You must know that old expression 'Man's best friend', well, that's what Dandy is to me.

A lot of my life used to be spent looking for eight-balls at gigs, but these days it's more like dog balls in park bushes, and I wouldn't have it any other way.

I don't get to see my brother as much as I'd like to these days, mainly because we just never seem to be available at the same time to enable us to hook up, but he is always in my thoughts.

What else...

Well, West Brom are still under/over achieving in the premiership and I'd like to say thanks to the people all over the world who've supported me and my music, and give a 'big up' (see I can be modern!) to Paul Miller, Ian Morris and Ruth Williams for shall we say their 'technical help' with this book. I can't tell you how much it means to me.

And as for me...

It's been forty years since I played my first professional gig and I'm still chasing my musical dream, although as time marches on I'm not quite sure what that even means any more. I think if I ever did have my dream in the palm of my hand, I would probably just move the goalposts and keep searching for something else that is out of my reach. I have finally realised that that's just the way I am. At least I no longer get those 'black dog' feelings, wondering why I'm not more successful than I am. Thankfully, I came to terms with that a few years ago, when I concluded that maybe I just wasn't in the right place at the right time. I'm not complaining, I know I've done better than some, and not as well as others.

I still gig, and will do until the day life finally gives me the elbow. I keep to the promise I made to myself a few years ago: to always keep it fresh and interesting. Which is why, in the last few weeks I've performed in:

- **A schoolhouse in the back streets of Barnsley**
- **A show on top of a mountain in southern Italy**
- **A tent at an acoustic weekender**
- **A ska festival in Costa Rica**

Yeah, you heard right... Costa Rica baby!

I've just got back, and hand on heart I can only describe the experience as being one of the most memorable of my life. It was another one of those countries that I never thought I'd get the chance of visiting. When I got the call to invite me over I couldn't believe it. The thing that turned me into a reggae Victor Meldrew was when the promoter told me I would be the first British ska man to ever perform there.

Besides being a fucking beautiful place, the locals really do love their ska and reggae. At the show, they gave me a gift of a night that I will never forget. On my last day there, I was invited by a ska-core band, Red Numbers, to guest on a track of theirs. I was familiar with the genre, and it's never been my kind of thing, but I accepted their offer. I really enjoyed doing my bit on their track, which is why I also agreed to appear in their promo video with them ... on a motorbike!

As far as recording goes, I'm just putting the finishing touches to a brand new King Hammond album, "Diggin' Love... Ditchin' Hate", which is without doubt the King's finest effort to date. The tracks "Out Of Control" and "Protest Song" have a theme of 'What the fuck's happening to the world?' while on "I Need An Ace" and "This Babylon", it's more of a case of 'What the fuck's happening to me?'.

"To say the things he really feels and not the words of one who kneels."

I think I'm gonna leave you with this...

Writing this book has been a very emotional experience for me. I've done it the only way I know how, and that's honestly and in my own voice.

Obviously, there are hundreds of other stories that I could have included, but as I wrote each chapter I went for whichever story sprung to mind first, because that must be what best defines that period of my life.

And finally, ...

The world has always been a bit of a scary place, but these days it really does feel like the lunatics have taken over the asylum.

At least, on a personal note, I'm cleaner and happier than I have been in years.

It's just a shame that it's taken me so long to get there. X

Mans best friend x

JUDGEMENT DAY

I've been pleasure,
I've been pain,
I've been the dog out in the rain.

I've been shallow,
I've been deep,
I've been the dark end of the street.

But what am I gonna do on Judgement day,
What am I gonna do on judgement day,
On judgement day.

But the thing that's killing me is the endless mystery

I've been stupid,
I've been smart,
I've been the guy who can break your heart.

I've been shallow,
I've been deep,
I've been dancing while the speed freak sleeps.

But what am I gonna do on judgement day,
What am I gonna do on judgement day,
On judgement day.

But the thing that's killing me is the endless mystery

Brian Smith (Friend and Waster)

It would be impossible for me to say anything good about Nick that he hasn't already said a million times before, which is just one of the reasons why I think he's been very fortunate to be able to write a book about the one subject he's truly obsessed by.

I think it should be a good read because it's fair to say that he's tried to live his life in the same manner as some of the great men I know he admires...

Caligula, Nero, Machiavelli and Stalin.

We were both born at the Bearstead Memorial Hospital in Stoke Newington.

It's no longer there so don't look for it, because when you find it you'll see that it doesn't exist.

The two of us were in adjoining cots and even at that early age I can remember Nick saying to me, "Don't worry, we're gonna make it out of here."

Although I could be mistaken.

The Bearstead's policy was for all babies to be kept together in one large industrial sized crèche and on more than one occasion some parents would try and take advantage of this situation and swap their children for ones they considered better.

I don't know if this happened to Nick but he remains proud of his Pakistani heritage.

We were in quite a few bands together when we were younger.

In 'The Livid' we had some songs we thought showed promise but when we went into the studio to record them Nick's unique individual style caused quite a few problems within the band.

At one point on the tape, you can clearly hear the engineer's voice say "That's fine lads but do we really need the cannon?"

"We told him not to bring it."

It was ultimatum time. We all knew the band couldn't carry on after a heated argument like that and Nick stormed out of the studio leaving his cannon behind.

Still, we met up a bit later and had a right good laugh about it, and there were a lot of laughs to be had back then because Nick was always full of comic invention. I was close to tears the first time I saw him lying between two slices of bread performing his now celebrated cheese sandwich impersonation, and then there was his hilarious soup routine where he talked about Tomato, Vegetable, Chicken and Oxtail being the classic soups and how people were always trying to get the other soups promoted and....

Well, I suppose you had to have been there.

Many people have spoken about Nick being restless and discontented.

He once asked me, "Do you think I'm restless and discontented?"

"No."

"What about my dark moods?"

"I haven't seen any."

"Well, you must be blind then because everyone else has."

Nick was a natural risk taker who seemed to get high on danger.

I remember my mother saying, "Have you spoken to that Nick? Well when you do, tell him we want our cushions back."

Of course, he denied it.

It wasn't all fun and laughs though.

When we were 15 we went on a camping holiday to Wales where for a prank we decided to cause an avalanche, but the joke backfired on us because we became trapped in a network of caves of which there seemed to be no way out for us and we vowed that if we ever managed to escape we would one day finger a girl together.

After leaving school Nick had grand dreams but harboured inner doubts.

"I could swim the channel," he said, "but I'd only frighten the fish, especially if I played my accordion."

"That's all very well Mr Welsh, but have you done any paid work in the last 14 days?" replied the woman behind the counter at the Unemployment Benefit Office.

Some of Nick's behaviour was quite baffling and remains so to this day.

For instance, he believes it's okay to indecently expose himself to a woman if she has impaired vision and described himself as an 'ethical sex offender' when he appeared in court for committing the offence.

And why did he steal a limbless man and plant him in someone's garden?

"I thought he would grow back," he said with his customary childish reasoning.

Imagine that sinking feeling you get when you're told you're about to meet a real "larger than life character" well let me tell you, that certainly wouldn't be the case if you were to see him when he's holding court in his Islington local.

I recently went along to meet him there, and with Nick in party mood I have to say it really was a non-stop roller coaster of an evening.

"Has he done the cheese sandwich impersonation?" said a latecomer.

"Yeah, he's done that."

"What about the…."

"Yeah and all the soup stuff."

And that was the last time I saw Nick. (There probably should be some kind of film montage thing here, maybe a little sentimental music over it, that kind of thing, you know "The Way We Were" or something like that; this is for a documentary right?)

A few weeks ago the phone rang, it was Nick. Somehow, I knew it would be.

"Brian, it's about those cushions."

Researched from Nickipedia.

Paul Williams (Specialized)

I'd been involved in the ska scene for about ten years promoting ska and reggae gigs in the north of England when I decided to travel down to London for a ska festival at the Sir George Robey pub in Finsbury Park.

Now back then the scene was for want of a better word 'underground' but it did spawn some great new bands like Maroon Town and Potato 5 and you still had a few legendary reggae stalwarts like Rico Rodriguez and Laurel Aitken plying their trade on the circuit, but it was at this festival that I first slapped my eyes on a confident young buck…

Nick Welsh.

He was playing bass in the newly reformed Selecter, and having a big 2-Tone name back up and running was a real buzz for all us fans, because this was before the Madness reformation at Madstock and as for the idea of ever seeing The Specials back together again, well, you'd have to be a nutter to ever think that was gonna happen.

Anyway it was a cracking weekend and The Selecter were absolutely brilliant.

I couldn't believe I had Pauline Black and Neol Davies standing right in front of me, backed by a band including ex-Bad Manners keyboardist Martin Stewart, drummer Perry Melius and of course Mr Welsh.

Now although Nick wasn't an original Manners member he had been a key figure in the bands late 80s resurgence and responsible for the majority of the songs on their brilliant "Return Of The Ugly" album that I'd bought and played to death, and that's exactly what I wanted to tell him when I saw him standing at the bar having a well earned drink after the gig. When I eventually got my chance to do so all that came out of my mouth was a load of old bollocks but he was still very gracious towards me.

Now I don't think for one moment he'll remember signing my ticket that night, but he did, and as we chatted my impression was that he was a very funny man, although it has to be said he did have a bit of a swagger about him which is something us from the north regard as being part and parcel of being an archetypal 'gobby cockney'.

I warmed to him immediately, although his constant jokes about northerners eating everything with gravy did make me want to push him into a huge vat of the stuff.

I'd just written a book about The Specials and now I wanted to do something similar on The Selecter, and so a few days later I rang Nick to ask him about it (he must have given me his number) and I'm glad to say that he was more than happy to help, and offered to discuss his involvement with the reformed band at his home in Islington the following Saturday, which by a strange piece of luck coincided with The Selecter doing a show at the Mean Fiddler in Harlesden.

Nicks place was well cool with huge gig posters on the walls and great retro furniture (I'm sure he had a leopard skin print sofa?) in every room.

He was on top form that day telling me stories that frankly were unprintable…

I can't remember laughing that much in years.

The show that night proved one thing to me: just like when he was in Bad Manners, he was obviously (along with Pauline) the driving force in this 90s version of The Selecter, making everything tick over.

The icing on the cake was when Nick invited my childhood hero John Bradbury (who was now playing drums for the band) to come over and join us to add his thoughts. I also talked to Pauline and Gaps that night but because Nick, Martin and John had already got me in stitches (and drunk) it became a totally pointless exercise and it was that evening me and Nick became firm friends.

I've always admired Nick's talent as a songwriter, producer and arranger so much that in my opinion since he left Bad Manners and The Selecter I don't think either have made a decent record, which is a very sad state of affairs; but as I said that's only my opinion.

After leaving The Selecter he went on to form his own band Skaville UK who I had the pleasure of putting on a couple of times in York and it was always a brilliant night.

I know sometimes people see Nick as a larger than life character and maybe in some respects he is but I'm lucky to say that I know the real Nick.

He is a man who will go out of his way to help anyone. He is a man with a big heart and a tremendous generosity. And then there is the work he does for Specialized.

What's Specialized?

Specialized is a charitable music project I started in 2010 with the aim of raising money and awareness for The Teenage Cancer Trust.

In life you can sometimes have something people call a 'lightbulb moment' and mine was to put together an album of today's ska and reggae artists covering Specials songs that I wanted to call "Specialized – A Modern Take On Specials Classics" with the aim of raising money for the TCT.

I started calling around some of the bands I knew to see if they would be interested in donating their time and talent although to be honest I didn't expect to get too much joy from my cold calling, but do you know what? Musicians can be very warm hearted people and pretty soon I had enough artists offering their services to make a six CD album!

Right from the start Nick was at the top of my 'wants' list and was extremely excited to see what he would do with "Friday Night Saturday Morning", the song he chose to do, and what a brilliant version it turned out to be. Of course it was no surprise to me because the one thing I know about Nick is that he will never let you down, his trademark is professionalism and he will never do anything half hearted.

Specialized takes a lot of time out of the lives of people involved in it but as busy as he is the man always seems to be there for us, and let me tell you support like that is priceless.

He has gone on to become an ambassador for the charity spreading the word wherever he goes and it's through his connections in the music industry that we managed to get former Specials guitarist Roddy Byers and Stiff Little Fingers frontman Jake Burns to jump aboard to help record "Get Specialized!" Nick's song that has gone on to become Specialized's anthem.

People tend to see him as King Hammond more than Nick Welsh but what I will say to you is that this man has worked with some of the biggest names the ska and reggae scene has ever brought us. Prince Buster, Laurel Aitken, Rico Rodriguez, Dave Barker, Susan Cadogan, Judge Dread & Lee 'Scratch' Perry are just some of the legends who have chosen to work with him which shows you how highly he is thought of and respected as a musician.

For Christ's sake he's won a Grammy Award!!!

He's an altruistic man, he's a caring man

And I love him dearly.

Jake Burns (Stiff Little Fingers)

I met Nick on the first "3 Men & Black" tour in 2001. Of all the musicians involved he was the only one I hadn't previously met and yet by the end of it he was definitely the one I was closest to. We bonded over a shared love of bad comedy programmes, average football teams and a passion for the music we played and listened to.

Nick is undoubtedly one of the most talented people I've been lucky enough to know and the fact he's not a household name is quite frankly a matter of national shame.

I'm constantly amazed, not just at the quantity of his output, but the quality of it.

Melodies seem to fall effortlessly from him and if I'm being honest that makes me more than a little bit jealous, and if I also add that he's one of the funniest and most genuine guys I know, well, I really should hate him but it's impossible to.

I've been helpless with laughter on many a late-night drink up with Nick telling me some of his outrageous stories and so now I'm looking forward to reading a few more in this book.

Nick I hope I have many more nights spent in the company of a true gent; even though you do always sting me for a double brandy to my humble pint!!

Cheers mate.

Jennie Matthias (Belle Stars)

I first met Nick properly in the early 90s not long after my boyfriend had passed away and he recently reminded me that it was backstage at a Trojans gig in Camden Town, which jogged my memory into remembering how we'd talked that night about the pain of having someone close to you departing this earth far too soon.

Our friendship then escalated over a few after show drinks when we discovered a mutual love of glam rock, ska and soul music and these were the influences we used when we started writing songs together a few weeks later.

These creative sessions would usually start off with us singing old Donovan, T.Rex or Mott The Hoople songs over a cup of tea and end up a few hours later with a finished song of our own under our belts, many of which ended up on the two Big 5 albums "Popskatic" and "In Yer Face".

I think it's safe to say most band's stories come from when they are 'on the road' and during the short but exciting time Big 5 were together we did our fair amount of that, performing all over Europe, but it was a show on our doorstep at The Robey in Finsbury Park that makes me smile the most. It was the first time my dad had ever come to see me perform and on this occasion the band were joined by our good friend the legendary trombonist Rico Rodríguez.

After introducing a very respectful Nick (I like that) to him Dad spotted Rico sitting on his own in the corner of the dressing room and went over to join him and that was it...

For the rest of the evening me and Nick sat watching the two of them laughing at each other's stories about their early life in Jamaica and in the end we just left them to it.

Another funny time was when we were asked to play at a gay club in London, which was something neither of us had done before. A few weeks before the show the promoter asked me to do an interview with a gay magazine to help promotion for the gig and when the reporter asked me if any of our band were gay I immediately put Nick's name forward.

You should have seen his face when I told him, it was priceless, and on the night of the show he spent most of the time looking sheepishly over his shoulder. It was so funny.

Another memorable show we did together was in 2007 when I guested with his band Skaville UK at the Guildford festival in front of a huge audience who totally submitted to our ska and reggae sounds, and when we received some exceptional write ups from the dailies the next day I was so happy to see Nick sporting the proudest look I'd seen him have in a long, long time.

As I said before it's on the road where you gain experiences that years later make great fodder for nostalgic tour bus chat and Nick would always be first in line to share his memories. Nick's storytelling is legendary in ska and reggae circles, his fast wit providing musicians with the most belly laughs I've ever witnessed, although there were times (depending on his mood) where some of his stories were a little 'close to the bone' and were obviously being told with the intention of just shocking anyone within earshot, but thankfully those anecdotes were always outweighed by his more tasteful reminisces.

I have enough fond memories of Nick to fill up a book of my own!

There have been days that have begun with us in a tight spot where the only solution to get us out of it was to simply just do a runner but would then end up with us partying in some club after playing another one of our wild gigs.

Nick is an extremely accomplished musician often playing every instrument on his little masterpieces, and let me tell you when he plays the bass, he doesn't just play it, he owns it. This is all backed up with a natural proclivity of creating the catchiest melodies to accompany those bass lines of his perfectly.

Our relationship has been a long one and a learning process for both of us, sometimes emotional but always fun which is why in 2017 we are still working together.

Nick has added greatly to my life's journey in a myriad of ways and for that I am forever grateful.

Jen xx

Garry Bushell (Journalist)

What's the best way to describe Nick Welsh?

Well, if Judge Dread had knocked up Millie Small in Arthur Daley's lock-up, he would probably have been the result.

Nick is one of the most prolific ska musicians of all time, a brilliant songwriter and one of the scene's funniest characters.

An afternoon spent with him in some West End boozer is like being transported back to a long lost England where *Carry On* films still reign supreme, Desmond Dekker is Number One and *The Sweeney* bang up 'blaggers' and 'wrong 'uns' with a passion that makes AC-12 look like hapless amateurs.

Much of the best ska & reggae music released in Britain over the last few decades will have his fingerprints on it.

Nick has worked with and produced such A-list artists as Prince Buster, Laurel Aitken, Dave Barker, Susan Cadogan, Rico Rodriguez, Alex 'Judge Dread' Hughes and the legendary Lee 'Scratch' Perry on his Grammy Award winning album "Jamaican ET".

He was also the bassist and songwriter in Bad Manners and The Selecter helping to shepherd both bands' post 2-Tone careers by bequeathing them with gems like "Skaville UK", "Cruel Brittania" and "Skinhead Love Affair".

As King Hammond, he towers over the ska scene like a bluebeat Harold Shand, knocking out top notch quality street anthems that stick in your nut from the very first time you hear them; and if you don't believe me go and check out "The Rudest Girl In Town", "Rocking On Ridley Road" and "Riot In London Town".

Oh, and a word of warning…

Don't stray too far from the khazi while reading this hilarious anecdote-packed autobiography because I guarantee you that you will piss yourself on every page.

Roddy 'Radiation' Byres (The Specials)

The first time I met Nick was in Hollywood in the mid 90s while I was there recording The Specials MK2 album "Guilty Until Proven Innocent" at a studio in Van Nuys.

We'd been hard at it without a break for a few weeks and so when we heard The Selecter were in town playing The House Of Blues we all downed tools and went out on a Specials school outing!

I remember taking over their dressing room which put the band's keyboard player Martin out a little bit because I helped myself to all the beers in their fridge.

Nick seemed a bit reserved but he recently told me that he was just off his face and to be honest I probably didn't notice because we were partying pretty hard too!

A few years later we worked together as part of the 'Two-Tone Collective' alongside Pauline Black, Ranking Roger, Neville Staple and

301

Gappa Hendrickson which was always great fun and I still play with Nick today doing guest spots at his King Hammond & The Rude Boy Mafia shows.

Nick's always a fun guy to be with and a great pal too...

Well he must be because he always lets me crash at his flat every time I'm in London!

Wendy Jane Bridger (The Rude Girl Mafia)

I'm not a natural writer and so in the hope that it would give me the necessary literary inspiration I needed to write this piece I decided to go to the nearest kebab shop for some chips and gravy but for fuck's sake they didn't even know what gravy was.

Hurry up Brexit eh?

The first time I spoke to Nick I was working as a carer when he rang me to arrange an amp share for a gig I was doing with my band The Skanx supporting his mighty Skaville UK. We had a nice chat but unfortunately during the middle of it the person I was looking after started screaming at the top of his lungs and so I walked away from our conversation thinking that maybe Nick thought I was totally insane, but luckily it turned out that he didn't mind at all.

From the moment I joined The Rude Boy Mafia I felt at home even though I have to say that sometimes Nick would say some slightly inappropriate things onstage which is why I'd like to take this opportunity to let him know that now I've reached the grand old age of thirty two I think his onstage line of "It's her birthday tomorrow, she's gonna be fifteen" is getting a little bit tired.

Although to be fair to him it's not as 'rapey' as it used to be.

I love travelling the country with Nick because it's always such great fun to be with him.

One gig memory that sticks out in my mind was the time we were booked to play at a ska weekender in a holiday park.

When we arrived at our caravan/dressing room we found Nick, and our sorely missed drummer Al, indulging in the kind of behaviour you'd expect from a couple of rock stars...

Watching the Jeremy Kyle show laughing their heads off while eating Heinz tinned soup and ravioli!

Nick is the best friend a girl could ever ask for and will always be on hand to let me know if my Bristols have gotten any bigger and for that alone I will always be his little bit of 'Penge Minge' x

Dave Wakeling (The Beat)

Off the cuff, straight from the hip,
Always genuine, never flip,
If you want the real thing, well this is it,
Go and listen to Nick Welsh and give it some stick x

Sue Golding (Bolanite)

The first time I met Nick was outside the offices of Marc Bolan in Bond Street, London in 1975.

I used to bunk off school with my friend Ollie and go there in the hope of seeing or even better meeting Marc, which was something that happened many times, and it was on one of those occasions that we met Nick who was doing exactly the same thing as us. From that first day we became friends and partners in crime (well partners in bunking off school anyway).

We were all of a similar age and I suppose that's why when we'd see all the older girls who were also hanging around outside Marc's office that we never really had much to do with them because we were a tight little gang of three.

The hours would fly by with Nick keeping us entertained with his fantastic sense of humour, and the only problem with our friendship was that we were all from different areas of London. Ollie and me were south London girls and he was from north London which made it difficult for us to meet up other than at the office and get this...

Nick was the only one of the trio who had a telephone in his house which is why I can remember many evenings spent in our local phone box ringing him up and asking him to call us back (which he always did) so we could spend many hours on the blower laughing, joking and planning the next time we'd all meet up in Bond Street to see Marc.

When Marc died so tragically in 1977 it signalled the end of an era for us because the times they were a changing and Nick had started making music of his own. I guess you can say that this was the beginning of his lifelong musical career and even though we lost touch I would always think about him and wonder how he was and what he was up to.

And then out of the blue nearly thirty years later thanks to Facebook I heard from him again.

I was impressed to find how well he'd done for himself in our wilderness years and when he invited me to see him perform at a London club I felt so proud watching my long lost mate onstage in his role as King Hammond; but more importantly I was back in touch with Nick and he still makes me laugh just like he used to do all those years ago.

Long live our King x

Paul Miller (Chancer)

Nick tried to stripe me up on our first meeting by trying to knock me out a moody copy of his "The King & I" album in his second home, The King's Head, a boozer that would soon become our regular watering hole to meet up for a cuff.

Fuck me that was seven years ago.

Seven years of listening to all his shit.

Seven years of trying to teach a Chimpanzee how to do tech stuff. And I know fuck all! I just press buttons until one works, so how the hell this book ever got to the printers is a mystery to me, but at least I don't need to buy it because I've heard all his fucking stories week in week out when we are out 'on the piss' together and so although I'd like to take some of the blame you know how that old saying goes...

"There's One Born Every Minute."

And if you don't believe that then why the fuck are you reading this?

Roydon Stock (Road Manager)

I was lucky enough to go to Woodberry Down school alongside some very talented musicians, amongst them most of the members of Bad Manners who I eventually went on to work with in the role of roadie and sound engineer, but the one that sticks out most in my mind is my lifelong friend Nick Welsh who is without doubt one of the most versatile musicians I have ever known, a multi-instrumentalist and a wonderful songwriter.

In my opinion Nick could've been a household name, but he decided to stay true to his ska and reggae roots and remain loyal to his die-hard fans that he has all around the world who continue to support him in his incarnation of King Hammond.

Aidan Sterling (Feckin Ejits)

The first time I saw Nick Welsh he was playing bass for Buster's All Stars.

Now I could be wrong here but I'm pretty sure it was at the Dublin Castle but what I can remember is thinking "Fucking hell that geezer can play the bass".

I'm pretty sure our paths had crossed sometime before during that third wave ska revival of the late 80s but a lot of those nights for me were lost at the bottom of a bottle of Newcastle Brown and a haze of Moroccan black. I'd seen him many times giving it plenty onstage with Bad Manners and also my least favourite ska band The Selecter but it wasn't until one night when I was backstage with him drinking brandy and rum in the company of Rico and Prince Buster that I really got a proper insight into the man.

On first meeting I don't always think Nick comes over as the clued up decent man he is, in fact my first impression was that he came over as a bit too cocky and sure of himself, so much in fact that I was more inclined to wanna chin him than buy the fecker a drink!

But all these years later I now know…

1. What a gifted musician and writer he is particularly in his persona of King Hammond playing skinhead reggae as well as anything that was released back in 69 and certainly better than any of the live acts I've seen recently and fuck me I've seen a few.

2. How ska and reggae is in his blood and unlike so many artists who have turned their backs on the genre Nick has stuck to it.

3. And last but not least what a big heart the man has, always generous with his time, advice and friendship.

In my book Nick Welsh is a 'Ska Man' unequalled in modern times.

Ian Taylor (Writer)

Nick first came to my attention during the late 80s ska revival when he was bossing it with Bad Manners providing the band with some of the best material they'd had in a long time.

Why?

Because he had the innate sense of what made Manners tick and was able to tap into the group's DNA and produce music that was perfect for the band.

He also pulled off the same trick a few years later when he helped shape (along with Pauline Black) The Selecter's revival of the early 90s.

But it's Nick's own music that I really find fascinating.

It doesn't matter if I'm listening to his skinhead reggae alter ego King Hammond or one of those deep and introspective acoustic tracks that he puts out under his own name, the music will always come out of leftfield and sweep you up into a new and different world.

Over the years Nick has worked his magic in and on more bands and projects than I have fingers and toes to count.

In the last decade alone he's released at least a dozen albums while still finding the time to tour all over the world, and throughout it all has remained a man of the people, a straight shooter with a heart as big as his talent. For ska and reggae lovers everywhere he is undoubtedly and will continue to be the King.

Ian Morris (Fan)

I first became aware of Nick in the early 90s during his time with The Selecter but I can also remember a few years before in 1989 when a friend of mine played me "Revolution 70" an album by someone called King Hammond, and although I really loved it for some strange reason I never bought it (after many years of looking I finally managed to get a copy on eBay). It wasn't until 1992 when the "Blow Your Mind" CD was released that I finally managed to get some King Hammond music of my own but when I did it was never out of my CD player.

I wanted to find out more about him but in those days there was no internet where you can just type in a name and find out everything about an artist and so the King disappeared off my radar and it wasn't until 10 years later that I found out that the reggae royalty behind the music was none other than Nick Welsh.

In 2007 Skaville UK released their debut album "1973" and it was this record that relighted my interest in ska music, but I had to wait a year after its release before I got the chance to see the band in action. When I did two things stood out for me: their great songs and Nick's extremely bright bleached blonde hair!

306

He came to Middlesbrough in 2014 to perform his one man show "The Life And Times Of A Ska Man" and I first had the pleasure of meeting and chatting with him properly. It was also the first time that my wife Denise got to witness his musical talents in the flesh after which she immediately became an instant fan.

Since then we have followed Nick all over the country and we've never left a show disappointed and I'm proud to say that over the years the three of us have become friends.

Nick is one of the most talented artists in ska and reggae, a brilliant songwriter and performer, but away from the limelight he really is a truly wonderful and genuine man.

Tim Wells (Poet)

Nick Welsh and I are both big reggae fans.

The two of us are totally obsessed with 70s British horror films and I think it's fair to say that *Dracula AD1972* is as big an inspiration to Nick's early King Hammond records as someone like Lee Perry.

Nick recorded his songs as if they were throwaway reggae singles that you'd first hear in Ridley Road market in 1974 and it was this sound that formed the backbone of his "Revolution 70" album.

And then there were the gigs.

The early shows were basically Nick singing over backing tapes with me and Steve Friel providing dodgy backing vocals while throwing in some equally dodgy kung fu bootboy moves. But fuck me it was great fun.

There was one gig we did in Brighton where Nick, after an afternoon's fun and games with some Richard he'd pulled in a boozer, overslept and so it was left to yours truly to take to the stage on my own and being well pissed I spent the whole of the first two songs styling it out with patter like…

"Ladies free before 11."

"No jeans, no trainers."

Eventually when Nick arrived at the venue he took to the stage and apologised to the packed-out audience by way of giving them some piss poor excuse that he was sorry but he'd been 'resting' due to all the touring he'd recently been doing which they thankfully swallowed and he went on to save the show; and I guess that's the way it's always been for the king.

307

Allan Finnie (Fan)

After spending a few years of gigging anywhere they could just to pay off a huge tax bill Bad Manners made a sensational comeback in the late 80s with a new energy and more importantly some great new songs and the man behind this was Nick Welsh who in just eighteen months took the band from being 'yesterday's men' to the front of a tabloid predicted 'Ska Revival'.

With an amalgam of original Manners members alongside members of the recently formed Buster's All Stars the new and improved Manners began selling out venues up and down the country, thrilling fans old and new while at the same time releasing some of the best material the band had done since the early 80s.

Who can forget the magnificent "Eat The Beat" album that morphed into the blistering "Return Of The Ugly" with a brand new western inspired sleeve courtesy of Steve Friel.

The atmosphere at their gigs made electricity seem like candle light, especially at the ones I went to at Dingwalls, Electric Ballroom and numerous others in London. Unfortunately a serious intake of lager has clouded my memory of their names!

Student shows were also home to scenes of absolute mayhem as this 17 year old skinhead will testify to after being kicked out of a packed Reading University for invading the stage during one particularly lively Manners performance.

And then there was the gig on the back of a lorry in Clerkenwell and I'll never forget the secret show they did in a tiny pub in Islington as a 'warm up' for another one of their US tours where they were billed as 'The Psychedelic Skinheads'.

I went to the gig after losing an arm and leg on a dead cert at Kempton Park and so I was more than happy to bump into a certain bass player who, after I'd told him my story, put me and ten of my friends on the guest list just so we could hear them play "Non Shrewd".

Great days.

Steven Friel (Artist)

I was with Nick the day he went to meet Rupie Edwards at his record stall in Ridley Road market for the first time and believe it or not I could see that he was visibly nervous about it, but after shaking hands with the 'skanga' man he was back to his normal self chatting away like they were lifelong friends and it wasn't long before there was talk about a future possible collaboration and phone numbers were exchanged. As we walked down Kingsland Road together I could see Nick was as pleased as punch that it had gone so well.

I'm sure this book will give you the impression that Nick is a confident and assured guy but I know him as a shy passionate reggae and glam-rock fanatic; although he's done really well on his chosen path he's still in awe of his idols in the music world and it's that paradoxical low-key approach coupled with his immense musical knowledge and undoubted talent that makes him so affable and approachable.

He's such a prolific and professional musician, songwriter and producer I think he should be hitting the big time but he insists on remaining loyal to his roots and his fans and for that we should be thankful.

Richard Girling (Fan)

Picture a cold night in a seaside town.

I'm walking towards the pier when I hear, "Oi Mate, is that a Chrissie Hynde shirt you got on?"

The voice is coming from the driver's side of a large white van and within seconds I found myself inside the vehicle chatting with a fellow fan who turns out to be Nick Welsh, front man and leader of Skaville UK, the band I'm on my way to see.

I'd seen Nick in concert many times before with Bad Manners and The Selecter but now he was centre stage with his own band playing his own songs and I'm happy to say they went down a storm with the audience that night taking the room full of dancing bodies to a temperature of near boiling point.

These days he's back in his role as King Hammond creating an amazing amount of wonderful new music and if that's your thing, then Nick Welsh is the man to look out for.

I'm proud to call him my friend and would like to thank him for taking me on a unforgettable and exciting trip on his "Memory Train"!

Andy McGowan (friend)

Despite having listened to Nick's music for more years than I care to remember I didn't actually get to meet him until 2009 at a Skaville UK gig in Camden Town and while we stood there chatting we found out that we'd grown up pretty close to each other in East/North London and had gone to a lot of the same clubs/gigs during the punk era.

The two of us had a right craic that night and to be honest, it hasn't stopped since.

We live about 20 minutes away from each other and along with Paul Miller, we still meet up whenever we can for a few beers and a good old slagging match and I always come away from these nights with sore ribs from laughing at/with Nick, as he recounts stories from his past with all the different bands he's played with, the people that he has met and the escapades that have ensued along the way.

The banter is sometimes quite brutal and often at Nick's expense but he doesn't give a fuck about the piss being taken out of him because and I know this may sound soppy but the geezer is truly one of the good guys and someone I'm proud to call a friend (even if he can be a right cunt at times Ha Ha).

Love ya matey!

Richard Wayler (Brother)

Mmm…What can I say about my brother?

Even as a child he had a passion for music.

I would often find him sitting cross legged on our bedroom floor in an almost hypnotic state staring at the records that were going round and round on the family Dansette, or lying on his bed with his head stuck inside *Disco 45* a monthly magazine he'd buy religiously to learn all the lyrics to the hit songs of the day.

And then there was Dial-A-Disc…

Now for those of you too young to remember Dial-A-Disc was a telephone service provided by the GPO that played chart records on a continuous loop. Our dad had recently put a padlock on the dial in an attempt to stop both of us using the phone but Nick found a way of 'tuning in' by tapping out the number and Dad never did find out why the phone bill was still so high!

When he was twelve or thirteen Nick told me he wanted to be a bassist and pretty soon, armed with a natural aptitude, genetically inherited musicality and determination it became apparent to everyone he was going to be a force to reckoned with, and it wasn't long before I was going to see him play with his band The Dead at the famous punk venue The Roxy in Covent Garden and ever since then he's not looked back.

I've had the pleasure and privilege of working with him as a vocalist on stage and in the studio and I have to say he's always a consummate professional, and as a musician, songwriter, producer and performer he has brought (and continues to bring) pleasure to ska and reggae music lovers all over the world.

You make me proud bruv and long may you continue to do so.

I love you x.

Me and Richard – The photo booth generation

JUST ANOTHER SONG

Here's another song I wrote for you,
A little something just to see you through,
I even wrote it in my favourite key,
And now the song belongs to you and me,
You and me.

Oh, it's just another song for you.

Here's another thing I want to say,
A little song can go a long, long way,
And don't you worry that the cupboard's bare,
I've always got a little going spare,
Going spare.

So, when you get lonely,
You know how you do,
You don't have to phone me,
'Cos here's another song for you.

Oh, it's just another song for you.

DISCOGRAPHY

All songs written by Welsh. Except where indicated *.

"2016"

"21st Century Poison Pen"

"22 Bullets From A Rude Boy Gun"

"A Man Always Wants (What A Man Can't Get)"

"Algebra" * (Welsh/Black)

"Am I Going Mad?"

"Amphetamine Rush" * (Welsh/Matthias)

"At Any Time At All"

"Baby Version"

"Baby's Got A Death Wish"

"Bad Til I Die" * (Welsh/Ska Beat City)

"Bad Dog" * (Welsh/Black)

"Bad Karma" * (Welsh/Matthias)

"Bad Man Version"

"Ballad Of A Bad Man"

"Beast Of The East"

"Beautiful World" * (Welsh/Matthias)

"Beer Garden"

"Better Days"

"Big Organ" * (Welsh/Hughes)

"Big White Lies"

"Black & White" * (Welsh/Black)

"Black Is" * (Welsh/Black)

"Black King '78"

"Black Sheep"

"Black Ska Liner" * (Welsh/Black)

"Bless You"

"Blind Leading The Blind" * (Welsh/Black)

"Blood Run Cold"

"Bluebeat Boogaloo"

"Bluebeat Christmas '64"
"Bongo Ska Fever"
"Bring Me The Head Of The Musical Grifter"
"Cactus Rock"
"California Screaming" * (Welsh/Black/Haynes)
"Can U Hear?"
"Checker Chucker"
"Chicken & Chips"
"Chocolate Whip" * (Welsh/Black)
"Christmas Time (Again)" * (Welsh/Trendle)
"Chula Vista Ska Man"
"Chutzpah!"
"Confessions Of An Organist"
"Cool Down Your Temper"
"Cruel Britannia" * (Welsh/Black)
"Cuban Missile"
"Dance Little Rude Girl Dance"
"Dancing In The Garden of Evil"
"Dave & Ansell"
"Dead Men Can't Skank" * (Welsh/Gudge)
"Die Happy" * (Welsh/Black)
"Digging My Own Grave"
"Dignity & Pride"
"Do I Love You Or…?" * (Welsh/Dakar)
"Do It Right" * (Welsh/Black)
"Don't Throw Your Toys Out Of The Pram"
"Downbeat On Upper Street"
"Dracula AD 72"
"Dub Movement #1"
"Dume Batty"
"Easy Lovin'"
"Easy Up"
"Ebbaway" * (Welsh/Dakar)
"Enter The Dragon"

"Escape From The Human Jungle"
"Everyone I Love Is Going To Die"
"Everyone's Playing Ska (Nowadays)"
"F**k Off Christmas"
"Fat Cat Splat" * (Welsh/Bushell)
"Floorshaker!"
"Forbidden Fruit"
"From Bennie Bish" * (Welsh/Dakar)
"From The Hip"
"Fuck Art Let's Dance"
"Fun In The Sun"
"Get Specialized (A Rock 'N' Roll Prayer)"
"Gimmie Some Juice"
"Gimmie Some Soul" * (Welsh/Soul Syndicate)
"Girl I Want You" (Welsh/Cotter/Ferreyra)
"(Girl) I'm Losing My Grip"
"Go Go Girl" * (Welsh/Dakar)
"Gone, Gone, Gone (Gone)" * (Welsh/Black)
"Government Man" * (Welsh/Black)
"Groovy Times"
"Hairspray" * (Welsh/Black)
"Hammond Rides Again"
"Hammond's Showdown"
"Hammond-Delic!"
"Hang My Head In Shame"
"Hate Culture"
"Hearsay" * (Welsh/Black)
"Heart & Soul"
"Heavy Science" * (Welsh/Black)
"Hey You"
"Hole In My Pocket"
"Homebound Train" * (Welsh/Black)
"Hot Skin Music"
"How Can I Win?" * (Welsh/Black)

"How Do You Get To The Palladium?"
"I Am Your King"
"I Don't Need This Shit Anymore"
"I Hope You Find What You've Been Looking For"
"I Need An Ace"
"(It's All About The) Bassline"
"I Want U" * (Welsh/Matthias)
"I'm Sorry" * (Welsh/Hughes)
"It Sucks!" * (Welsh/Matthias)
"Jacknife" * (Welsh/Barker)
"Jacuzzi"
"Jesse James" * (Welsh/Matthias)
"Jet Black Tourniquet"
"Jimmy Saville"
"Ju Ju Eyes"
"Judge Ded"
"Judgement Day"
"K.M.A."
"King Hammond Shuffle"
"King Hammond Vs The Exorcist"
"Kingston Affair" * (Welsh/Barker)
"Kingston Excursion" * (Welsh/Barker)
"Kinky Kinky"
"Kinky Version"
"Ladders" * (Welsh/Black/Haynes)
"Landlord" * (Welsh/Dakar)
"Let Me Go" * (Welsh/Dakar)
"Licks" * (Welsh/Wilson)
"Live For Today" * (Welsh/Dakar)
"Lonesome Road"
"Loonie Tune" * (Welsh/Dakar)
"Love Is Stronger Than Hate"
"March Of The Skinheads"
"Mash Dem"

"Maskaraid"

"May Your God Go With You"

"Memories & Guilt"

"Memory Train"

"Mighty Love"

"Monkey Boots"

"Monkeys Uncle" * (Welsh/Black)

"Monochrome Drome"

"Mother Knows Best" * (Welsh/Black)

"Move Along"

"Move Me, Groove Me, Touch Me, Hold Me, Soothe Me"

"Mr DJ"

"Mr Easy Talk"

"Murder On The Disco Express"

"Musical Postcard"

"Musical Servant" * (Welsh/Black)

"My Beautiful Friend"

"My Favourite Things"

"My Perfect World" * (Welsh/Black)

"Neurotica!" * (Welsh/Black)

"Never Said I Love You" * (Welsh/Black)

"New York Doll" * (Welsh/Dakar)

"No No No" * (Welsh/Matthias)

"Non Shrewd"

"Not So Tall" * (Welsh/Black)

"Nutty Boyz"

"Oh Lorna!"

"One Dollar Hotel"

"One More Drink"

"One Step Forward"

"Organ Grinder"

"Out Of Control"

"Outrageous" * (Welsh/Matthias)

"Parallel Road"

"Pass De Peyote"
"Prayer"
"Private World" * (Welsh/Dakar)
"Protest Song"
"Psychedelic Pum Pum"
"Punk Rock Holiday Camp"
"Pussy Got Nine Lives"
"Pussy O' Clock"
"Pussy Whipped" * (Welsh/Matthias)
"Reggae Mantra"
"Reggae Movement #1"
"Reggae Movement #2"
"Reggae Movement #3"
"Reggae Riot"
"Reggay Train"
"Re-Infected" * (Welsh/Bushell)
"Requiem For A Black Soul" * (Welsh/Black)
"Reselecterization" * (Welsh/Black/Haynes)
"Return Of The Kung Fu Skinhead"
"Return Of The Ugly" * (Welsh/Trendle/Perry)
"Rewind The World" * (Welsh/Black)
"Right On King Hammond"
"Riot In London Town"
"Riot Version"
"Rise Up Hooligan"
"Rock Me"
"Rocking On Ridley Road"
"Rocksteady Breakfast" * (Welsh/Trendle)
"Rosemary" * (Welsh/Trendle)
"Rude Boy Rock"
"Rudie's In Jail For Christmas"
"Scorpion Hits Back" * (Welsh/Barker)
"Scorpion Rising" * (Welsh/Barker)
"See Ya"

"Self-Medicating Man"
"Shake To Go"
"Shock to the System" * (Welsh/Black)
"Since You've Gone Away"
"Skalet Fever"
"Skapache"
"Skaville O'le"
"Skaville UK"
"Skin 2 Skin"
"Skin Lake" * (Welsh/Hughes)
"Skinhead '69"
"Skinhead A Suffa"
"Skinhead Love Affair" * (Welsh/Trendle)
"Skinhead Revolution"
"Skinheads In Space"
"Soho Blues"
"Space Trippin'"
"Spaced Out Cowboy"
"Spirit Of '69"
"Spirit Of '79" * (Welsh/Black)
"Stampede" * (Welsh/Trendle/Perry)
"Stay With Me Baby"
"Suck/Lick It Up"
"Sweet & Funky" * (Welsh/Matthias)
"Sweet Like Sugar"
"Sweet Mortal Sin"
"Talkin' Ska Man Blues"
"Tattoo Girls"
"Ten Years" * (Welsh/Black)
"The 1970's Nonce Club"
"The Ballad Of Judge Dread" * (Welsh/Hughes)
"The Beat Is Blue"
"The Devil In Me"
"The Dubwiser"

"The Freak Show In Your Head"
"The Hanky Panky"
"The Liar, The Bitch & The Warzone"
"The Life & Times Of A Ska Man"
"The Loop"
"The Outsider"
"The Rich Get Richer"
"The Satanic Rites Of King Hammond"
"The Soho Skank"
"The Viper" * (Welsh/Barker)
"The Wreck" *(Welsh/Dakar)
"Then She Did" * (Welsh/Black)
"They Will Rise"
"This Babylon"
"This Is Today"
"This War Will Never Cease" * (Welsh/Dakar)
"Three Card Trick"
"Three's Up" * (Welsh/Bushell)
"Tick Tock… You're Dead"
"Tighten Up"
"Torn" * (Welsh/Dakar)
"Train To Dreadville" * (Welsh/Hughes)
"Trout" * (Welsh/Black)
"Turn To Dust"
"Two Tone Party" * (Welsh/Trendle/Stewart)
"Ultra Viper" * (Welsh/Barker)
"Universe" * (Welsh/Matthias)
"Vicky's Magic Garden * (Welsh/Black)
"Vinyl Junkie"
"Viva Le Ska Revolution" * (Welsh/Trendle)
"Voice Of The People"
"Way Of Life"
"We Are The Jacamo Skins"
"When Boy Meets Girl"

"When We Were Young"
"Where Are All My Friends Today?"
"Where Have All The Rude Boys Gone?"
"Whip Them Down" * (Welsh/Black)
"Who Left Their Crombie At The Scene Of The Crime?"
"Wicked & Brutal"
"Will It Be Tomorrow"
"Wired To The Moon" * (Welsh/Matthias)
"X Rated"
"You & I"
"You Can't Get Those Sweet Things Anymore"
"You Fat Bastard" * (Welsh/Trendle)

There are hundreds more sitting in the vaults waiting to be let out so as Shaw Taylor used to say on Police 5 "keep 'em peeled".

Lightning Source UK Ltd.
Milton Keynes UK
UKOW01f0844270917
309957UK00001B/17/P

9 781910 705292